FENG SHUI THAT MAKES SENSE

Easy Ways to
Create a Home that FEELS as Good as it Looks

FENG SHUI THAT MAKES SENSE

Easy Ways to

Create a Home that FEELS as Good as it Looks

by

Cathleen McCandless

Two Harbors Press

Minneapolis, MN

Two Harbors Press
212 3rd Avenue North, Suite 290
Minneapolis, MN 55401
612.455.2293
www.TwoHarborsPress.com

For further information about the contents of this book and more, please visit
www.FengShuiThatMakesSense.com

Cover design by Cathleen McCandless

ISBN-13: 978-1-936401-56-7
LCCN: 2011926120

Distributed by Itasca Books

Printed in the United States of America

This book is dedicated with the deepest love possible, to my mother, Mary, whose wisdom, love, and sense of humor fashioned me into the person I am today. As she looks down from Heaven, I owe her not only my life but also the way I have chosen to live it. She is part of me forever and always.

I have been blessed because of her.

Contents

Part I
Feng Shui Fundamentals

Chapter 1   *An Introduction to Feng Shui*

Chapter 2   *Four Basic Principles of Feng Shui*

Part II
Practical Feng Shui for Your Home

Chapter 3   *Outdoor Feng Shui*

Chapter 4 *Feng Shui Basics for Home Interiors*

Chapter 5 *Feng Shui Tips for Every Room*

Part III
Energetic Aspects of Feng Shui

Chapter 6   *Energizing Your Home with Compass School Feng Shui*

Chapter 7   *Home Numerology*

Chapter 8   *Space Clearing and House Blessings*

Acknowledgments

This book was created from countless requests over many years from clients and students who said that my approach to feng shui worked so well and made so much sense that I had to write a book. Well, all that nagging finally paid off!

With loving thanks to my wonderful students and clients, your inspiration has guided me along my path. I have learned as much from you as you have from me. For those lessons and for your persistence, I humbly thank you. I would also like to thank Rebecca MacDonald for helping me get this book out of my head and onto paper, and to Julie Wheaton for her keen eye and superb editing skills; without you, this book would still be a pipe dream. A special thanks to Denise Linn, who lit a flame of inspiration in me many years ago that continues to shine just as brightly to this day.

Wishing you great joy and many blessings,

Cathleen McCandless

Preface

Would you like to create a home that *looks* beautiful and *feels* inviting, comfortable and relaxing? Do you have an interest in feng shui but have become frustrated or discouraged by confusing, conflicting, and sometimes downright silly information and suggestions? Are you searching for an approach to feng shui that's easy to understand, easy to implement, and easy on your budget? If you answered "yes" to any of these questions, this book was written for you!

In my twenty years as a feng shui consultant, people have often told me that they were interested in feng shui but had become turned off to the subject by the complicated, contradictory, and occasionally ridiculous concepts sometimes associated with it. This is unfortunate because, when applied properly, the system of feng shui can transform an ordinary space into an environment that relaxes our bodies, inspires our minds, and lifts our spirits.

Through experience, I've found that most of my clients and students are looking for a common-sense approach to feng shui—one that can be easily and inexpensively applied to their environments. This book provides just that. As much as possible, I will present the rationale behind many feng shui suggestions and dispel several of the myths and misconceptions associated with this beautiful and often misunderstood system. I will then show you ways in which you can easily integrate these concepts into your home to create a nurturing, comfortable, and inspiring living space.

Feng shui concepts range from gracefully simple to dazzlingly complex. It would be impossible to cover all aspects of feng shui in one book. This book focuses on sharing practical, basic feng shui information that you can easily apply to your home. And speaking of home, you will find that I refer to the place where you live as "home," even though you may reside in an apartment or a condo. No matter where you live, when you're returning to that place, you don't say, "I'm going apartment" or "I'm going condo." No, you say, "I'm going home."

Whether you rent or own your home, live in a small apartment or a sprawling mansion, have a large budget or are living on a shoestring, feng shui has something to offer you. In these pages, you will discover an abundance of ways to apply feng shui principles to your home, no matter what your current circumstances may be. In order to get the most out of this book, I recommend that you read the chapters in order.

Part I introduces the fundamentals of feng shui and explains how human instinct has influenced the foundation of feng shui principles.

Part II is the first step on your feng shui journey and begins outdoors. The way you experience the area surrounding your home greatly influences how you feel when you step inside. This section offers a wealth of practical ideas and feng shui decorating tips to create comfort and beauty within each area of your home.

Part III addresses the more energetic and esoteric aspects of feng shui. This information may not be easily understood from a practical or logical point of view, but it can help improve the energy in your home.

And finally, the appendix provides a website that can help you in finding many of the items mentioned in this book.

Feng shui can lead to fascinating self-discoveries, as you begin to understand the powerful influence of your surroundings. It is an honor to help you on this segment of your feng shui journey. I sincerely hope that, once you've read this book, implemented its suggestions, and experienced the benefits, you will not only have created a more optimal home environment but also a more optimal life.

PART I

FENG SHUI FUNDAMENTALS

Chapter 1
An Introduction to Feng Shui

Believe nothing, no matter where you read it, or who said it, no matter if I have said it, unless it agrees with your own reason and your own common sense.

— *Buddha*

What Is Feng Shui?

"*I don't believe in feng shui.*" I can't begin to count how many times I've heard this statement throughout my years as a feng shui consultant. Yet every time I do, it always amuses me. You see, saying you don't *believe* in feng shui is like saying you don't believe in air or gravity. Whether you believe in it or not, feng shui is all around you and affecting you *all the time.*

Take a moment to observe your environment right now. Are you curled up in your favorite chair or propped up against soft pillows in your bed? Maybe you're relaxing on a tropical beach or sitting in an airplane at 35,000 feet on a long flight to London. How are you feeling right now? Relaxed or tense? Focused or distracted? No matter where you are or what you are doing, how you are feeling right now is influenced by the way you are experiencing the *feng shui* of that environment.

Feng shui [pronounced "fung shway"] is the study of the environment and how it affects people. Contrary to what you may have heard, feng shui is *not* a belief system, a religion, superstition, or magic. You don't need to "believe" in it in order for it to work. Feng shui has nothing to do with changing your luck and everything to do with helping you create a space that promotes feelings of happiness and well-being.

How Does Feng Shui Work?

The fundamental premise of feng shui is really quite simple and makes perfect sense: *When you live and work in places that feel good to you, your attitude becomes more positive, and the quality of your life improves.* Feng shui, at its most basic level, is a set of principles that you can apply to your surroundings in order to experience greater pleasure and satisfaction in whatever it is you're doing.

Feng shui gives you specific guidelines that can be applied to any environment in order to increase your feelings of relaxation and comfort. The automotive, hotel, and airline industries all recognize that if people can afford it, they will pay more for greater comfort. These businesses know that generous seating, more legroom, and luxurious amenities are things that people want if they can get them, so companies charge more accordingly. When people are paying for luxury, they are often paying for a greater level of comfort, in other words, for better feng shui.

Similar to the modern-day fields of environmental psychology and ergonomics, feng shui is an ancient system used to identify features in your surroundings that make you feel relaxed or uneasy, calm or irritable. Sometimes these features are obvious; sometimes they are very subtle. When your environment feels nurturing and supportive, you're better able to relax and concentrate on what you're trying to accomplish, whether it's working, resting, or just socializing with friends. Feng shui helps you experience your everyday surroundings in new and more meaningful ways.

In order to have an optimal life, you must have optimal surroundings. All living things practice feng shui. Plants, animals, and people have specific requirements for their respective environments in order to thrive. An unfavorable setting may bring disease and illness, causing living things to degenerate and possibly even die. Just like plants and animals, your relationship to your surroundings is fundamental to your health and well-being.

What Can Feng Shui Do for You?

Feng shui is often credited with creating miraculous changes in people's lives. Many people attribute improvements in relationships, finances, health, and well-being to applying feng shui principles to their homes and offices. The benefits that are achieved with feng shui are not the result of magic, belief, or luck. They occur because feng shui helps people adjust factors in their environment in order to accentuate the positive and minimize the negative. When you're happier in your surroundings, you experience greater happiness and satisfaction in your life.

In this book, you'll find an abundance of practical, easy-to-implement feng shui tips and techniques to improve the look and feel of your home and outdoor surroundings. Feng shui may help you to:

- Create a garden or landscape that welcomes you home

- Make every room a place of beauty and relaxation

- Find more balance and peace in your life

- Increase feelings of joy and contentment

- Enjoy happier, healthier, and more loving relationships

- Arrange spaces to promote health and well-being

- Identify and improve aspects of your personal or professional life

- Relax in a home that supports your goals, wishes, and dreams

- Bring vitality and fresh energy into your life

- Become aware of the deep, instinctive relationship you have with your surroundings

A Brief History of Feng Shui

The exact time when feng shui became an organized system is shrouded in history. The earliest evidence of the practice of feng shui dates back approximately four thousand years ago to ancient China.

The early Chinese lived in a predominately agricultural society in a location subject to earthquakes, floods, and hurricanes. Completely dependent on the land for their livelihood, these people lived at the mercy of nature to bring them either abundance or devastation.

In order to minimize their exposure to the destructive forces of nature and to maximize the benefits of its bounty, the ancient Chinese created basic feng shui principles as guidelines for choosing the best areas in which to plant crops and build homes.

Feng shui helped people optimize their living and working conditions in the natural world. For example, a farmer would need to be close enough to water to nurture his crops but far enough away to be protected from floods that might wipe out his harvest. Feng shui principles also helped people understand where to build their homes in order to be protected from the extremes of heat, cold, wind, and rain.

Over time, the system of feng shui evolved and was applied to a variety of circumstances. For example, early feng shui masters were schooled in the discipline of feng shui in order to determine the best locations for burial sites. It was believed that the perfect burial site would please the deceased, and in turn, they would "thank" their descendants by bestowing blessings upon them.[1]

Interestingly, the compass (known in feng shui as the "Lo Pan") was invented by the Chinese to make feng shui analysis more precise. Early compasses were made from magnetic stones carved in the shapes of fish or spoons and oriented toward the south instead of the north. South was considered a more favorable direction because the warmth of the sun came from the south, while cold winds and extreme weather came from the north.[2]

Feng shui techniques were later expanded to include building guidelines for palaces and temples. There's evidence that suggests the early Chinese Bronze Age

---

[1] David W. Pankenier, "The Cosmo-political Background of Heaven's Mandate," *Early China* 20 (1995): 121-176.

[2] Suzanne Williams, *Made in China: Ideas and Inventions from Ancient China* (Berkeley: Pacific View Press, 1997).

culture of Erlitou (2100-1500 BC) used feng shui for palace architecture. Further archeological research points to evidence that the capital cities in China during this period followed feng shui principles for their layout and design.[3]

Because so many of the tenets in feng shui are universal, they have withstood the test of time. With slight modifications, these principles are just as pertinent to modern lifestyles as they were at their origination. While life today is obviously very different from how it was in ancient history, our instinctive reactions to the world around us are the same as they were for our ancestors.

Feng Shui Today

The popularity of feng shui in western culture today is partly a response to the development of technologies that began in the late 1800s. Beginning with the Industrial Revolution and particularly in the years following World War II, a dramatic shift took place in developed countries. People began moving from farms and open countryside to the city for its jobs and burgeoning opportunities.

In the mid-twentieth century, the invention of air conditioning gave human beings the ability to completely control a building's environment. As they stepped out of the natural world and into a completely artificial setting, more and more people spent their days living and working indoors for longer and longer periods of time.

You wouldn't take a wild animal from its natural habitat, put it in a windowless room, install artificial lighting, pump in recycled air, and expect the animal to live a happy and healthy life. When the people who lived and worked in these unnatural settings didn't thrive, work productivity decreased while illness and stress levels increased. Scientists and psychologists scratched their heads and began to wonder why.[4]

---

[3] Li Liu, *The Chinese Neolithic: Trajectories to Early States* (Cambridge: Cambridge University Press, 2004).

[4] Winifred Gallagher, *The Power of Place: How Our Surroundings Shape Our Thoughts, Emotions, and Actions* (New York: HarperPerennial, 1994).

Scientists in the fields of biology, psychology,[5] and even physics conducted studies and found evidence to support what feng shui has known for centuries: that the environment directly influences emotional, mental, and physical health.[6] Furthermore, studies by cellular biologists indicate that even body cells can be affected by the way you experience your surroundings.[7]

Technology and the Rise of Feng Shui

Technology has made "home" much more than just a place to retire to at the end of the day. For many, home is also a workplace where they connect electronically with coworkers instead of having to be physically present. Home entertainment systems have replaced trips to the movie theater, and the Internet allows you to shop for just about anything while sitting at home in your pajamas. Even dating is done electronically!

With greater numbers of people spending more time than ever at home and with the home serving more functions than ever before, there has been a huge interest in learning how to make it as comfortable as possible. Home improvement stores are springing up in neighborhoods all over the country, and home-and-garden television shows can be found in abundance. It's no coincidence that the interest in feng shui has increased along with the interest people have in creating an optimal home environment.

Feng Shui Myths and Misconceptions

The misconceptions that people have about feng shui range from silly to downright absurd. A few years ago, while giving a lecture to a very large group of gardening enthusiasts, a woman sheepishly raised her hand to ask me a question. She

---

[5] A.H. Maslow and N.L. Mintz, "Effects of Aesthetic Surroundings: Initial Effects of Three Aesthetic Conditions Upon Perceiving 'Energy' and 'Well-being' in Faces," *Journal of Psychology* 41 (1956): 247-254.

[6] DAK Kopec, *Environmental Psychology for Design* (New York: Fairchild Books, 2006).

[7] Bruce H. Lipton, PhD, *The Biology of Belief, Unleashing the Power of Consciousness, Matter, & Miracles* (Carlsbad, California: Hay House, 2008), 19-43.

explained that she had hired a feng shui consultant a couple of years before and was concerned about something the consultant had told her to do.

This woman's bedroom was directly above the garage, and the consultant said that this was a very negative placement for the bedroom due to the "unstable energies" of the garage. The consultant's advice? Place aluminum foil covered with a red sheet between the box spring and the mattress to deflect the "negative energy" emanating from the garage. As the woman told her story, a round of giggles rippled through the room. Suppressing a smile, I asked, "How is that working out for you?"

"Well," she said, "the foil is so noisy that every time we move, it wakes us up. My husband wants me to take the foil out, but I'm afraid to, in case something bad might happen." Her husband thought feng shui was ridiculous, and I can certainly understand why based upon this silly recommendation! I reassured her that there was no legitimacy to the idea that having a bedroom above a garage was a portent to catastrophe. Furthermore, not being able to sleep at night was detrimental in itself—certainly much worse than sleeping above a garage.

The woman was relieved and said she would go right home and remove the aluminum foil and red sheet from under her mattress. Weeks later, she emailed me to say thank you for putting her mind at ease on the bedroom-over-the-garage issue. She wrote that, since removing the aluminum foil, she and her husband were sleeping well once again. She was very relieved to learn that the original advice she had received was well-meaning but inaccurate. She later hired me to redo the feng shui of her home because she appreciated the practical nature of the information given in my lecture. Even her husband was happy with the results this time!

It is exactly this type of misinformation that perpetuates incorrect assumptions regarding the practice of feng shui. If it sounds like nonsense, it *is* nonsense and certainly not feng shui.

Sources of Misunderstanding

Many feng shui practitioners inadvertently perpetuate misinformation that was never intended to be part of the system. They accept this information at face value and unquestioningly pass it on to their clients, students, and readers without considering the source or validity of what they are communicating. Such information ranges from ineffective to absolutely comical and has done a lot of damage to the integrity of this ancient environmental system.

Centuries ago, feng shui knowledge was passed verbally from teacher to student through many generations. Over time, the original meanings for some feng shui principles were changed or lost in translation as the information was handed down from one person to the next. The end result is that some of the original feng shui principles have been misinterpreted and misunderstood.

One of my biggest challenges as a feng shui consultant has been rectifying these misconceptions. Throughout this book, I point out many of these fallacies and offer insights on how these ideas may have originated. These "Reality Checks" will hopefully shed some light on a few of the strange and incorrect things you may have heard about feng shui.

Reality Check

Myth: Sleeping above a garage is considered bad feng shui.

Let's look at our first Reality Check in the context of the case mentioned earlier, where a bedroom was located above a garage. There's a notion in some feng shui circles that it's unfavorable to have a bedroom situated over a garage. The idea is that such a placement creates unstable, negative energy and promotes sleeplessness and/or negative experiences.

Not only is this untrue, but it also makes absolutely no sense. The time that it takes for a car to move in or out of a garage is, at most, a few minutes per day. The rest of the time, the garage is a room like any other room, whether or not it has a car in it. During sleeping hours when the bedroom above is occupied, chances are there's no movement at all in the garage below. It's no more active than the family room or the living room and has no more of an impact on the people sleeping above than any other room in the house.

Where did this idea come from? Remember that the original intention of feng shui was to help people live in harmony with nature. It's possible that the issue of having a bedroom over a garage was inferred from an early feng shui principle stating that it was unwise to build a home hanging over a moving stream or a river. It's easy to understand why this was sound advice and still is. However, the differences between building a home over a constantly flowing river and pulling a car in and out of a garage a few minutes each day are clear, and one really has nothing to do with the other.

Feng Shui Trinkets, Gimmicks, and Talismans

I once received a phone call from an excited young man telling me that he had invented "feng shui dog collars." He wanted to know if I was interested in marketing them for him. They were essentially dog collars with a decoration of a Chinese character on them. The marketing angle was supposedly "feng shui for dogs."

When I asked him what the point of the collars was, he replied, "Well, you know, it's feng shui." I asked him what he thought that meant.

He said, "You know, feng shui … it's supposed to bring you good luck."

"So the dogs will have good luck if their owners buy these collars?" I asked, thinking that "good luck" for a dog might be more like finding the right fire hydrant at just the right time.

"Yeah, I guess so," he offered. After a lengthy explanation on what did and what did not constitute feng shui, the man hung up, and I never heard anything about him or his dog collars again.

Unfortunately, this is not the only example of ridiculous marketing techniques based upon the exploitation of feng shui principles. As a consultant, I've received well-meaning gifts ranging from "feng shui" candles and soap to three-legged frogs and glass crystals. I was even given a pair of "feng shui" eyeglasses once. What they were supposed to do is still a mystery to me.

Every time I see a product marketed with a feng shui angle, I wince. It's sad to see the concept of feng shui reduced to a cheap gimmick, a get-rich-quick scheme, or a talisman for good luck. It's a shame that this incredible environmental system has become diminished and exploited by so many. With all the nonsense out there, it's no wonder that people become easily confused and misguided regarding the subject of feng shui.

Reality Check

Myth: *Faceted glass crystals, coins on a string, three-legged frogs, eight-sided mirrors, and wooden flutes will improve your luck.*

Let me make something very clear: feng shui has nothing to do with luck. Luck implies something that occurs randomly and accidentally, and there's nothing random or accidental about feng shui. I'm sorry to burst anyone's bubble, but hanging a glass crystal, an eight-sided mirror, a rope with coins on it, an ugly, plastic three-legged frog, a wooden flute, or any other trinket in your home or office does no more for your life's circumstances than rubbing a rabbit's foot or keeping a four-leaf clover in your pocket. None of these items has inherent mysterious powers that can dramatically improve your life or your fortune. If they could, everyone would be using them, and no one would experience loss or misfortune again! If only life were that simple!

The truth is, when you purchase these so-called "feng shui" items, you're only adding to the luck and prosperity of the person who sold it to you while diminishing your own fortune.

Feng shui has nothing to do with symbolic figurines, glass crystals, flutes, or coins and everything to do with creating a space of beauty and comfort. Certainly designing an environment that feels peaceful and serene will take more time and effort than hanging a glass crystal sphere, but the effort is well worth it.

Fortunately, this book will teach you how to incorporate good feng shui without cluttering your home with a bunch of meaningless knickknacks and unsightly good luck charms.

Building Design and Feng Shui

I frequently give presentations to building industry professionals and their design teams to educate them on how crucial a proper understanding of feng shui principles is to the building process. During my presentations, I point out scientific research that indicates how the layout and design of homes and office buildings have powerful, long-range effects upon the quality of life of the people who live and work there.[1]

I conclude each presentation by saying, "No other industry that I can think of has more of an impact on the daily lives of people in our society than the building industry." For many of the builders, this is a sobering thought and the very first time that they've ever considered the long-term human consequences of what they've created.

I often wonder whether there would be less stress, disease, crime, and dissatisfaction if more builders, architects, and home designers considered the far-

[1] Joan M. Campbell, "Ambient Stressors," *Environment and Behavior* 15, No. 3 (1983): 355-380.

reaching effects that their creations have on people and the environment. Hopefully as feng shui becomes better understood and requested by the public at large, homes and public buildings will be designed and constructed to support and nurture body, mind, spirit, and planet.

Schools of Feng Shui and My Approach

As I mentioned earlier, feng shui has evolved and changed over many centuries. Variations in methodologies and philosophies have entered the picture, and as a result, there are now many different "schools" or approaches to feng shui. Some are simplistic and rely more upon intention and belief, while others are more complex, utilizing advanced mathematical and astronomical calculations in order to arrive at recommendations for a space.

This book is not intended to debate the superiority or merits of one approach over another. While I do have my personal opinions and preferences for what works in feng shui, I honestly believe that each person needs to decide which approach works best for his/her specific space. Here's a brief overview of several well-known schools of feng shui.

Form School Feng Shui

Form School feng shui is thought to be the oldest system of feng shui. This method examines the layout of landforms (such as mountains, bodies of water, or canyons); street configurations; nearby buildings; architectural designs; and other physical factors that may affect how people experience a space. On a smaller scale, this method also considers room arrangement, décor, design, furniture placement, and flow within a building. Form School feng shui pays close attention to the physical features around and within a location that most directly impact our experience of that environment.

In my opinion, Form School feng shui is the most fundamental type of feng shui and the easiest to understand and implement. A great deal of this book will fall under the Form School approach.

Form School feng shui helps determine what it is about a space that makes it feel "right" to you. Without good form, the other approaches to feng shui fall short of the mark. It's absolutely essential that you feel comfortable and safe in your surroundings, if you are going to thrive. Form School feng shui helps you do just that.

Chapters 2 through 5 explore in detail how Form School feng shui can be applied to your home environment. In fact, if you decide to put into practice *only* the Form School approach to feng shui, you'll still be well on your way to creating an optimal living space. It is my hope, however, that once you've experienced the benefits of Form School feng shui, you'll be inspired to explore the more energetic aspects of feng shui described in chapters 6 through 8.

Compass School Feng Shui

Compass School feng shui utilizes a compass to determine areas in a structure that pertain to aspects of our lives, including Wealth & Prosperity, Family, Fame, Love & Partnership, Creation, Synchronicity, Career, Knowledge, and Health.

These nine areas correspond to the nine compass directions: southeast (Wealth & Prosperity), east (Family), south (Fame), southwest (Love & Partnership), west (Creation), northwest (Synchronicity), north (Career), northeast (Knowledge), and center (Health). These compass points are activated by specific placement of the five elements: water (north), wood (east, southeast), fire (south), earth (southwest, center, northeast), and metal (west, northwest).

In Compass School feng shui, it's thought that when the five elements are placed properly in their assigned locations, the energy of those areas of our lives improves. In a way, Compass School feng shui is like acupuncture for a building; however, instead of inserting needles to increase the flow of energy, specific elements are used.

Chapter 6 teaches you the basics of Compass School feng shui and presents fairly easy ways to integrate its principles into your home. While this is an aspect of feng shui that's more esoteric and energetic than the Form School approach, I've found it to be very effective, especially when coupled with Form School feng shui.

Flying Star Feng Shui

Flying Star feng shui is one of the most complex schools of feng shui. Flying Star utilizes numerical formulas based upon the year a building was built, the direction it faces, the location of its front door, and the birth information of its occupants (or potential occupants) to determine whether a home is optimal.

Much like an astrological chart is used to identify strengths, weaknesses, and trends in a person's life, Flying Star feng shui also integrates time and space calculations to help determine the positive and negative aspects of a home and the experiences that the occupants may have while living there.

Flying Star is what I'd call advanced feng shui. While this approach is effective in determining whether a structure is well-suited to someone, it's also very complex. For the sake of simplicity and out of my desire to provide you with an easy-to-understand foundation of feng shui, I will not be covering Flying Star feng shui in this book. However if you're interested in continuing your research, I encourage you to find out more about this intricate and fascinating approach and all of its various applications.

Black Hat Feng Shui

Perhaps the least scientific form of feng shui, Black Hat feng shui—also known as Black Sect Tantric Buddhism or BTB feng shui—is a more recent type of feng shui that was developed and popularized in the West in the late twentieth century.

One of the main differences between Black Hat feng shui and the more traditional approaches is that it does not use a compass to determine the feng shui qualities of a space. Instead, the building is analyzed based upon the location of the front door. Black Hat feng shui focuses on intention and symbols more than the traditional approaches and uses objects such as mirrors, crystal spheres, flutes, and other items not previously used or associated with feng shui.

My Approach

In this book, I will teach you the fundamentals of Form School feng shui and introduce you to the basics of the Compass School approach. Bear in mind that feng shui is a complicated subject with many different philosophies and techniques. Therefore, you'll have to discover what feels and works best for you.

I suggest that you examine and integrate the ideas that resonate with you and proceed from there. If something sounds odd or makes you uncomfortable, don't force yourself to implement it. Instead, take what feels right and give it a try. You have nothing to lose and everything to gain.

After twenty years as a feng shui consultant, my advice to all of my students and clients can be summed up in one sentence: "If it feels good, then it's good feng shui." As you seek to improve your surroundings, remember to do what feels best to you and know that it's good feng shui.

Chapter 2
Four Basic Principles of Feng Shui

A house is a home when it shelters the body and comforts the soul.

— *Phillip Moffitt*

Creating an Optimal Home Environment

Does your home feel nurturing and relaxing? Are there areas of your home that just don't feel right, but you don't know why or what to do about them? Have you ever wondered what it is that makes you feel more comfortable in some places rather than others? Would you like to know how to create a more positive, beautiful, and comfortable living space? In this chapter, you'll discover how to transform your living space into a place of beauty and comfort and learn why doing so is important for both your physical and emotional well-being.

One of the most powerful ways in which feng shui can help is by reducing environmental stressors. When you reduce the stressors in your environment, you reduce the stress in your life. When anything in your environment aggravates you, threatens you, or irritates you, it creates stress responses in your body and in your emotions.

Feng shui reduces stress by addressing the instinctive need to feel safe in your surroundings. When your survival needs are met, you feel safe. When you feel safe, you feel comfortable. When you feel comfortable, you feel a sense of well-being.

When you feel a sense of well-being, you feel empowered to accomplish positive things in your life. When you accomplish positive things in your life, you are able to thrive and prosper.

Stress comes in many forms and from countless sources. One of the least obvious but most important sources of stress can be found in the places where you spend the most time: your home and workplace.[1] Since the time of the cave man, human beings have related to their environment based upon an instinct to survive. When you perceive any threat to your safety, your body and emotions react instinctively to protect you from harm, thus ensuring the survival of the species. The survival mechanisms your body uses to keep yourself safe in the wild are now triggered by many features found in man-made settings.

Feng shui employs basic principles to address specific features in your surroundings that contribute to your well-being or to your detriment. When you feel uncomfortable in a space, your survival instincts are alerting you to potential situations that aren't good for you. You experience this negative response as stress.

In nature, a human being's instinctive response to stress is either fight or flight. In man-made surroundings, these responses are frequently impractical or impossible. Many people must live and work in stressful environments over long periods of time, perhaps even years. Experiencing stress over long periods of time wears down the immune system and can have a detrimental effect upon your quality of life. The epidemic of stress-related illnesses and diseases in modern society exemplifies the disastrous effects of long-term exposure to physical and emotional stress.

Feng shui provides guidelines that help identify and reduce environmental stressors and increase factors that promote health and well-being. An environment that is optimized for our safety and survival is actually optimized for our comfort, health, and happiness.

The basic principles of feng shui can be applied to any environment. Once you understand the basics, you'll be able to apply them easily at home or work in order to create more comfortable, relaxing spaces. You may be surprised to learn

---

[1] Joan M. Campbell, "Ambient Stressors," *Environment and Behavior* 15, No. 3 (1983): 355-380.

that how an environment feels to you is less about personal choice and more about your basic instinct to survive. Survival instincts play a crucial role in determining whether or not a location feels good to you. Once you understand that, you have the ability to make *any* space feel better.

Basic Principle #1: Protect your back.

Have you ever walked into a restaurant with a group of people and been the first one to approach the table? Chances are, you instinctively walked around to the far side of the table and took a seat that provided you with a view to the rest of the room. I'd even venture to say that you may have felt guilty for doing so. Conversely, you may have taken one of the first seats you approached (so that your back was to the rest of the room) and felt as though you were being gracious by taking a less favorable seat at the table. You know which seat feels the best at a restaurant, but you may not know exactly *why* this is so. While seat selection is often done non-verbally, every person involved in the group understands what's going on at some level.

When given a choice, people prefer to sit with their backs to a wall and with a view to the rest of the room. When your back is protected, you feel safe enough to relax and enjoy yourself because your basic survival needs for safety and protection are being met. Figure 2.1 illustrates the seats that people tend to choose when they're able to choose any seat.

To carry the restaurant scenario a step further,

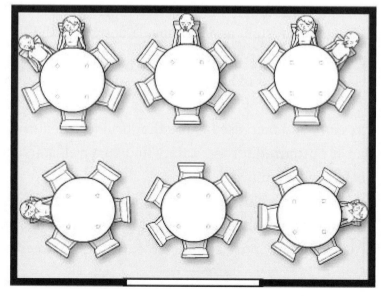

Figure 2.1

consider this situation: You walk into the restaurant, and the hostess asks whether you'd prefer a table or a booth. What's your usual response? Most likely, you will answer "booth." If I ask you why you prefer a booth, you might say that it's more comfortable, cozy, or private. While those words may describe how you feel when sitting in a booth, they don't explain *why* you feel that way. The *why* in this case refers to a fundamental feng shui principle that stems directly from your basic instinct to survive.

Both people and animals prefer to sit with their backs to a wall in order to have a view to the rest of the room. You can observe this same instinct in the animal kingdom. Watch your pets when they sleep. When a dog or cat is going to sleep, it instinctively positions itself to face out toward the rest of the room and bolsters its back up against another surface, be it furniture, each other, or even you! The survival instinct that your pet uses to protect itself while sleeping is no different from the impulse that guides you when selecting a booth rather than a table in a restaurant. When your back is protected, you feel safe because your basic survival needs for safety and protection are being met. When choosing to sit in a booth, you're ensuring that you and your dining companions will share the same level of comfort by having your backs protected during the meal. With your backs protected, survival instincts relax, and you and your companions are better able to enjoy the experience of dining together. However, if your party is seated at a table in the middle of the room, none of you will relax as much as you could because you can't be sure of what's happening behind your back. The vulnerability of having everyone's back "exposed" rather than protected may distract from fully enjoying the experience of dining together.

While you may have always known that sitting in a booth is more comfortable, now you know *why* it's more comfortable. Feng shui translates human survival mechanisms into a basic design principle that can help create an environment that's relaxing and comfortable. Following are some ways to use this basic principle in your home.

Seating

Select chairs, sofas, and headboards with sturdy backs that are high enough to provide a feeling of safety but not so high that they feel oppressive. With seating, be sure that the back isn't too high to see around if you turn your head. Chair backs that come up to the shoulder or neck level while seated feel best to most people. Also, chairs and sofas with arms offer a greater feeling of protection than seating with open sides.

Homesites

Avoid choosing a house on a lot that has a downward slope or a drop-off behind the house, such as a cliff, a hillside, or a canyon. A house such as this does not provide an adequate feeling of protection. This sense of vulnerability can adversely influence your life. If you already live in a home like this, refer to chapter 3 for more information.

Headboards

Add a significant, solid headboard made of wood (with no slats or openings) to your bed. Upholstered headboards also can provide a protective feeling. The headboard should be connected to a bed frame. Footboards are optional. A headboard provides a greater feeling of protection and security while you're sleeping than simply having a wall behind you. This is true for adults as well as children. You'll learn more about beds and bed positioning in chapter 4.

Furniture Arrangements

Arrange furniture to provide a clear view of the main door to a room. This is especially important with desks and task-oriented seating. When you're seated with your back to a wall and with a clear view of the door as well as the rest of the room, this is known as the "Command Position" in feng shui. This position eliminates the element of surprise. No one can sneak up behind you or enter your space unnoticed. Such an arrangement allows you to feel more empowered, more relaxed, and more in control of your surroundings.

Basic Principle #2: Minimize sharp edges, points, and corners.

Consider this: In almost every culture throughout the world, it's considered rude to point at someone. The reason for this custom is based not solely upon etiquette or something that your mother taught you but rather on the instinctive human response to danger. When things are pointed at us, we feel defensive. In this same way, sharp points, corners, and angles in our surroundings can be interpreted as threatening, and our bodies respond to the threat with tension.

Right angles and straight lines don't exist in nature. Even the horizon, which may at times appear to be a straight line, is technically an arc. Because of the way most buildings are constructed, we're constantly surrounded by right angles and sharp corners. When sharp corners protrude into a room, the space may not feel very relaxing because our survival instincts are on high alert to keep us safe. Our instincts are warning us that bumping into a sharp corner can hurt. This awareness keeps us from completely relaxing in the space.

Many builders have responded to this issue by rounding off the sharp edges of corners in newer homes. These "bullnose" corners, as they're called, instinctively feel more comfortable because, on a subtle level, the home feels *safer*. Our survival instincts know that if we bump into a rounded corner rather than a sharp edge, we won't be harmed. Rounding off sharp corners in a room may not seem like a big deal, but it makes a huge difference in how comfortable we feel in a home.

Let's apply this concept to a room arrangement. A square room with sharp-cornered furniture and little else may feel uninviting and uncomfortable. However, when the room's corners are softened by adding plants and furniture with curved edges, the atmosphere feels calmer and more welcoming because subconsciously we perceive it as safer and less threatening. You can easily soften or minimize sharp angles and pointed objects in your space by doing the following:

- Avoid plants with spiked leaves and thorns,
  both inside and outside your home.

- Place round objects, such as sculptures, plants with soft
  leaves, circular tables, and lamps, in the corners of a room.

- Position furniture with sharp edges, such as tables, desks, and cabinets, diagonally in corners to make a room feel more inviting.

- Opt for furniture pieces that have rounded lines rather than sharp angles. This choice makes a huge difference in how comfortable a room feels.

- Frame windows with drapes to soften the edges.

- Choose floral or non-geometric patterns for rugs and upholstery.

When you make these simple changes in your home, you'll be amazed at how much more relaxed and comfortable it feels. Remember, anything you do that allows your survival instincts to perceive a space as safe will increase feelings of calm and relaxation, one of the main goals in feng shui.

Basic Principle #3: Incorporate images and materials from nature.

Scientific studies have proven time and time again that plants, images, and materials from nature reduce stress, promote healing, increase productivity, and provide a greater sense of well-being in humans.[2,3] It's not difficult to understand why this is so. Human beings have lived in nature far longer than in their man-made environments. We are hard-wired to respond to all aspects of the natural environment: its shapes, materials, smells, and colors. When we integrate plants, images, and materials found in nature into our living and working spaces, we're including features that resonate with us on a deep level. These features connect us to the favorable surroundings that resonate with our bodies and minds.

Spaces that lack natural images and materials are often described as feeling cold, impersonal, and uncomfortable. We usually don't want to spend any more time in these spaces than we have to. Many airport terminals exemplify this concept. The

---

[2] Stephen Kaplan, PhD, "Aesthetics, Affect, and Cognition," *Environment and Behavior* 19, No. 1 (1987): 7.

[3] V.I. Lohr, C.H. Pearson-Mims, and G.K. Goodwin, "Interior plants may improve worker productivity and reduce stress in a windowless environment," *Journal of Environmental Horticulture* 14, No. 2 (1996): 97-100.

lack of natural images and materials, the harsh lighting, and the sensory overload keep us from feeling relaxed and comfortable, while adding to our stress levels.

This is one reason why airlines offer special lounges for their VIP passengers. These lounges feature soft seating, calming music, and good lighting. Often, they integrate textures, plants, colors, and other materials from nature into the décor to provide an atmosphere of comfort and relaxation for weary travelers. These VIP lounges are offered as escapes from the stress and chaos of the main terminals. They help to lower anxiety levels and calm ragged nerves.

If only the entire airport industry would follow suit in applying natural materials and comforts throughout regular terminals, then the masses could benefit as well. In doing so, the industry would be doing itself, its employees, and its passengers a great favor by reducing passenger stress, improving passenger/staff interactions, and offering a more relaxed atmosphere at the airport.

Thankfully, most of us don't live in airport terminals, but there are still plenty of features in our homes that can make us feel as uncomfortable and uneasy as we feel in airports. You'll find that by adding more natural materials into your home, you'll increase the feelings of comfort and relaxation. No matter what your design preferences are, there are some simple ways to bring nature into your home.

Plants

Add live plants. It's a simple idea, but sometimes just the addition of a plant or two can transform an area from a place where no one feels comfortable to a place where people want to be all the time. Plants are, by far, the one item I recommend to clients more than any other when improving the feng shui of a space.

If you cannot or do not wish to take care of a live plant, consider a silk plant as an alternative. Many silk plants are now so realistic that it's difficult to tell whether or not they're real. Just remember to clean them periodically by taking them outside and hosing them off. See chapter 6 for more information about adding plants to enhance the feng shui of a room.

Scenes from Nature

Display artwork that depicts scenes from nature. Seascapes, landscapes, and other outdoor scenes help to bring the natural world indoors, promoting a feeling of calm. This is an especially good choice if the windows of your home don't look out onto peaceful views.

Materials from Nature

Choose materials that come from nature. Wood, stone, jute, hemp, bamboo, and cotton feel better and are better for you than synthetic or man-made materials. They're also better for the environment because they're often renewable and sustainable.

Our Instinctive Attraction to Water

The most prized real estate throughout the world almost always has a water view or is in close proximity to water. A home that features a view to an ocean, lake, stream, or river usually commands a higher price in the real estate market than a comparable home without a view of water. In order to explain this fondness for water, we must once again look to basic survival instincts.

The human affinity for water is primal. We need water to survive and being close to water or being able to see water causes us to react favorably. Not only is water calming for us to look at, but the negative ions it produces have a relaxing effect on our bodies.[4],[5]

Feng shui uses water a great deal in its application partially because our nervous systems, survival instincts, and pleasure centers are soothed by water. Water is a wonderful natural element that you can add to your living spaces, both indoors and outdoors. There are specific areas in the home, however, where water is optimal and other places where it should be avoided. I cover this in more detail in chapter 6. Here are several ways to integrate water into your home environment:

---

[4] Christopher Alexander and others, *A Pattern Language* (New York: Oxford University Press, 1977), 323.

[5] Roger S. Ulrich, "Aesthetic and Affective Response to Natural Environment," *Behavior and the Natural Environment*, Irwin Altman and Joachim F. Wohlwill, eds. (New York: Plenum, 1983), 104-105.

- Indoor tabletop fountains have become very popular in recent years. They come in many sizes, types, and prices. Shop online or in stores to find one that appeals to you.

- Aquariums are beautiful and fun as long as they are kept in tiptop, healthy condition. Consider hiring an aquarium service if you wish to have an elaborate aquarium or exotic fish.

- Pools, ponds, and even birdbaths (as long as they have water in them) add water to an outdoor setting.

- Outdoor fountains add a great deal of charm and ambience to yards and patios. Home improvement and garden stores sell fountains as well as kits for creating and installing your own.

Basic Principle #4: Create balance between extremes.

The term "feng shui," loosely translated, means "wind" (feng) and "water" (shui). Instead of taking these words literally and separately, it's more beneficial to consider them conceptually and together. Combined, they capture the essence of feng shui, which is *balance* and *flow*.

To illustrate this concept, imagine a breeze coming into the room where you are now. If the breeze actually had a color, you could see it as it moved throughout the room. You would notice it curling around chairs, swirling around table legs, and floating past your body. If there was too little air flowing through the room, the atmosphere might feel thick and stuffy. If too much air was flowing, the force of it could be destructive. The same idea applies to water. Picture water flowing in a river or a stream. In your mind's eye, watch as the water gently moves past reeds and stones, traveling gently around the curves and bends in the riverbed. If there's too little flow, the water becomes stagnant and foul; too much flow may cause flooding and devastation.

The concept of balancing between two extremes is the essence of feng shui's approach to optimizing an environment. I like to think of it this way: The balance and flow in feng shui equate to standing up in a canoe while it's moving. You must be mindful moment-to-moment of keeping your balance while also looking ahead to make sure that you're heading in the best direction. It's about being balanced and focused in the present moment while paying attention to, and preparing for, what lies ahead. When you apply feng shui principles to your surroundings, you're helping your environment, and your journey through life becomes more balanced and positive.

Yin and Yang in Feng Shui

 Do you recognize this symbol? Most people have seen it, but many don't understand its meaning. I'm going to present you with a simplified explanation of this universal symbol and the important role that it serves in the practice of feng shui.

Yin-yang theory assigns everything in the Universe two energies: Yin represents energy that's feminine, dark, damp, soft, and still. Yang represents energy that is male, bright, dry, hard, and active. When these two energies are equally present, harmony and balance are also present. Over time, the balance of yin and yang energies ebbs and flows within an environment, a person, a place, or a thing. As it changes, so does the prevailing energy of that environment, person, place, or thing. Yin-yang theory holds that creating and maintaining balance is a dynamic, ongoing process rather than a static state.

The yin-yang symbol is a combination of two teardrop shapes: black represents yin energy; white represents yang energy. There is a dot of white within the black teardrop and a dot of black within the white teardrop to symbolize that these two energies must coexist simultaneously in order to exist at all. That is, yin cannot exist without yang, and yang cannot exist without yin. In the same way, day cannot exist without night, hot cannot exist without cold, and hard cannot exist without soft.

The swirling shape of the yin-yang symbol signifies the Universe's constant quest for balance through the unending cycles of time. As yin energy increases, yang energy decreases. As yang energy increases, yin energy decreases. The changing of the seasons provides a perfect example of the shifting between yin and yang energies over time. Summer, with its heat and sunlight, is a yang season. As summer's heat and sunlight slowly yield to the approaching cold and dampness of winter, we experience the transition as autumn. The autumnal equinox marks the point at which light (yang) and dark (yin) are balanced. As the cold and dampness of winter increase, we experience the winter solstice, where dark (yin) prevails over light (yang). As winter's cold and dampness slowly yield to the approaching heat and sunlight of summer, we experience the transition as spring. The spring equinox marks the point at which, again, light (yang) and dark (yin) are balanced. As the heat and sunlight prevail, we experience the summer solstice, where light (yang) prevails over dark (yin). Summer and winter represent the extremes of the seasons, with spring and fall providing the transition times between the two, endlessly flowing into one another.

In feng shui, we use yin and yang to help balance the way we experience an environment. Using yin and yang energies to guide us, we're better able to determine what needs to be added or removed in order for a space to feel better. When there's too much of one energy present, the area will feel unbalanced. When yin and yang energies are represented equally, our surroundings will feel more harmonious and pleasing.

The Goldilocks Principle in Feng Shui: Getting It Just Right

I like to joke that Goldilocks was the first really famous feng shui consultant. Goldilocks knew that anything that was too hard, too soft, too hot, or too cold just didn't feel good. Goldilocks couldn't relax until everything felt just right. "The Goldilocks Principle," as I call it, is really a just a contemporary version of basic yin-yang theory. When clients and students tell me that their spaces don't feel right but that they don't know why, it's often because there's an imbalance between the yin and yang energies.

Just like Goldilocks did when she visited the home of the three bears, whenever you use the word "too" to describe something about a room, as in too cold, too hot, too hard, too soft, or too *anything*, you're pointing out an area of imbalance. Using "too" in describing a space in your home is a heads-up that the space needs to be counterbalanced by its opposite. For example, if you describe a room as "too dark," then you need to bring in more light. Along with adding actual light (natural or artificial), you can also use light paint colors, mirrors, bright fabrics, light-colored furniture finishes, or light-colored floor coverings to lighten up the space.

The Goldilocks Principle and the Flooring Business

I have a friend who owns a successful carpet and flooring business. One evening, we were discussing the resurgence in popularity of area rugs with dramatic textures, like shag, cable, and faux fur. He asked what I thought about the increase in demand for these types of rugs.

I told him that the popularity of these rugs made perfect sense to me from a feng shui perspective. In the past few years, tile and hardwood flooring had become more popular in homes than wall-to-wall carpeting. I surmised that people were now instinctively trying to balance the hard, smooth surfaces of their floors with softness and texture.

My friend became very excited when he heard this because it made perfect sense to him, too. This new understanding and insight inspired him to create a fresh marketing strategy. He put together a package deal for his customers, pairing the sale of hardwood flooring and tile with selected, textured area rugs. Weeks later, he reported back to me that the concept had been a tremendous success, and his business had dramatically increased as a result.

As you consider the exterior and interior aspects of your home's feng shui, use the Goldilocks Principle and yin-yang theory to help create an environment that feels harmonious and balanced. While chapter 3 addresses the outdoor spaces of your home, chapter 4 goes into more detail on how you can use yin-yang theory and the Goldilocks Principle to balance interior rooms. You may find that the more balanced you make your surroundings, the more balanced and peaceful you will feel.

PART II

PRACTICAL FENG SHUI FOR YOUR HOME

Chapter 3
Outdoor Feng Shui

The goal of life is living in agreement with nature.

— Zeno of Citium,
Greek philosopher, 300 BC

First Impressions

How do you feel when you drive up to your home? Do your spirits rise with anticipation or sink with despair? Does your home feel like a place of rest and rejuvenation or a source of stress and exhaustion?

Thanks to countless home improvement shows on television, you're probably familiar with the term "curb appeal." Curb appeal is the first impression that a home makes when seen from the street, and this impression can make or break a real estate transaction. Realtors find that many buyers decide whether to make an offer on a home within the first ten to fifteen seconds of seeing a property, and this happens even before they've stepped foot inside the door! First impressions are lasting impressions, and once made, they are very difficult to change.

Certainly you can understand why curb appeal is important when selling a home, but how does your home's curb appeal affect you on a daily basis? The exterior surroundings of a home are crucial to the quality of a home's feng shui. One of the most important exercises you can do when evaluating your home's feng shui is to notice how you feel when you arrive at the front of your house. Your home is supposed to be a place that nurtures, protects, and rejuvenates you. If you feel anything but positive feelings when you arrive home each day, it's important to reassess what it is about where you live that's contributing to a negative mind-set.

Often when people buy a new home, they initially spend their time, money, and efforts fixing up the interior. They carefully pore over paint swatches, evaluate furniture choices, and seek out pieces of art to decorate their walls. Usually the outside of the home—the yard, the landscaping, and the walkway— are left until the inside décor is complete. Sometimes attending to the landscape takes months or years, and sometimes it's put off indefinitely and never happens at all. You may think that focusing on the inside first makes more sense because that's where you spend the most time, but from a feng shui perspective, this sequence is actually backwards.

Consider this scenario: You and your spouse have bought a home. You've scrimped and saved to add paint, flooring, rugs, furniture, and artwork in order to create a place of beauty and comfort. Gardening really isn't your thing, and you've been so busy getting the inside just right that you've left the exterior for a later date when you have more time and money to put into it.

You know you should be excited to come home at the end of the day, but as you approach your home, you feel overwhelmed with a sense of lethargy and frustration. This wonderful home that you've spent so much time and money on feels like a huge job that will never end. After working all day, you feel as though you're just coming home to more work, instead of a place to rest and relax. This feeling of frustration may carry over into the relationships you have with your spouse or children. Instead of greeting everyone with a happy hello, you may snap at them. You may wonder why you don't feel better about your house after all you've done to improve it. The reason doesn't lie within the house at all; the answer is actually right outside in the front yard.

From a feng shui perspective, the best approach to improving a home is to take care of the front exterior *first* and then work your way through the rest of the house. When the front of the home looks and feels good, you experience a sense of pride, order, and accomplishment, rather than frustration and annoyance. These positive feelings influence your overall experience of your home and result in a much better attitude toward tackling whatever it is that awaits you on the other side of the door. With the importance of first impressions in mind, let's look at some ways in which feng shui can help you create an optimal front yard and a great first impression.

Healthy Landscapes Encourage Healthy Attitudes

As I just mentioned, whether or not you have a green thumb, the area surrounding your home has a definite influence on how you feel about living there. The healthier and more attractive your landscaping is, the more positive you and your family will feel when arriving home. Feeling positive about your living space significantly impacts both how you experience your home and your personal interactions with others.

For Apartment Dwellers, Condo Owners, or Homeowners with Strict HOAs

Sometimes you have little or no control over your home's exterior due to ownership issues. However, this doesn't mean that you can't add a touch here and there to make it feel better. If you live in an apartment or a condo, usually you're able to place your own doormat outside the door. Be sure to pick an attractive one to welcome you home. Some associations permit residents to personalize exterior spaces with pots of flowers, plants, wind chimes, and small statuary. Adding these personal touches can make your apartment or condo feel less generic and more like home.

Plants and Feng Shui

Although plant types are subjective depending upon your personal preferences and what part of the world you live in, feng shui offers some specific guidelines to use when choosing plants for the exterior of your home.

Avoiding Plants with Sharp Points and Thorns

As we discussed in chapter 2, one the basic principles of feng shui is to minimize sharp angles and points. When something is pointed at you, your survival instincts kick in and make you feel defensive. The more defensive you feel, the less relaxed and comfortable you are.

The same concept applies to the types of plants we choose for our indoor and outdoor environments. Plants with sharp spikes or thorns create subtle feelings of apprehension in people as they approach your house. If your goal is to create a home that feels welcoming and peaceful, it's important to eliminate any sharp or thorny plants growing in your yard, particularly ones located near the front door.

Almost all plants have a point at the end of their leaves called a "drip tip." Drip tips channel water off of leaves to keep them from rotting, and they help direct water to the ground where it can be absorbed by the roots. Most plants have leaves with points at the end, but not all plants are sharply pointed or threatening because the shape of their leaves is, for the most part, soft and rounded.

Examples of spiked plants include yucca, flax, aloe, cactus, holly, and some palms. Softer plants include ficus, boxwood, pittosporum, and most flowering plants. I'm sure you can think of many other examples. Use your own judgment when deciding whether or not a plant feels sharp to you and keep those plants away from your front door.

For those of you in desert climates, spiked or thorny plants aren't your only choices. There are many succulents and other native plants that are softer alternatives to prickly cactus, while still being drought-tolerant.

Using Spiked Plants Purposefully

Sleeping Beauty's castle wasn't surrounded by thorns for nothing! While we want the front of our homes to feel welcoming, there may be times when you wish to keep people away. In this case, you can use spiked or thorny plants to serve as deterrents or protective barriers, but try to keep them as far away from the front door as possible. If you love roses, by all means, grow roses. However, it feels best to keep those pretty (but thorny) plants away from the front walkway and the doorway of your home.

The Tale of the Unwelcoming Walkway

Several years ago, a very frustrated homeowner asked me for advice on how to sell his home. This particular home had been on and off the market for a couple of years, and the owner had become quite discouraged. The house was beautiful and priced well for the market. Still, no matter what he did, the owner hadn't received a single offer. People who toured this beautifully decorated, ocean-view home said they liked the house, but they would also tell the realtors that something about the house just didn't *feel* right. No one could figure out what was going on or what to do about it. In desperation, the client called me.

I almost laughed out loud when I saw the house. It was no mystery to me as to why it hadn't sold. The walkway leading up to the front door was lined with planters overflowing with large, scraggly cactus. The prickly cactus was provoking an uncomfortable, defensive reaction in visitors as if to say, "Go away!" These same unfriendly plants that greeted people when they first arrived also reinforced the negative impression when they left. The first impression and the last impression that the spiked plants created were off-putting for anyone interested in buying the house. The house may have been pretty, but there was something about it that left people uneasy.

I told my client that while the house itself was lovely, those sharp, hostile-feeling plants were making a negative impression on prospective buyers. I suggested that the cactus be replaced with soft, beautiful flowers, ferns, and other welcoming plants. Desperate, the client set to work that day making the changes we had talked about.

The next weekend, the realtor held another open house. This time, the house sold in three days after a bidding war between two interested buyers. It even wound up selling for much more than the asking price! The most incredible part of this story is that the plants were the only things that had changed. First impressions are powerful indeed. The subliminal messages we receive from our environment are very influential in affecting thoughts, behaviors, and decision-making.

Flowers Soothe Our Spirits

Flowers are a wonderful accent to any front yard and make a positive first impression. Behavioral scientists at Rutgers University[1] found that human beings are predisposed to reacting positively to the sight and smell of flowers. Think about it. What do we give when we want to cheer someone up or celebrate a special occasion? Flowers, of course.

The scientists theorize that we're programmed to respond positively to flowers based on our prehistoric interrelationship with nature. When human beings lived outdoors, flowers provided a rare glimpse of color and a pleasant respite from the abundance of browns, greens, and blues found in the natural landscape. Perhaps that's also why a rainbow gives us so much pleasure. The cheerful colors of flowers uplift us and provide an appreciation for the gifts from nature.[2]

Pretty pots of flowers on either side of the front door can go a long way to perk up your mood and raise your spirits. If you live in a place that's too cold for year-round flowers, a colorful red pot with a small evergreen near the front door will bring some color to the front of the home during dreary winter months.

Flowers can provide a wonderful distraction when there's something in your yard that's unsightly and cannot be changed. For example, many people living in newer housing developments have large, unattractive electrical boxes in their yards. To draw attention away from these eyesores, plant a colorful splash of flowers in a location a bit away from the box, and suddenly the box won't seem nearly as noticeable.

Winter Landscapes

If you live in a colder climate, snow and ice may limit your landscape options during winter months, but all is not lost. Here are some ideas to bring zest to your outdoor landscape during the dormancy of winter:

---

[1] Jeannette Haviland-Jones and others, "An Environmental Approach to Positive Emotion: Flowers," *Evolutionary Psychology* No. 3 (2005): 104-132.

[2] Ibid.

- Plant evergreen trees and shrubs to lend greenery
  and interest to winter landscapes.

- Vary the height of evergreen plants. If evergreens are not tall enough,
  they may lay hidden under blankets of snow for much of the winter.

- Add bird feeders to trees that can be seen from indoors.
  The birds will be grateful, and they're fun to watch.

- Consider trees that produce non-toxic berries during winter
  to add color and attract birds and animals to your yard.

- Select trees with beautiful bark patterns, which look
  especially nice during winter months. When their leaves are
  gone, the texture of the bark creates visual interest.

- Break up the monotony of a winter landscape with trees that have complex
  branch patterns. These will collect snow in unusual shapes and patterns.

- Plant bulbs. Anyone who has lived in a cold winter climate knows
  the delight of seeing bulb flowers poke their heads up out of the
  ground each spring, signaling the end of the dormancy of winter.

In addition to evergreen trees and shrubs, the following plants may offer variety to your winter landscape: Viking black chokeberry, yew shrubs, birch trees, winterberry holly, bayberry, Red-Oster dogwood, and plume grass. Check with your local garden center to find out which plants are best for your particular area.

Pathways: Straight versus Curved

Read through this exercise first and then try it: Close your eyes and relax. Imagine yourself walking on a forest path. Notice any birds, sounds, smells, and feelings you experience along the way. Imagine yourself walking a little further down the path. Notice the sunlight coming through the leaves, the gentle breeze stirring the branches, and any bird songs or other sounds filling the air. Keep this awareness as you "wander" along the path for a few more minutes. Eventually, your path opens to a meadow. When you get to the meadow, open your eyes, and "come back" to where you are now. After completing this exercise, look at figures 3.1 and 3.2.

Figure 3.1

Figure 3.2

Which path most closely resembles the one you envisioned? While there's no right or wrong answer, the vast majority of people will say that the path they envisioned was a meandering or curved path. The interesting thing to remember is that I never mentioned what *shape* the path was, whether straight or meandering. I just said "a forest path." Yet without being given the exact description of the path, 98 percent of people doing this exercise will say that they envisioned a curved path rather than a straight one. Try it with your friends and family. It's a fun way to see a basic feng shui concept at work. Let's explore this a bit more to discover how it can be applied to the feng shui of your home or yard.

Reality Check

Myth: Straight pathways are like poison arrows and bring bad luck.

When practicing feng shui, curved, meandering pathways are generally preferred over straight, linear ones. Some feng shui literature takes this principle to an extreme, warning that a straight path leading to one's front door is a portent to all sorts of calamities and should be avoided at all costs. Explanations for this fearmongering range from the humorous to the absurd. While it is, indeed, preferable to have a curved pathway rather than a straight one leading up to your door, the rationale is actually based on common sense and basic human nature—not on superstition or luck.

One of the most common explanations given for avoiding straight pathways in feng shui is that a straight pathway is like a "poison arrow" that sends negative energy toward the house and may potentially do harm to its occupants. Rest assured, there are no malevolent energies shooting toward you, should your front walkway be straight.

A few years ago, a feng shui "expert" informed me, in all seriousness, that meandering pathways are preferred because ghosts have no knees and cannot negotiate a curved pathway. He went on to say that, in order to keep ghosts out of your home, you must make sure that the walkway to your front door is not straight. He actually said this with a straight face!

While it's true that a curving path feels better to most people than a straight one, it's not because of superstition, "poison" or "silent" arrows, ghosts, or any other unseen force that perpetuates negative energy. The simple, logical reason that curved pathways are preferred is that the organic shape of a meandering path mimics migration routes found in nature. Your subconscious recognizes this natural shape as familiar and comforting.

In order for people and animals to navigate through a natural landscape, they must wander around boulders, trees, waterways, and other natural obstacles. A river, too, must curve as it winds its way around the barriers on its banks and in its bed.

A meandering pathway also forces you to slow your pace and relax while taking time to notice your surroundings. I'm sure Dorothy's journey to the Emerald City would have been much less interesting if the Yellow Brick Road was a straight line rather than a meandering path through the cornfields and forests of Oz.

Contrary to warding off bad luck, imaginary arrows, and the like, a meandering pathway offers another symbol of our intrinsic relationship to nature.

More Reasons for Curves

On a scientific note, another interesting explanation for the preference of meandering pathways over straight ones is supported by the research of psychologists Drs. Stephen and Rachel Kaplan of the University of Michigan. The

Kaplans explain that the human preference for winding paths is due to a natural attraction to mystery in one's environment. The concept is that, as human beings travel further into a natural outdoor setting, there's an innate curiosity that propels them along in order to find out what lies ahead.[1] Whatever the explanation, it's clear that most of us prefer the visual effect of curved, winding pathways to straight ones. The shape feels more agreeable, comfortable, and welcoming to most people.

If you already have a straight path or a sidewalk leading up to your front door and you can't or don't want to remove it, here are a few things you can do to visually soften the effect:

- Plant low-growing flowers along the edge of the sidewalk. The flowers add visual interest and slow down the approach to the house. Flowers also soften the straight lines of the walkway.

- Choose irregularly shaped stones for the path, such as slate and flagstone. Geometric patterns, like squares and rectangles, emphasize the straight lines of a walkway. Natural, irregular

Figure 3.3

[1] Stephen Kaplan, PhD, "Perception and Landscape: Conceptions and Misconceptions," *Environmental Aesthetics: Theory, Research and Application,* Jack L. Nasar, ed. (Cambridge: Cambridge University Press, 1988), 50.

shapes add more interest to the path. Stamped concrete with non-geometric patterns is an alternative to natural stone.

- Plant bushes or shrubs at irregular intervals along a straight walkway so that it feels more like a meandering pathway as seen in figure 3.3.

Street Configurations

In addition to the areas surrounding your home, the street on which you live also has qualities that contribute to either good or bad feng shui. Some of them are obvious. For example, no one says to a realtor, "I want to live on the busiest street you can find." It doesn't take a brain surgeon to figure out why living on a busy street isn't as desirable as living on a street that carries less traffic. Safety, noise, congestion, and a feeling of community are going to affect the way you feel about your house. So what *is* a desirable street configuration in feng shui?

Given the preference that most people have for curved, meandering pathways rather than straight ones, the same concept applies to residential streets. Ideally, all houses would be located on quiet, gently curving, well-marked streets that open onto other streets (that is, no dead ends). Like a gentle stream, the curve of the street slows traffic down, making the neighborhood feel more peaceful. A quiet street provides a feeling of comfort and safety. The positive feelings that such a street promotes can result in more favorable interactions between neighbors and a greater sense of community pride and satisfaction.

Cul-de-sacs

A cul-de-sac is a dead-end street with only one entrance and exit. In feng shui literature, much of the information on cul-de-sacs is confusing and misunderstood. Often, feng shui experts warn against the hazards of living on a cul-de-sac, striking fear in the hearts of families living in housing developments everywhere.

Builders know that families with small children often prefer the safety of cul-de-sacs and will pay a higher price, as much as twenty percent higher, for homes located on cul-de-sacs. The added benefit to builders is that cul-de-sacs allow

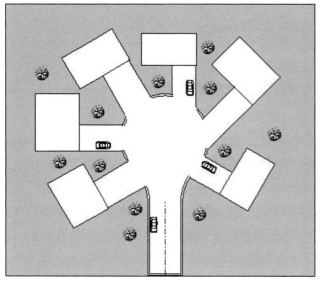

Figure 3.4

builders to fit more houses on oddly shaped pieces of land. Both of these reasons have made cul-de-sacs very popular in planned communities.

With the popularity of cul-de-sacs, the question looms: do they have good or bad feng shui? In answering this question, the first consideration is how tight the cul-de-sac is. Are there too many homes crowded into the cul-de-sac? Look at the available parking. If there's no room to park a car between the driveways on the cul-de-sac, then the cul-de-sac is too tight and therefore undesirable. Figure 3.4 illustrates a tight cul-de-sac. This configuration forces too many people to share too small a space, which forces social interaction and increases tension, often resulting in confrontations between residents.

When houses are built too closely together and when there's no outlet on a cul-de-sac, there can be a loss of privacy. When we feel a loss of privacy, we may experience increased feelings of vulnerability and may become more protective of our space. When animals' territories are encroached upon, they may become aggressive, and

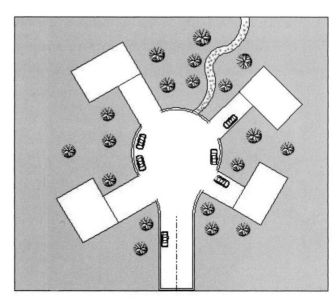

Figure 3.5

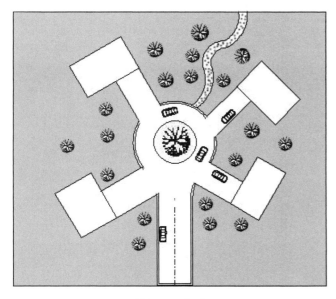

Figure 3.6

we can find the same response in humans. On the other hand, some cul-de-sacs are designed with large, open areas that give a feeling of expansiveness as seen in figure 3.5.

This extra space can alleviate the closed-in feeling of a cul-de-sac. Still other cul-de-sacs, like the one shown in figure 3.6, are large enough to provide a small circular park or roundabout that also gives a feeling of flow and spaciousness to the otherwise dead-end feel of a cul-de-sac. In these cases, a cul-de-sac can be a positive street configuration for residents. By taking into consideration the things that I mentioned above, you will be better able to decide whether or not living on a cul-de-sac is the right move for you and your family.

Reality Check

Myth: T-junctions, Y-junctions, and dead ends bring misfortune.

One street configuration that you should avoid at all costs is having your home positioned at the *end* of a T-junction, at the top of a cul-de-sac, or at a dead end.

This is another one of those feng shui requirements that's practical but often has some silly jargon associated with it, like this: If a "poison arrow"

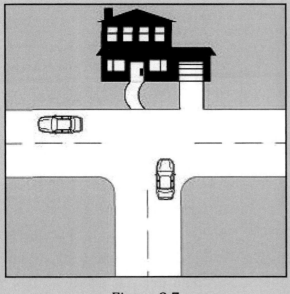

Figure 3.7

is directed at your house, then the house will attract "evil spirits." Or, the "energy" of the oncoming traffic will weaken the inhabitants of the house.

If you live in a home at the end of a junction or a cul-de-sac, do not be concerned that there's an arrow (poison or otherwise) coming at your home. What you DO need to consider is that vehicles, weighing *several thousand pounds each,* are coming toward your house several times a day! Forget the "poison arrows" and other explanations. The fact is that you are potentially very unsafe when cars are coming directly toward your home. How often do we turn on the news and find out that someone lost control of a car and went hurtling into the living room or bedroom of some poor, unsuspecting resident? It's not hard to imagine why people living in homes with these street configurations feel more vulnerable and uneasy in their everyday lives.

If you already live in a house that's positioned at the top of a cul-de-sac, T-junction, or dead end, the solution is to place a wall, a fence, dense shrubbery, or large trees between the home and the street. These objects will literally and figuratively lend a feeling of protection and safety to the home, which in turn will create more positive associations and experiences for anyone living there.

Home Proximity and Positioning

Proximity to Neighbors

One aspect that you need to consider when choosing where to live is how the proximity of others will affect you. The closer that homes are to each other, the greater the need for physical boundaries between the properties. If your home is built close to your neighbor's home, it's important that you and your neighbor respect each other's boundaries and needs for privacy. High fences, hedges, and window treatments can help to maintain feelings of autonomy.

If you're a person who requires a lot of space and privacy, then this type of arrangement may not be the best choice for you as you may always feel a sense of tension while living there. These feelings will increase the likelihood of negative interactions with your neighbors.

Proximity to the Street

In feng shui, homes that are built too close to the street often promote feelings of being exposed. When there's not a lot of space between the street and the house, privacy is diminished and feelings of vulnerability increase. If you're in a home like this, as with a home at the end of a cul-de-sac or T-junction, it's important to have a solid barrier such as a hedge, wall, or fence between the home and the street. This buffer adds much-needed privacy and safety, both important components of feeling comfortable in our homes.

Homes At or Below Street Level

Feng shui also recommends that a home be situated slightly above street level. This positioning enables the occupants to have a clear view of what's going on around the outside of their home, and it provides a greater sense of privacy and protection. Additionally, homes that are located at or below street level need to have exceptionally good drainage to avoid problems with dampness and flooding.

The Health and Safety of Your Home

Feng shui is about creating spaces that are safe and comfortable. Good feng shui encompasses many aspects, not the least of which are environmental concerns that you may have about pollution of the air or ground. Be sure to carefully inspect your home for mold, electromagnetic energy, radon, asbestos, chemicals, or other hidden and potentially harmful elements. The old adage, "better safe, than sorry," definitely applies here. There are experts in many communities who can come out to your property to determine the environmental safety of a home or building. If you suspect a problem, it's well worth the investment to have it checked out. With a proper assessment, you can then make informed choices about how to remedy the issue(s).

Power Lines

An important, but often overlooked, feng shui consideration is to make sure that the home is positioned away from any large power lines. High-voltage power lines create invisible areas of energy known as electromagnetic fields (also known as EMFs) that studies[1] have linked to health issues, such as cancer and childhood leukemia. Brain researcher, Dr. Eric Braverman states, "There is no question EMFs have a major effect on neurological functioning. They slow our brain waves and affect our long-term mental clarity. We should minimize exposures as much as possible to optimize neurotransmitter levels and prevent deterioration of health."[2]

An Electromagnetic "Field of Dreams"

Years ago, one of my former students called to share her excitement: after much searching, she'd finally found her dream home. This woman had attended several of my classes and was pretty sure she'd chosen a house with excellent feng shui. The

---

[1] National Institute of Environmental Health Sciences – National Institutes of Health, "Electric & Magnetic Fields," Health & Education webpage; http://www.niehs.nih.gov/health/topics/agents/emf/.

[2] Eric Braverman, MD, *The Edge Effect: Achieve Total Health and Longevity with the Balanced Brain Advantage* (New York: Sterling, 2005).

home was brand new and beautiful, had an excellent floor plan, and was located on a quiet street in a lovely neighborhood. The housing development had a lot of other families in it and good schools nearby, so my client was overjoyed at finding such a wonderful home in her price range. Before signing the final papers, she wanted me to make sure that she hadn't overlooked any feng shui issues the house might have.

When I approached the housing development, I noticed a row of huge, high-voltage power lines looming overhead. Many of the homes in this new community had been built either very close to or directly under these massive structures. When I met my client at the sales office, I had some serious reservations about the home even before I saw it, based on its proximity to those lines. When we arrived at the home she had chosen, I was dismayed to see that it was, indeed, built directly under the power lines.

My client eagerly showed off all the features of the home and explained what she was planning to change, once she and her family were moved in. Finally, she asked what I thought about the feng shui of the house.

I told her that, at first look, the home had excellent feng shui. The street location, the footprint of the home, and the flow throughout the home were excellent. She had certainly done a great job in applying what she had learned in class. However, she had forgotten this important lesson: always check the electromagnetic field reading in a house, especially with power lines so close to the property. I saw her face change from joyful to anxious.

I bring an EMF meter to all consultations. (Refer to the appendix for more information). This is a sensitive device that measures levels of electromagnetic energy in an environment. Unfortunately for my client, the meter showed dangerous levels of EMFs throughout the home, especially in the bedrooms at the back of the house. My client desperately asked if there was anything that could be done to alleviate the danger of the power lines. I had to tell her that, short of removing them, there was nothing she could do to make the house safe from their energy. I felt bad about disappointing her but also knew that it was better that she find out now, rather than after moving into the house. With a deep sigh, she resigned herself to continue searching for a better and safer home, which she eventually found.

Ideal Landforms in Feng Shui

In chapter 2, you learned the basic Form School feng shui principle of protecting your back. This same rule applies to the land surrounding your home. Just as you feel better when sitting with your back protected, you also feel better when there's a protective hill or support behind your home. You always want your back and sides protected while still being able to see what's coming from either side or directly toward you.

In feng shui, the ideal landform for a building is one that has a hill behind the structure, smaller hills on the left and right sides of the building, and the smallest hill in front of the home. This configuration is frequently referred to as "Armchair Position" as shown in figure 3.8. When a building is protected from the rear and the sides with a low barrier in the front, the home will feel more secure, protected, and comfortable, much as we feel when sitting in a comfortable armchair. This protection can be found either in the natural topography of the landscape or in man-made forms, such as raised areas, fences, walls, embankments, or hedges.

Figure 3.8

Reality Check

Myth: *A house located with a slope behind it will cause your money to roll down the hill.*

Several feng shui proponents state that, if a home is unprotected from the rear or has a drop-off behind it, all the money and fortune of the occupants will fly away or slide down the hill. While I personally don't believe in such a specific correlation and outcome, I do feel that living in a home that's unprotected from the rear can increase feelings of insecurity and vulnerability among the people who live there. It's hard to be all you can be and feel happy and productive when you're also feeling a nagging sense of vulnerability in your life. A home that feels exposed or unsupported from the rear will undoubtedly create a higher level of anxiety in residents, which can have an impact on the quality of life they experience while living there.

In order to have good feng shui *in* your home, it's important to have a feeling of protection *behind* your home. This feeling can be achieved by adding a secure wall, a fence, some low bushes, a dense hedge, or a hill behind the home, especially when it backs up to a downward slope or a drop-off. Many of my Southern California clients have homes situated on canyon rims. These clients tell me repeatedly that, although they love their home and the feeling of openness behind it, they can't figure out why they don't want to spend more time in their backyards. After I explain the effect of the drop-off, they suddenly understand their reluctance.

You *can* increase the sense of security in a home that backs up to a slope or canyon without sacrificing your view. Install a low wall, a fence, or some bushes along the edge of your property where it borders the slope. The barrier doesn't have to be high—two feet is enough to remedy the issue. This way, you'll still able to enjoy your view and have an added feeling of protection. Adding a visual barrier can change the way you experience your backyard and change the overall feeling of security and comfort within your home. In the same that way a frame or a mat around a picture makes it more interesting, the solid, low barrier along the back edge of the yard will, in turn, make the view more interesting.

Figure 3.9

The Goldilocks Principle in Gardens and Landscaping

In order to have a yard that feels "just right," you need to balance the extremes in your outdoor surroundings. Consider the following ideas to increase the good feng shui in your garden:

- Create areas of shade mixed with areas of sunlight. Place seating or a hammock in a shady corner of the yard where you can get out of the heat to relax or read a book.

- Keep trees and shrubs to scale with other landscape elements, including the house. For example, a tree that's too close to a home and that towers over it will make the inhabitants of the home feel oppressed by the tree's massive size, not to mention anxious over the possibility of it falling on the house.

- Balance hard and soft materials. A stone pathway, for example, may be softened with a border of flowers, and patio furniture with soft cushions will be more inviting and comfortable.

- Use color to add interest to monotonous landscapes. A healthy, green lawn may be beautiful, but the addition of flowers will really make the landscape "pop."

- Vary the topography of your landscape. Small hills or raised areas can add interest to a completely flat yard. You can also plant flowers and hedges that will grow to a variety of heights.

- Try to avoid planting any deliberately stunted plants such as bonsai, pygmy palms, dwarf palm trees, or any dwarf fruit trees. In feng shui, the energy of growth and expansion is preferred to the energy of a plant that is in any way limited.

One of the best indicators of whether or not your environment needs balancing is to be aware of the words that you use to describe it. If you want to find out what specifically needs to be balanced in your landscaping, make a list of sentences or words that best describe your yard. Anytime you find yourself using the word "too" in describing a feature in your home or garden, it's a strong indicator that you need to remedy the situation. If the yard is "too" boring, liven it up with some color. If the garden is "too" dark or shady, clear some foliage to bring in more light. If a backyard has "too much" concrete or "too many" hard surfaces, soften it with plants, and so on.

Your Five Senses in the Garden

Your physical senses connect the inner self to the outer world. The five senses of smell, taste, hearing, sight, and touch are the avenues by which you gather information from the environment. Sensory information helps you know whether or not a place makes you feel good. In order to enhance your environment, it's important to consider the impression that your surroundings are making on each of your senses. When you place items in your garden or yard that positively stimulate your five senses, you are working to optimize your outdoor space.

Scent

When planning your garden, pay attention to plant fragrances, especially with the plants that will be near the front door. Your sense of smell is the strongest and most primitive link to memories. In the garden, scent can be employed in delightful ways. Each climate type offers an abundance of choices for scents that will please and refresh your spirit. Consider jasmine, lavender, lilac, lemon geranium, lily of the valley, freesia, sweet pea, sage, pine, and even freshly cut grass to transport you to another level of awareness and feeling. Scents are highly subjective, and not all people find the same scents pleasing. Be sure that *you* will enjoy the scents of the plants in your yard before you commit to them.

A "Scents-able" Way to Welcome Guests

A wonderful way to welcome guests to your home is to plant fragrant flowers near your front door. Then, right before your friends arrive, rub the leaves or flowers of the scented plants in your hands to release their oils and sprinkle the plants with water. Your guests will arrive at your door to a pleasant aromatherapy experience and feel uplifted even before they get inside your home.

Texture

To appeal to your sense of touch, consider adding textures to your landscape that you can feel underfoot or with your hands: smooth stones, pebbles, river rock, flagstone, or textured surfaces. Plants like kangaroo paw, bottlebrush, lamb's ear, delicate ferns, and other sensual foliage will give interest and variety to your landscape. Consider adding trees with interesting textures on their bark and branches such as birch, poplar, maple, or apple trees.

Taste

There's a certain amount of respect that fruit trees command. When asked what kind of tree this one or that one is, people will proudly declare, "It's a pear (or orange, lemon, apple, pomegranate) tree." Fruit trees, herb gardens, and vegetable plots are terrific additions to any landscape. When choosing plants for your yard, be sure to appeal to as many senses as possible. Rosemary, mint, oregano, thyme, sage, and basil not only taste good but smell wonderful. Flowers such as nasturtium, lavender, and honeysuckle are beautiful, and certain varieties are edible and delicious.

When growing plants and trees that you plan to eat from, avoid pesticides and grow organically. Growing your own fruits, vegetables, and herbs brings satisfaction and puts healthy, low-cost food on your table. Even the White House has a vegetable garden!

Sight

For most people, sight is the dominant sense when it comes to experiencing the environment. Repeat after me, "Ugly, bad. Pretty, good." It's really that simple. If something in your garden does not please your sense of sight, it must be addressed.

Flowers enhance most any landscape. Place flowers along pathways, near the front door, and along the edges of larger gardens to create a pleasing feast for the eyes. The visual appeal of the colors can lift your spirits and positively impact the rest of your day.

Be sure to fix, repair, clean, or paint anything that's unsightly. Your garden and yard should be places to relax and regroup, which is pretty hard to do when a bunch of unfinished chores are staring you in the face!

Sound

Adding sound to the landscape is as easy as adding a wind chime, a bell, or a gently babbling fountain. If there's an unwanted sound source nearby, such as a road, a playground, or an airport, the gentle bells of wind chimes or the trickling of water will help to relax and refocus your sense of hearing. Chapter 6 presents the best locations for water features and wind chimes.

Wayfinding and Feng Shui

Have you ever gotten lost while looking for a home or a place of business? The frustration and confusion of not knowing where you are or how to get somewhere can be very stressful. Environmental psychologists have a term for the way people navigate their environments: it's called *wayfinding*. When wayfinding becomes overwhelming because house or building numbers aren't clearly visible or street names are unmarked, poorly marked, or too similar, stress levels increase, and feelings of insecurity take over. On the other hand, when wayfinding is easy, stress levels are lowered, and you're more likely to arrive at your destination feeling positive and relaxed.

In feng shui, it's important that the entry to your home be clearly visible. If the main door to your home isn't obvious, guests may become frustrated and uncomfortable. A home without a well-defined entrance can create problems for guests and occupants alike. A couple of years ago, friends of mine bought a beautiful new home and were eager to show it to me. When I arrived, I parked in front of the house, got out of my car, and proceeded to walk to the front door. The problem was, there was no front door. The home had a garage on one side, a side gate on the other, and windows along the front facing the street—but no front door. I didn't know quite what to do. I began to feel awkward and uncomfortable. Finally, I called my friends on my cell phone to tell them that I was standing outside and couldn't figure out how to get to their front door. They laughed and told me that it happened all the time. It turned out that the side gate led to a door around the corner that was the entry to the home.

Once inside, I was given a tour of the home. I brought up the fact that it wasn't good feng shui for people to not know where the front door was when they arrived. I explained that, by not having an obvious front entrance, visitors would likely experience an increased sense of anxiety and tension—feelings that are not conducive to a happy social experience. I asked my friends whether they had noticed anything different about their social interactions since moving into the home. They admitted that their friends and guests seemed to be tense when they arrived, and they felt as though they had to work extra hard to put them at ease. Their social gatherings didn't seem to be as much fun, and they were having a hard time understanding why they had begun to entertain less and less.

My friends were motivated to sit down with me and brainstorm ways to solve the problem. We spent over an hour discussing how to draw the eye from the street to the location of the front door by installing a clearly marked pathway, planters, markers, and signage. After I left that evening, my friends got right to work remodeling their entrance. They still used the same gate, but for security, they installed an intercom doorbell system that made it easier to find out who was arriving. After clearly demarcating the entrance to their home, my friends told me how much better they felt about living there. They no longer had to apologize to irritated visitors about the difficult-to-find entrance, and friends no longer felt confused or frustrated when they arrived at the house for the first time. My friends discovered that the entry to their home had been creating more stress than they initially realized. Once the problem was solved, their enjoyment of the home and their love of entertaining vastly improved.

Tips for Streets with the Same Names

In feng shui, streets that repeat the same name over and over again in a neighborhood are undesirable. For example, if one neighborhood includes Maple Street, Maple Lane, and Maple Road, it can be very confusing for friends and visitors to decipher which "Maple" will lead them to your home. To make directions easier to follow, give lots of visual cues. "Turn left at the yellow house on the corner of Maple Drive and Maple Street." People tend to remember visual cues more easily than non-visual cues. Following are some simple ways to improve the wayfinding experience for visitors and friends.

House Numbers

Make sure that your house or building number is clearly visible from the street. Trim bushes and trees that may be blocking the numbers, and apply a fresh coat of paint if the numbers are faded. Friends, mail carriers, delivery drivers, and emergency personnel will appreciate your efforts. Plus, knowing that your home or office is clearly marked can make you feel safer and more at peace. In feng shui, we are always striving to maintain that sense of peace and calm.

Giving Directions

Mention landmarks, street configurations, and any other pertinent bits of information when giving directions to first-time visitors. Remember that the *fastest* way may not be the *easiest* way for someone who's unfamiliar with where you live or work.

Type up a sheet of directions that you can email or fax. If you know that online mapping sites or GPS navigation systems usually come up with incorrect directions, *be sure* to mention this in advance to visitors.

Parking

Offer advice on where to park. Again, if parking is a problem, let people know in advance. For commercial areas, inform visitors as to whether they'll need to pay for parking or tolls. People are less stressed when they know what to expect when they arrive.

Front Doors

The front door is another focal point that impacts the first impression of any home. The look of a beautiful home can be marred by an ugly, faded, or worn front door. In fact, if you are trying to sell your home, your front door can actually influence a buyer either way on whether they want to own your home.

Reality Check

Myth: Red front doors bring good luck.

Have you ever heard that you must have a red front door in order to have good feng shui? Frequently, clients will ask whether or not they need to paint their front doors red. Usually, they've read or heard that a red door will bring "good luck." As I have shared with you, feng shui has nothing to do with luck, and painting your front door red or any other color isn't going to change that.

After hearing about the lucky red front door so many times, I decided to do a little investigating to discover how this practice began. Like many traditions, this one had very practical origins, which over time were lost and subsequently replaced by symbolism. Hundreds of years ago in rural China, people didn't have the luxuries of heating and electricity in their homes. In the cold regions of China, people would build dwellings that faced south to ensure the maximum number of sunlight hours and warmth throughout the day. This, of course, makes perfect sense.

In China (and in feng shui), south is the direction associated with the element of fire. The color that represents the fire element is red. Therefore, it was reasoned that the color red on the front door would symbolize the benefits of the preferred southern exposure to the sun. If a home could not be built to face south, painting the front door red was considered the next best thing.

Over time, the practical aspect of southern exposure was forgotten, and all that remained was the symbolism and tradition that a red front door is more fortunate than any other color. This tradition has been passed on through time and has become a symbol rather than a practicality. With this information in hand, feel free to paint your front door any color you prefer, even if it is red. Just know that if you choose red and expect something wondrous to happen, you may be disappointed!

Choose a front door that's both safe and attractive. As you're learning, feelings of safety and comfort go hand in hand. A solid door is preferable to a door with glass included. Glass is less resistant to break-ins and gives visitors a view into the home from the outside. Even frosted or beveled glass doors show shadows and movement inside the home. For a greater feeling of safety (and in turn, comfort), opt for a solid front door. If you need a window to add light to your entry, select a door with a window placed up high where it's difficult to easily see inside your home. The window must also be too small for a person to crawl through or reach through to turn your doorknob. These features will enhance safety and comfort while allowing natural light into the entry.

Reality Check

Myth: A sticky front door blocks opportunities.

One frequently misunderstood idea in feng shui is that a sticky front door will cause obstacles in your life and block opportunities. The underlying message is that the energy of the door itself is creating blockages. This, of course, is untrue. What is true, however, is that anything in our surroundings that doesn't work properly can create frustration, tension, and anxiety. Sometimes those negative feelings can have dramatic repercussions.

For example, let's say that your front door sticks and is very hard to open. You have an important meeting at work first thing in the morning. On your way out of the house, you have to spend a couple of minutes wrestling with your front door. The sticky door creates a delay, increases frustration, and raises your level of tension. Now preoccupied with being late for your big meeting, you run a stop sign, get a ticket, and arrive twenty minutes late for the meeting, landing you in a heap of trouble with your boss. Did the sticky front door actually *cause* your problem? Of course not, but your reaction to it did play a part in the way you experienced the rest of your day.

It doesn't just have to be a sticky front door. Feng shui encourages us to attend to and alleviate anything in our lives that's a source of frustration, negativity, or tension. Something as seemingly unimportant as a front door that sticks can in turn, have a snowball effect on the way you go about your day and the interactions you have with others, sometimes in profound ways.

In chaos theory, the cause and effect between one seemingly small event and far-reaching consequences is known as the butterfly effect.

The butterfly effect theorizes that the beating of a butterfly's wings on one side of the world can change airflow patterns around it enough to result in a tornado or a hurricane on the other side of the world.

So if your door squeaks or sticks or is hard to open, fix it, along with anything else in your home that needs repair. Saving yourself moments of frustration and irritability throughout your day are important aspects to living a well-balanced life, and a well-balanced life is the goal of good feng shui.

Chi, Life Force Energy, and Their Effect on Our Surroundings

In feng shui, life force energy is known as *chi* [chee], which is also spelled *ch'i* and *qi*. When surrounded by beauty, healthy plants, and animals, you experience positive emotions and feelings of vitality. In this case, a space is considered to have good chi. When the surrounding area lacks life force energy, you may feel depleted, lethargic, and depressed.

There's a community just a few miles from where I live that always depresses me. Whenever I pass through this part of town, I feel drained, even though it's a normal, middle-class neighborhood. One day while driving to a consultation in this community, it dawned on me why I feel this way every time I go there: this neighborhood has almost *no* trees! Although it's a fairly old community, for some reason, trees are not included in the landscape. The effect is a feeling of dullness and lethargy—something that many of my friends also mention when driving through this area.

Without trees to shade the streets, sidewalks, and yards, there are very few children playing outside or people walking in the neighborhood. There are almost no birds or any other signs of life, except for cars moving up and down the streets. It simply doesn't feel like a nurturing or happy place. It's fairly safe to say that an area like this doesn't promote vibrant life force energy. This neighborhood is certainly not a place with good feng shui or good chi.

When the area surrounding your home is healthy and vibrant, that energy impacts the way you experience your space and your life. Beautiful healthy plants and animals increase positive feelings of vitality and improve our energy levels. Trees provide oxygen, help clean the air, and provide a place for birds to nest and sing. Colorful flowers provide beauty and encourage butterflies to flit from blossom to blossom. Plants provide food and dwelling places for animals. All of this life force contributes to your own vitality and vibrancy. Without healthy chi around you and inside of you, you may experience depression and even illness. Therefore, it's very important to keep your landscape and the area surrounding your home as healthy and as vital as possible.

You may be unable to change the landscape in your entire neighborhood, but you can change the landscape around your home. And maybe if you set an example, the trend will catch on! To help bring more vitality to your yard, try the following:

- Include plants that attract butterflies and birds.
- Provide birdbaths and bird feeders.
- Add koi ponds.
- Provide bat houses. Bats are very beneficial in areas with large mosquito populations.
- Avoid toxic chemicals and fertilizers. Opt for healthier alternatives.
- Plant trees that will beautify the area and provide shade and shelter for birds and animals.
- Add items that provide movement such as fountains, wind chimes, and weather vanes.

The Soothing Properties of Water

Flowing water provides a soothing, auditory source and can mask undesirable sounds such as traffic, barking dogs, or neighbors. When adding water to an environment, it's best to consider the following:

- Keep the water clean and the water fixtures in excellent working order. Clean up any stagnant water, and fix or remove broken spas, hot tubs, and unused fountains.

- Avoid vanishing-edge pools. While these pools have a certain visual impact, they also contribute to feelings of vulnerability. A vanishing-edge pool exaggerates feelings of being unprotected and unsafe.

- Avoid using bleach or other chemicals in fountains and pools. Water features attract wildlife, so opt for one of the many non-toxic alternatives for treating water.

- Locate pools and water features preferably in the east, southeast, and north portions of the yard. Try to avoid placing water in the south, if possible. Details on placing water features are covered more extensively in chapter 6.

Getting Organized Outdoors

Too often, I meet with clients who use the exterior areas of their homes as storage for neglected and unwanted items. I've seen everything from old box springs to kitchen sinks dumped in the yard or alongside the house by owners who meant to dispose of these items but never quite got around to it.

I met with a lovely client several years ago who had, what appeared to be, a neat and attractive home. As we toured the house, I asked why she kept the curtains in her dining room closed, as they made the room feel dark and oppressive. She became self-conscious and replied that the large, dining room window looked into the side yard where she and her husband had stored many unwanted objects over the years. I asked her to open the curtains, so I could get a better idea of what she was talking about. Reluctantly, she opened the curtains and revealed a side yard filled with an old bed frame, stacks of lumber, piles of bricks, a washing machine, two broken sinks, and even a toilet!

When I asked how she felt about having all that stuff piled alongside her home, she let out a long sigh and told me that it depressed her and made her feel embarrassed and frustrated. She admitted that this stuff had been sitting out there since they'd completed a home remodeling project almost five years ago. Her drapes had been not opened in all this time.

Out of sight is *not* out of mind. I reminded my client that feng shui is all about feeling happy and uplifted. Anything that brings you down needs to be remedied. I pointed out that the decision to dump all the unwanted objects into the side yard was making her feel bad about her home and was affecting the way the house felt on the inside as well.

As we'll discuss in more detail in the next chapter, holding on to clutter contributes to a whole host of problems that could easily be avoided with just a little effort. Instead of using your yard as a dumping ground, roll up your sleeves, and get rid of that stuff. Rent a dumpster, call a junk removal company, have a thrift store pick it up, or sell it all at a garage sale. Whatever you do, give yourself a deadline. Once the space is empty, you'll feel such freedom and joy that the effort it took will have been more than worthwhile.

Here are some more ways to help you get organized outside: Get rid of or fix anything that's broken or needs repair. Set up storage containers (available at your local home improvement center) for items such as rakes, lawn mowers, potting soil, and garden tools. Remember that out of sight does *not* mean out of mind! Make sure that everything you own is something you love, want, need, or use. Provide storage solutions for trash containers. I've seen the exteriors of many homes ruined by a jumble of trash containers littering the area. Keep trash areas clean and organized and preferably out of view. You don't want them to be the first thing you see when you drive up to your home. By consciously integrating feng shui principles into your outdoor environment, you're increasing the positive energy inside your home. Remember that when you create an optimal first impression outside, you're going to have a more positive outlook toward whatever awaits you on the other side of your front door.

Chapter 4
Feng Shui Basics for Home Interiors

Feeling is the language of the soul. If you want to know what's true
for you about something, look to how you're feeling about it.

— *Neale Donald Walsch*

N ow that you've spiffed up the front yard and your spirits are rising as you reach the front door, let's keep the positive energy flowing through the rest of your home. Before I get into the specifics for each room, there are some important basics to keep in mind as you implement feng shui changes inside your home.

Let Your Feelings Be Your Guide

When people ask me what feng shui does, I reply that feng shui helps to create a space that **feels** *as good as it looks.* Whether or not you have an intuitive sense of good design, you do know how you feel within a certain setting. When a space feels good, your body and mind relax into a greater sense of well-being. When a space doesn't feel good, you avoid spending any more time in it than you have to. Paying attention to how you *feel* as you pass from room to room is a good indication of the feng shui of that space. Sometimes it's obvious why a space doesn't feel good, and sometimes the reasons are subtler. Imagine yourself sitting on a hard, plastic seat in an airport waiting area. Now, imagine sitting in your favorite lounge chair at home. It's clear that these two settings produce very different moods. But, what about deciphering why everyone seems to congregate in the family room rather than in the living room? The answer to this question takes a bit more exploring.

Nature's Role Inside Your Home

Until very recently, human beings depended solely upon nature and natural resources to stay alive. Even now, this intrinsic relationship with nature carries over to the way you experience your surroundings. Homes that include natural shapes, colors, images, textures, and materials in their design feel better than homes that do not. By integrating nature into your surroundings, you are strengthening this instinctive connection to the natural world.

Of all the elements found in nature, people generally have the greatest fondness for wood (including plants and flowers). Most likely, this affinity for wood comes from the instinctive knowledge that plants provide survival elements in the form of oxygen, food, shelter, and clothing. Adding wood elements to a space can do wonders to increase feelings of beauty, relaxation, and comfort—unless a room is located in an area where feng shui suggests that wood elements be minimized. (This is covered in chapter 6.) Here are a few suggestions on integrating wood into your décor:

- Add houseplants, remembering to keep them healthy and to avoid plants with spiked leaves.

- Install flooring and floor coverings made from renewable and recycled materials, such as hardwood, bamboo, and sisal.

- Consider wood wall coverings (such as grass cloth) as well as wood molding and trim.

- Furnish your space with wood furniture, including wicker.

- Accessorize with woven baskets and trunks.

- Display fresh flowers.

- Incorporate cloth items made from cotton, bamboo, and hemp.

- Emphasize windows that have a view to a forest, a garden, or trees.

- Add wood décor in the form of figurines, picture frames, wall hangings, or screens.

- Hang artwork depicting plants, flowers, and forests.

As a side note, please make sure that the wood materials you're using are *not* from rare or endangered plants or trees!

Feng Shui, Décor, and Interior Design

Feng Shui and Décor Styles

Many people mistakenly believe that when a space has good feng shui, it's been decorated in a Chinese theme or style. You don't need to decorate your home with Chinese knickknacks, objects, or artwork in order to practice good feng shui, although you're certainly welcome to if that's your preference. Feng shui is an *approach* to design and can be applied to any décor, whether contemporary, traditional, or eclectic, but it's not a design *style* in and of itself.

I was once asked to consult on the design of a large, upscale sushi restaurant. I'd done the feng shui for the client's first restaurant, and his business became so successful after the consultation that he wanted to ensure the same success for his next restaurant. During the planning and design phase, I met with my client's architect. The architect made it very clear that he wasn't thrilled about having input from anyone, least of all "the feng shui lady."

Before we had even started to discuss the project, he said to me in a rather snide tone, "I don't know why they're asking for *your* advice. This is a Japanese restaurant, not a Chinese one." I explained that feng shui has nothing to do with Chinese themes and everything to do with how customers experience the space. It took quite a bit of convincing, but eventually the architect became inspired by the suggestions I made, and we ended up with an incredible design as a result of our collaboration. The new restaurant was not only beautiful but also tremendously successful.

Feng Shui and Interior Design

Feng shui and interior design are interconnected and strongly influence one another. I've seen interiors where feng shui principles have been completely ignored in order to make a certain visual statement, but these interiors certainly aren't places where people feel comfortable or relaxed. I've also seen interiors where feng shui principles have been incorporated incorrectly, with no consideration for aesthetics, and these spaces are neither beautiful nor comfortable.

People often become interested in feng shui because they want their homes to be attractive and peaceful but have no idea how to go about creating that special atmosphere of relaxation and comfort. Together, good design principles and feng shui can create spaces where your body feels safe, your mind can be set free, and your senses delight in all that the space has to offer. There are many simple design principles that anyone can practice to create a more pleasing environment, and you don't have to go to school for years to learn them. The remainder of this chapter is devoted to décor tips and techniques that can improve the interior design of your home, which will help to create better feng shui.

Natural and Artificial Lighting

Sun Exposure, Natural Light, and Room Positioning

An important but often overlooked component of determining whether a home feels good is how much sunlight travels through the rooms throughout the day. Lighting and light patterns have a strong influence on the way people experience a home. The famous architect Frank Lloyd Wright carefully integrated the play of sunlight throughout the designs of his homes to make them more architecturally interesting.[1]

Short of picking up the home and turning it around or adding additional windows and skylights, natural light patterns cannot be changed, so they must be considered carefully. Many people buy a home after visiting it just once or twice and

---

[1] Grant Hildebrand, *Origins of Architectural Pleasure* (Berkeley: University of California Press, 1999), 58-59.

with little or no consideration of the flow of natural light in the home throughout the day. Think of the rooms in your home where natural light is emphasized, either because there's too much or too little. The way you experience specific rooms—such as kitchens, bedrooms, and gathering rooms—is strongly influenced by the amount of sunlight they receive during the day.

The ancient Chinese acknowledged the importance of sunlight patterns in their homes. Without the luxuries of indoor heat and electric lights, the ancient Chinese carefully positioned their homes to optimize the natural light and heat received from the sun. If you're deciding whether or not to move into a new home, take time to ask yourself the following questions:

- Is having a sunny kitchen in the morning important to me?

- Which rooms will receive the most heat and light during the day, and which rooms will be cooler and darker?

- Do I prefer a gathering room with an abundance of natural light, or do I prefer a cozier atmosphere?

- Would I prefer to have the sun wake me in the morning, or would I rather have a darker room for sleeping?

- Will my home office receive the quality and quantity of natural light that I prefer during the times that I'll be working in there?

- Is the backyard sunny or shady most of the day?

Above all, consider whether the home will provide adequate warmth and light for the climate. If you live in a colder northern climate, for example, you may require more direct sunlight to feel best. On the other hand, those living in warmer southern climates may prefer less direct sunlight entering the home, particularly in the afternoons. Remember that heat and light will also affect energy consumption during the winter and summer months.

I've met with clients who were dismayed to find out (after they bought their home) that the family room is shaded most of the day or that the kitchen doesn't receive enough direct sunlight to dispel a feeling of gloom. Some people are more sensitive to light than others, so this is an important factor in determining whether a home will actually *feel* good to you while you're living there.

If you're thinking of purchasing or renting a particular home, make arrangements to visit the home at least three different times: once in the morning, once around midday, and once in the late afternoon. Make sure that the electric lights are turned off so that only natural light illuminates the home. Note how the light moves through the rooms and how the mood in the rooms changes as the light changes. Experiencing the home's ambience at three different times during the day will give you a better idea of how it will actually *feel* to live in the home. By considering the movement of natural light through the home, you'll have one more piece of the puzzle to help determine whether this home would be a good fit for you and your family.

Artificial Lighting

Proper lighting in a room greatly impacts our physical and mental health. Sunlight is made up of many different wavelengths and frequencies that directly affect mood, body rhythms, the endocrine system, the immune system, and vitamin absorption—all of which contribute to general health and well-being. When natural sunlight isn't available, your physical and mental health can be adversely affected. Fortunately, there are many choices in artificial lighting for homes and offices. Artificial lights that mimic the natural-light spectrum can be an excellent alternative to traditional incandescent, partial-spectrum lights.

One comprehensive study, conducted over three decades by Dr. Fritz Hollwich, Professor of Ophthalmology at the University of Muenster, West Germany, demonstrated the long-term effects of working under partial-spectrum (artificial) lighting.[2] Dr. Hollwich and his staff determined that, "Subjects who spent the majority of their time under artificial fluorescent light had increased levels of cortisol [a hormone released in response to stress] and lower levels of mood-

---

[2] Fritz Hollwich, PhD, *The Influence of Ocular Light Perception on Metabolism in Man and in Animal*, Hunter and Hildegarde Hannum, trans. (New York: Springer-Verlag, 1979).

regulating hormones including melatonin and serotonin." When the study subjects were re-tested following exposure to full-spectrum lighting, their hormone levels returned to normal.

Neither partial-spectrum lights nor fluorescent lights emit the same spectrum as natural, full-spectrum light, providing only a very narrow range of light waves that prevent our bodies from achieving optimal physical and mental health.[3] Fortunately, lighting choices now include simulated, full-spectrum alternatives. I prefer to replace partial-spectrum bulbs with full-spectrum bulbs, which are healthier, energy efficient, and environmentally friendly. Exposure to full-spectrum lighting is said to do the following:

- Improve mood

- Increase mental awareness, concentration, and work productivity[4]

- Reduce eye-strain

- Contribute to better sleep patterns

- Provide accurate color perception and visual clarity

- Enhance the immune system

- Reduce stress

In addition to these benefits, energy-efficient full-spectrum lighting can reduce energy costs by up to 75 percent. From a décor perspective, full-spectrum lighting eliminates the dingy, yellow tones associated with partial-spectrum lighting, allowing the true colors of your paint, furnishings, and accessories to show.

One of my clients told me that she actually cried tears of joy after replacing the fluorescent light tubes in her kitchen with full-spectrum tubes. "I feel like I just installed a skylight for a fraction of the cost!" she said. She couldn't get over how

---

[3] John N. Ott, *Health and Light: The Effects of Natural and Artificial Light on Man and Other Living Things* (New York: Pocket Books, reprint edition April 1, 2000).

[4] Frank H. Mahnke, *Color, Environment, & Human Response*, (New York: John Wiley & Sons, Inc., New York, 1996), 121.

easy it was to change her once-depressing kitchen into a place that she actually enjoyed, just by changing some light bulbs!

While full-spectrum, indoor lighting can't replace exposure to natural sunlight, it is a huge step toward bringing the natural world indoors. If you can't find the bulbs that you're looking for at a local home improvement store, check out the variety of sources online for energy-efficient bulbs that mimic the natural-light spectrum. Once you've installed full-spectrum light bulbs throughout your home, you'll be amazed at the difference. Your home will not only look better, but it will feel better, too. (Note: Artificially simulated, full-spectrum lighting may be too bright for relaxing in the evenings, so consider installing dimmer switches or using bulbs with lower wattages for softer evening light.)

Full-spectrum lighting even plays a part in looking your best. When applying make-up in the morning, do so in a room that has plenty of natural light. Even if this means toting your cosmetics and make-up mirror into the kitchen or living room, applying make-up in natural light makes a huge difference in the way you're going to look when you step out the door. If you regularly apply your make-up in a room with artificial, partial-spectrum lighting, you're doing so in light that emits only a small portion of the light spectrum—the very unflattering, yellow spectrum, which changes the way colors and textures appear. When applying make-up at night, do so in a room with full-spectrum lighting. This will prevent you from looking like you're headed to a Halloween party, rather than out for a night on the town.

To look your color-coordinated best, add full-spectrum lights to your dressing area. For gentlemen, choosing which socks and tie to wear with a suit is a choice that should be made under full-spectrum lighting. You don't want to arrive at the party wearing brown socks with navy slacks!

Color and Paint Choices

The subject of color gets a lot of press with regard to feng shui. When clients ask me, "Which color is best for this room?" My answer is always the same, "Any color you love and will be happy living with." Color choice is highly subjective, and preferences are influenced by gender, past experiences, cultural backgrounds, and a host of other factors. Some studies indicate that people are instinctively attracted to decorating in colors that look good on them, so look to your closet for inspiration. Living only with what you love and what makes *you* happy is good feng shui.

One important point I'd like to make about color and feng shui is that you do *not* have to paint your home according to feng shui colors in order to have good feng shui! This is a very common misunderstanding that people have when integrating feng shui principles into their homes. In chapter 6, I share how the five elements of water, wood, fire, earth, and metal affect the feng shui of different areas of your surroundings and of your life. While it's true that these elements have colors associated with them, the colors were never intended to be the colors that you *had* to paint the rooms of your home.

Several years ago, a woman named Anne called me in tears. Anne told me that she had hired a feng shui consultant to advise her on decorating her home and was now devastated by how her home looked since making the enhancements. Anne was told that she absolutely *had* to paint the rooms in her home in specific colors so that the feng shui principles would "work." These colors included purple, blue, pink, gray, red, gold, and green. Anne protested, but the consultant stood firm, insisting that Anne paint these rooms as soon as possible in order to bring "good luck" into her home and her life.

After the rooms were painted with the "feng shui" colors that the consultant had insisted upon, Anne was horrified. Afraid to paint over the garish colors for fear of inviting bad luck, Anne called me for a consultation. I'd consulted for a friend of Anne's recently who had been delighted with the results. In particular, Anne's friend mentioned that I hadn't recommended anything extreme or silly and encouraged Anne to have her house analyzed once more by a different feng shui expert.

When I got to Anne's house, I could immediately see why she was so upset: Her husband's office was painted cotton-candy pink; the master bath was lipstick red; the master suite was royal purple; and the living room was apple green. It was truly awful. Anne's house looked more like a home for wayward clowns than a place of beauty and harmony.

I shared with Anne that the most important goal of feng shui is to create a space that *feels* good. In order to do this, she would need to repaint her home's interior in the soft neutral colors that she enjoyed. Anne was incredibly relieved, but it took a little convincing to reassure her that nothing bad was going to happen once she painted over the outlandish colors. I felt bad for Anne because she had wasted her time and money on a ridiculous recommendation. Once her home was repainted, she called to tell me how much better and happier she felt. Anne also mentioned that her husband, a fifty-year-old stockbroker, was delighted *not* to have his home office painted in a color that was better suited to a five-year-old girl!

Painting your home in colors that you dislike can increase feelings of depression, fatigue, and irritability, which is counterproductive to creating good feng shui in your space. Never live with colors that you don't like no matter what you may have read in a book regarding the "benefits" of those colors. Your intuition, likes, and dislikes are much better indicators of which colors are "right" for you, rather than a one-size-fits-all approach to color design. Certainly this concept makes more sense and is more meaningful than painting a room some bizarre color and expecting it to change your fortune.

Guidelines and Tips on Painting

Although your home doesn't have to be painted in specific colors to produce good feng shui, there are certain considerations to bear in mind when painting your home's interior. In general, most people feel comfortable when surrounded by neutral, non-distracting colors like those found in nature. Soft browns, greens, and blues are more soothing than bright colors. An abundance of white in a room can cause eyestrain and fatigue, while bold colors, which call attention to a room and bring excitement, should be used in moderation. Blue is generally an unappetizing color for a kitchen, as there's no naturally blue food (with the exception of blueberries), and red stimulates the appetite. Cold wet rooms, like bathrooms, often feel better in warm earth tones. In chapter 5, I go into more detail on each room and occasionally suggest a color palette, but ultimately how you *feel* in a room is the most important consideration when enhancing its feng shui.

Painting around Skylights

Skylights are wonderful for bringing in light and creating spaciousness in a home's interior. If you have a skylight in your home, consider painting the surfaces around it in a warm shade rather than a cool shade. If using white, a warmer hue of white will look better than a cool hue. This will make the light that comes in from the skylight feel warm and pleasing, rather than cold and uninviting.

Matching Colors for Furnishings

Let's say that you have a beautiful area rug in your living room and you'd like to find some throw pillows to match it. You go shopping, and you find pillows that you think are the right color. At home, however, you soon discover that the pillows are much too orange, too bright, too green, too something! Frustrated, you trudge back to the store to return the pillows (if the store will let you) and try again. It may take several tries—and plenty of irritation—before you find a color that's just right.

Instead of the trial-and-error approach, here's a simple way to take the guesswork out of finding the right color when matching something in your home: bring along a fabric swatch from the rug, drapes, or cushion that you're trying to match. This way, you'll be able to tell immediately whether something is going to work. If bringing the actual item or a swatch of it is impossible, go to your local paint store and select several paint swatches that are close to the color you're trying to match. Bring the paint swatches home and figure out which ones are the closest to the color you're shopping for. Once you've found a paint swatch that matches the color you're looking for, take it with you when shopping for accessories. You can also use this method to match things like tile, granite, furniture, carpet, and drapes.

You can even create entire color palettes for each room with paint swatches. This way, when you go out shopping for pillows, towels, furniture, drapes, artwork, or accessories, you'll know *for sure* that the color is the right shade because you'll have your swatches with you. I keep my color swatches in the glove compartment of my car. If I come across anything that I think *might* match something in my home, I can check it out before I buy it. This has saved me a LOT of frustration, time, and money over the years. Remember, most stores have partial-spectrum lighting, so the colors that you think you see in the store are going to look different when you get them home. Having color swatches with you will help you avoid all sorts of color-matching problems when you shop.

The Goldilocks Principle and Home Interiors

Sometimes, despite your best efforts, there are areas in your home that never feel quite right, and you just can't figure out why. Fortunately, feng shui provides a variety of techniques to help remedy the problem areas of your home. In chapter 2, you learned the basics of yin-yang theory and my modern-day perspective on yin and yang, which I call the Goldilocks Principle. In this section, you're going to learn ways in which to use these concepts to create a more balanced and comfortable home environment.

I once had a client named Lynn who had been trying to sell her home for several months. The house was reasonably priced for the market, yet no one had shown the slightest interest in buying it. Frustrated, Lynn called me to help her figure out and fix what it was about her home that was turning off buyers. When I met with Lynn, it was easy to identify what was going on. I knew right away that the living room was one of the biggest problem areas. The living room floor was polished, white marble; all of the furniture was upholstered in black leather; the windows were shaded with plastic, vertical blinds, and all the tables were glass with metal legs. This collection of hard, shiny surfaces made the home feel extremely cold and uninviting. Lynn knew that potential buyers were saying that her home felt "too cold," yet she had no idea how to remedy the problem.

It was time to utilize the Goldilocks Principle. The fact that potential buyers were using the word "too" to describe her home helped identify the problem and gave us clues on what needed to be done. The house felt too cold, so we needed to warm it up by balancing the hard, shiny surfaces with soft, matte textures. I suggested that Lynn buy some thick, textured rugs for the floors, soft drapes for the windows, and fabric throw pillows for the sofas and chairs. She also needed to add several healthy plants to create a more welcoming, natural feeling in her home.

After Lynn made the changes to her home, the results were staggering. Within two days, her house was sold. The new owners even commented on how "warm and inviting" the house felt! By using the Goldilocks Principle (creating balance between extremes) and feng shui, we quickly transformed her living room from a space that was cold and unfriendly to a home that felt warm and comfortable.

Balancing Your Home

Do you have a room or an area in your home that doesn't look or feel right, but you can't figure out why? The Room Descriptions Exercise and the Room Balancing Checklist that follow can help you unravel this mystery.

ROOM DESCRIPTIONS EXERCISE

Think about one problem area in your home, and complete the following sentences:

What's the name of this room and its function? _____

Use three words to describe this room: _____, _____, _____

There's too much _____ in this room.

There's too little _____ in this room.

The reason that it's important to identify the room's function is that the function influences what the room needs in order to feel comfortable. The requirements for comfort in one type of room may be very different from the requirements for comfort in another type of room. For example, a room used for sleeping has different requirements for comfort than a room used for entertaining. A room that's dark and quiet (a yin space) is conducive to sleeping but may not be good for entertaining. A room that's bright and active (a yang space) isn't restful but may be ideal for socializing.

Let's say that you write "guest room" in the space above and that this room functions as "a place for guests to rest when they visit." Three words that you use to describe the room are "stuffy, crowded, and drab." For the last two sentences, you write:

"There is too much <u>furniture</u> in this room."
"There is too little <u>color</u> in this room."

Now, find the opposite meaning for each descriptive word: stuffy/fresh, crowded/spacious, and drab/colorful. Your task now is to change this room from feeling "stuffy, crowded, and drab" to "fresh, spacious, and colorful." For clues on how to go about this, look at your answers to the statements regarding too much and too little.

This short exercise helps to identify what needs to be changed in order to make the room feel better. To bring in freshness, open the doors and windows more often, use an air purifier, add healthy plants, or diffuse therapeutic-grade essential oils. To create a feeling of spaciousness, remove some of the furniture. To add color, paint the walls, hang artwork, or change the comforter.

You can also use the Room Balancing Checklist for help in determining whether there's too much or too little of something in a room based upon its yin or yang qualities. You can then balance the room by adding or subtracting items according to what the checklist indicates. To use the Room Balancing Checklist, circle the quality (yin or yang) that best describes the details of the room. If both descriptions fit, then circle both. When you're finished, tally the circled items in each category. If the totals are close, the room is most likely balanced. Large discrepancies between the column totals indicate features that you may wish to adjust in order to create a more harmonious environment. Review the items you checked in each column to see what you may wish to remove from one column and add to the other to help make the room feel better. Remember, the balance of yin and yang energy differs based on the function of the room (that is, bedrooms tend to be more yin and kitchens more yang).

ROOM BALANCING CHECKLIST

Room Details	Yin	Yang
Main Function of Room	Resting/Sleeping	Working/Socializing
Main Room Colors	Dark	Light
Floor Covering	Carpet/Rugs	Wood/Stone
Size of Room	Small	Large
Ceiling Height	Low	High
Sound Levels	Quiet	Noisy
Organization	Cluttered	Orderly
Room Location	Back of Home	Front of Home
Natural Light	Low	Bright
Furniture Lines	Curved	Straight
Artwork	Complex	Simple
Windows	Few	Many
Window Coverings	Fabric/Drapes	Wood/Plastic Blinds
Plants	Several	Few or None
Tables	Wood	Glass/Metal
Upholstery	Fabric	Leather
Materials	From Nature	Man-made
Totals	_____ yin	_____ yang

Artwork in Feng Shui

More than just something to take up wall space, artwork plays an important role in the feng shui of a room. Art can tell a story, convey a mood or an idea, or stir the emotions. Art choices are highly subjective, and what inspires one person may be uninspiring to another. Although art preferences vary from person to person and home to home, there are still some basic rules to bear in mind when choosing art.

First, artwork should be appropriate in size for the wall, the room, and the furnishings. Choose smaller pieces for narrow walls and larger pieces for wide walls. Artwork and furnishings can complement each other if they're in correct proportion. When hanging art above a piece of furniture, the artwork shouldn't be longer than the width of the furniture. Also, be sure to hang the artwork at the correct height. Frequently, I visit homes where the artwork is hung much too high. In most cases, artwork should be hung so that the center point of the picture or grouping is at eye level for the average person.

When considering color, remember that neutral colors are calming and will blend with other features, while bright colors draw attention and add excitement to a room. When considering the number of art pieces to use in a room, remember that one large piece may be better than several small pieces. Unless grouped carefully, hanging many pictures together in one space can make the room feel jumbled and chaotic.

Landscape paintings or photographs can add dimension and depth to a room, especially to a room that lacks a beautiful view out the window. Artwork with depth can make a smaller room feel larger or less claustrophobic. Mirrors are another way to brighten a dark room. However in feng shui, there are certain places where mirrors are considered unfavorable: one is directly across from the front door and the other is in a bedroom—positioned in such a way that you can see your reflection when lying in bed. Otherwise, a beautiful mirror can be a great statement in a room when you aren't sure what kind of art to add. Just make sure that whatever the mirror reflects is a pleasing image. Mirrors are covered more extensively in chapter 5.

Unless you're an art connoisseur, choosing art for your home may be a real challenge. Too often when people shop for artwork, they become frustrated and end up buying something that they don't really like, just to cover a blank wall. Then every time they look at it, they feel dissatisfied on some level. This is contrary to what you're trying to accomplish with feng shui. If you can't find something that you really like, it's better to live with a blank wall.

The Internet is a fabulous way to shop for artwork (see the appendix). You can search by color, artist, theme, and more—with literally thousands of choices available. You can check dimensions and even see how a piece will look when framed. Even if you don't buy a piece over the Internet, doing some browsing online will give you a better idea of what you're looking for before you set out to shop.

Above all, choose pieces that inspire you. Artwork should be pleasing and uplifting and not remind you of anything that's painful or sad. Replace any artwork that doesn't feel good to you with something positive. In chapter 6, you will learn about the Life Aspiration Areas and how to enhance them. Artwork can be used as a visual reminder of the goals you wish to accomplish.

Establishing Kid-free Zones

We've all seen them, and perhaps you live in one: the house that looks like the adults are living in the child's house rather than the other way around. Over the years, I've seen far too many plastic kitchen sets in living rooms, toy car racetracks set up on coffee tables, and children's artwork hung in every available space around the house. Sometimes it's hard to believe that any adults live in the home.

From a feng shui perspective, this is always a portent to disaster. Most of the time when I am called to homes like these, the parents are overwhelmed and exhausted. Often, their marriage is suffering as well. Before I go into how to remedy this common problem, I want to share a story that clearly illustrates why it's not a good idea to let children's possessions have free rein over every room in the house.

The Story of Trish

A few years ago, I met with a woman named Trish. She was a darling, young mother with two small children, a boy and a girl. Her husband, John, was a successful businessman whose company had made a fortune in a short period of time. Trish and John lived in a large, beautiful home in a prosperous neighborhood. John worked hard to provide a lavish lifestyle for his family, while Trish stayed home to raise their children.

During my first meeting with Trish, I was shocked when she opened the front door. Tricycles, toys, shoes, and children's artwork filled the entryway. As I stepped carefully over the chaos, I noticed that the main living room of this luxurious home had no adult-sized furniture in it. It was filled with a miniature kitchen set, an enormous stuffed giraffe, children's books, games, and toys. Although the family had a live-in maid, the house felt chaotic and messy due to the quantity of brightly colored playthings scattered around every room. Even though the home was very large and expensive, its grandeur was greatly diminished by all the children's toys and artwork. The home felt like a gigantic playhouse.

As we toured the home, Trish went on and on about her children. It was obvious from her words and the state of her home that she was a very dedicated mother and that the children were her highest priority. Trish mentioned that her husband worked long hours and often didn't arrive home until after the children were in bed. John would frequently come home tired and irritable and criticize Trish for every little thing. Obviously there was tension in the marriage, and Trish slowly admitted that this was why she wanted a feng shui consultation. She was hoping that I'd be able to find a way to improve their marriage. From a feng shui perspective, it was obvious to me what was going on, and I knew what needed to be done to help Trish get her home and relationship back on track.

I began by telling Trish that having every room in the home, especially the main rooms (living room, family room, kitchen, and master bedroom), filled with children's possessions was a huge mistake from a feng shui point of view. I asked her how John felt about the house. She told me that he was often irritated by the mess, but according to her, he just didn't understand "how children are."

I asked Trish if John had any private areas in the home just for himself. She excitedly told me that her husband had a home office and a workout room. When she showed me the home office, I couldn't believe my eyes: Children's art filled the walls; a little desk and chair sat next to a big desk and chair, and there was a Diaper Genie® in the corner next to a huge bag of disposable diapers. This certainly wasn't how I'd envisioned this powerful CEO's home office to be. The home gym was no different. It was filled with the children's bikes, tricycles, and large toys. Once again, the walls were covered with children's artwork. Literally, there wasn't a single place in this large home to get away from the children's possessions.

As we made our way through the house, Trish admitted that her children could be "willful" and difficult to discipline. I explained that she'd given up too much of her authority as a parent by giving up so much of the home to them. It was obvious that Trish was a doting mother, but the mistake she was making by letting her children claim every room in their home was a huge one. By doing so, she was relinquishing her power and authority and was also putting her marriage in harm's way.

I explained to Trish that she needed to create some kid-free zones. By creating kid-free zones, there would be a greater feeling of peace in the home, and the children would have more respect for their parents with these established boundaries. These zones, I added, should be the main living areas of the home, including the family room, the living room, the master bedroom, and the home office. The children could, of course, *be* in these rooms and even play in them, but the décor and furnishings would be for adults. There would be no toys, games, or other children's things on display or stored in these rooms. By reclaiming the main rooms in the home as rooms for adults, John would likely begin to feel that he was a greater priority in Trish's life, and the house would feel more relaxing and welcoming when he came home at the end of his workday.

Trish listened carefully and reluctantly agreed that these changes needed to be made. As I drove away, I had doubts about whether she would actually follow through with establishing kid-free zones in her home. I feared that if she didn't do something soon, her marriage would suffer even more.

A year later, I received a tearful phone call from Trish. She told me that she'd discovered her husband was openly flirting with a young woman in his office. She didn't think he was actually having an affair yet but worried that that would be the next step. She asked me to come back to her house to see if there was something wrong with the feng shui of her home. When I arrived, I wasn't at all surprised to see that she'd made *none* of the changes we'd talked about a year earlier. Toys and kids' stuff still filled every room, and the old Diaper Genie®, while no longer needed, still occupied its corner next to the desk in Daddy's office. This time, when I explained to Trish what needed to be done and why, she listened. She asked if I would come back in a few weeks to check her progress and make sure that it was all done correctly. She was desperate to save her marriage.

When I returned to the house four weeks later, the changes were remarkable. It went from looking like a child's playroom to the elegant home that it was designed to be. The décor was beautiful and stylish, and all of the children's toys and other possessions were stowed away in cabinets in their bedrooms and playroom. Trish beamed with pride as she showed me all that she'd done. Establishing kid-free zones had had a powerful impact on John and Trish's marriage. John was astonished and overjoyed with the changes. He started coming home from work earlier and in a better mood. And, he was treating Trish with tenderness and affection again.

Another benefit of establishing kid-free zones was that the children were more respectful and better behaved. In fact, the entire family dynamic had improved. The feng shui changes resulted in a home that was more balanced and more peaceful. Trish could now see how she might have lost John if she'd waited any longer. When I checked in with Trish a few months later, she told me that she was still careful to maintain the kid-free zones in her home and that her marriage was better than ever. Trish said that she now shares with all of her friends the pitfalls of not keeping children's things put away in their own rooms and how integrating feng shui principles into her home helped save her marriage. Oh, and in case you're wondering, the young lady in John's office was "let go" soon after Trish made the changes at home.

Memories of Loved Ones

Where should you place the ashes or mementos of loved ones? I'm frequently asked this delicate question. Clients are often concerned about whether these cherished reminders bring any negative effects, and they want to know what location in the house is the most favorable for these items.

Reminders of those who've passed on can be a source of comfort or sadness, and there are no hard and fast rules as to where to place them. Mementos have no inherently good or bad energy of their own. Rather, the energy surrounding them is based upon our feelings toward the people or pets before and after they died. When deciding what to do with these items, consider this question: what was your relationship like with the deceased? If the relationship was positive and loving, mementos and photographs may be comforting. If the relationship was stressful and negative, having reminders of this person will only be a source of stress and should be avoided, if possible.

Avoid the mausoleum setting in your home. I've visited homes of people who've lost loved ones where they've turned their home into a shrine to the departed. There are huge photographs, mementos, untouched rooms, closets, and things left as if the loved one is going to return at any moment. Not only does this situation make the healing process more of a challenge, it's also very uncomfortable for visitors.

I've met with many grieving families who've lost spouses, children, parents, siblings, and pets. They call me for a feng shui consultation because they can't seem to stop grieving. From my own experience, I know that grieving is a very personal process and that it can take a long time to run its course. To help with this process, there are things that can be done from a feng shui perspective. One of the most positive things is to create a special place to hold your memories of a loved one. This can be a tabletop, a niche, a shelf, or the inside of a cabinet. Here, you can display photos, cherished belongings, and even urns.

When you set aside a special place as a memorial, you have both honored a loved one and allowed for areas in your home where you're not so intensely reminded of the absence. When photos and reminders of the departed are everywhere, it can be very hard for the living to go on living. I've helped many people with the creation of in-home memorials, and they tell me repeatedly how much it helped them with their grieving process.

Place the memorial in an area that feels right to you. It's usually best if the memorial isn't the focal point of a room. The idea is to honor a departed loved one while gradually healing your heart from the loss. If the memorial is too much of a focal point, it may make the grieving process more difficult.

Grieving takes time and is different for everyone. Over time, I've noticed that many people release their need to display or hang on to as many mementos of the loved one as they once did. This is a normal and healthy part of the healing process. Be gentle with yourself, and do what feels best. If this means displaying photos and items in a special place in your home, by all means, do it. If not displaying these items feels better, then that's what you need to do. Trust your heart, and you will know what's best for you to be able to heal. The main issue to pay attention to is how the possessions and memories of your loved one affect your emotions and daily life. Keep in mind that peace and happiness are what feng shui strives for and, most likely, what your loved one would wish for you, too.

Scents That Make Sense

Feng shui is a holistic process, and an important aspect of good feng shui is whether the home has any health dangers. Adding air fresheners to your home and even to your workspace has become very popular. Television ads are peppered with spots on how to "freshen" your home by using artificially scented products. What many people don't understand, however, is that these products fill the air with toxic chemicals.

I once met with a client who had artificial air fresheners plugged into almost every electrical outlet in her home. Within five minutes of walking into her house, my nose began to run, and I had a painful headache. I explained to my client that these products were actually quite unhealthy and could potentially cause health issues for her family. She told me that her 13-year-old son had been complaining of headaches the minute he got home from school. She promptly removed all of these products from her home and, lo and behold, her son's headaches went away.

If you enjoy adding scent to your home, use products that are natural and safe. Aromatherapy is an age-old practice of using essential oils to improve one's mood, health, and spirit. Pure, therapeutic-grade essential oils can be purchased online, through distributors, and in some health or retail stores. To diffuse essential oils in the home, use an ultrasonic essential-oil diffuser as a safe and effective way to distribute scent into the air. Because there's no heat involved, the therapeutic integrity of the oil stays intact. (Refer to the appendix for more information on purchasing therapeutic-grade essential oils and diffusers).

As to which scents to choose, remember that preferences are highly subjective. Floral scents are particularly personal—some people love them, some don't. The two scents that most people find pleasing are citrus and peppermint. Citrus can make a space smell fresh and clean, and peppermint works to clear the mind. Incidentally, peppermint is great when you're studying, taking a test, or in need of a pick-me-up. When I'm in traffic or driving long distances, I like to dab peppermint oil on a cotton ball and place it in the air-conditioning vents on the dashboard of my car. It helps me stay alert and feel less fatigued.

To make a simple, homemade air freshener, squeeze two teaspoons of fresh lemon juice into a cup of distilled water, fill a spray bottle with the lemon water and give the air a spritz. Your home will instantly smell fresh and clean, with no toxic chemicals to worry about! You can also do the same using distilled water with your favorite pure essential oils. For health and safety, avoid artificially scented sprays, candles, potpourri, and reed diffusers. Opt instead for natural alternatives. Aromas derived from pure essential oils are healthier and more pleasing than anything synthetic. You can learn more about the toxicity of air fresheners by doing an online search of "toxic effects of artificial scents and air fresheners." Even if a product claims to include "natural" ingredients, check the fine print before you purchase it, to avoid exposing yourself and your family to potentially toxic chemicals.

Clutter, Clutter, Everywhere!

Several years ago, I did what turned out to be a very memorable residential consultation. My client's name was Andrea. As with all clients, I had Andrea complete a detailed questionnaire before we met to assist me in preparing for our time together. In her questionnaire, Andrea went on at length about how she was feeling stuck and stagnant, how she and her husband had no energy, and how depressed and unmotivated she had become. In desperation, she hoped feng shui might hold the answer to her problems.

From years of experience, I've learned that any time a client mentions words like "stagnant," "lethargic," or "stuck," there's almost always a clutter issue. When I stepped inside Andrea's home, my suspicions were immediately confirmed. She had an overwhelming amount of clutter. Andrea and her husband, Joe, had lived in their two-story home for twenty-five years. Andrea was an avid fan of garage sales and online shopping. Slowly but surely, she and Joe had accumulated so much stuff that there was literally no open space left on the walls, the floors, or even the tabletops.

Andrea told me how they never entertained at home anymore, how embarrassed she felt about her home, how their home-based business had declined, how much weight she had gained while living there, and how unmotivated and despondent she had become. I explained to Andrea that, in order to manifest changes in her life, she would have to begin by clearing out and organizing her possessions. Dismayed, Andrea looked at me and asked, "Can't I just hang a crystal?"

"No," I smiled at her. "You have to do the work." Andrea was now faced with the overwhelming task of de-cluttering her home, and she had no idea where to begin. We started the process by walking from room to room and prioritizing what needed to be done. I explained to her how clutter was impacting her life.

One of the first areas of concern was a very large closet in the center of the house. It was crammed so full of stuff that the couple had placed hooks along the walls of the hallway in order to hang clothes that had nowhere else to be stored. I turned to Andrea and asked if anyone in her family suffered from heart problems. Her eyes grew wide as she told me that her husband had gone through two heart-bypass operations but was still experiencing serious heart problems. This was not something that she had mentioned on her questionnaire, so she was shocked by my inquiry. "How did you know that?" she asked. I told her that, in feng shui, the center of the house is the Health area and that the packed closet was symbolic of stagnant health issues. Suddenly, Andrea's energy shifted from reluctant to motivated. She began taking notes and asking questions. The realization that the clutter in her home was doing more than just taking up space finally had sunk in. As with so many people, Andrea needed a kick in the pants to get going and make the necessary changes. Her love for her husband was the incentive she needed to roll up her sleeves and begin the daunting task of de-cluttering her home, beginning with that center closet.

Three months later, I received a phone call from Andrea. She was brimming over with delight and enthusiasm. She told me that since our appointment, she had gotten rid of six *dumpsters* of stuff. She added that her husband had experienced what the doctors termed "an amazing recovery." Their home-based business was picking up, and they were both losing weight by walking every day. They had started inviting people over to their home again, and Andrea felt like she had a new lease on life. Although Andrea thanked me for the help I had given her, I reminded her that the credit was all hers. After all, it was she who had done the work. She said that anytime she's tempted to buy something at a garage sale or on the Internet, her husband says, "I'm going to tell Cathleen on you," and she reconsiders the purchase.

Clutter and Feng Shui

Clearing your clutter is imperative to the success of your feng shui efforts. You can make all the feng shui enhancements you want, but if clutter is bogging you down, you will experience few, if any, benefits.

Reality Check

Myth: Clutter has nothing to do with feng shui.

I once read a lengthy article written by a so-called feng shui "expert" in which the expert stated that clutter had nothing to do with feng shui. Furthermore, the author advised those in the feng shui community to stop recommending that clients clean up clutter. The expert backed up this position by stating that traditional feng shui teachings never mentioned clutter, so it should be eliminated from feng shui recommendations entirely.

Of course, traditional feng shui doesn't mention clutter! Clutter is a relatively recent phenomenon stemming from an affluent, consumer-driven society. Historically, the vast majority of people have lacked the means by which to accumulate material goods. They could afford only the most basic things for survival. To have *more* than one needed just wasn't possible. While this is still true in much of the world, those in affluent societies have the ability to acquire more than they need, which has resulted in an abundance of unwanted and unnecessary "stuff."

After two decades in this field, I can tell you that clutter has a profound impact on the feng shui of an environment. Clutter in and of itself is contrary to the very essence of what feng shui seeks to accomplish. The words "feng shui" represent the *balance* and *flow* of energy. When you have too much clutter in your home, the flow of energy cannot circulate and begins to stagnate. The more stuff, the more stagnation, and the less your life flows and flourishes. Clearing clutter unblocks the flow of energy in the home and makes way for the rest of your feng shui efforts. You simply cannot have clutter and good feng shui at the same time.

What's clutter? Clutter is anything that you don't want, love, need, or use. It's the pile of cooking magazines stored in the garage that you'll never read again. It's the rake with the broken handle that you never got rid of but have long since replaced. It's the obsolete computer now sitting forgotten in a closet.

The accumulation of stuff creates a ball-and-chain effect, bogging you down and impacting you in insidious and profound ways. Clutter has its own built-in sense of inertia. Having too much stuff sitting around can make you feel lethargic and unmotivated. Not knowing what to do with unnecessary-but-useful items results in procrastination. As one of my feng shui students aptly put it, "Clutter is postponed decision-making."

Having a great deal of clutter can wreak havoc on your mental and physical health. A closet full of clothes that one cannot hope to fit into again contributes to a negative self-image and a lack of self-worth. Finding places to store things, having to dust them, or vacuuming around them can be so much trouble that some people give up entirely on cleaning. Friends are no longer invited over, and the accumulation of dust can aggravate the lungs and sinuses, resulting in respiratory issues including asthma and chronic allergies. When you don't feel well mentally and physically, you're even less likely to take needed action to clear out what's bringing you down.

The problem is, the longer you ignore attending to things that need to be done, the worse they become. Clutter inherently creates a breeding ground for daily mental recrimination with an incessant stream of *shoulds*:

"I *should* clean out that closet."

"I *should* organize the garage."

"I *should* go through and discard some of these _____ (toys, clothes, tools, pictures, shoes, games, boxes, books, blankets, papers, baby things, craft projects, decorations, magazines, tapes, CDs, DVDs)."

Talk about a guilt trip! All of this incessant mental nagging can have a detrimental effect on self-worth and self-esteem. Have you experienced the sense of accomplishment, the swelling of pride, and the giddy feeling of satisfaction that comes from taking care of *shoulds*? Have you ever showed off your newly organized garage to a friend? Have you flung open the doors of a freshly cleaned closet or cabinet in sheer delight? Of course, your friend couldn't care less (unless your friend is also your roommate and is directly benefiting from the purge of possessions), but that's not the point. The point is that you feel good! No more guilt trip and no more disorganization. That feeling of jubilation is actually one of liberation. The end result of eliminating physical clutter is eliminating mental clutter as well. Not only have you gotten rid of unused belongings, you've also allowed balance and flow to come back into your life, making way for fresh new energy. If you have a clutter issue, it's sometimes hard to know where to begin. Here are some simple steps to help you get the situation under control:

Step 1. Mark a date.

Mark a date on your calendar by which to have a certain room or area of the house cleared. A very effective motivator is to schedule a donation pick-up with a local charity. You may also want to schedule a garage sale. This way, you know that you're committed to a specific date.

Step 2. Set up a system.

Set up a system for sorting items. Make three separate piles: one for trash or recycling, one for items to donate or sell, and another for items to keep. Have large bags and boxes on hand for the sorted items.

Step 3. Concentrate on one area at a time.

To keep the process from becoming overwhelming, concentrate on one area at a time. If your garage is full of unwanted stuff, start there. Once the garage is cleaned out, you'll have room to place items awaiting a donation pick-up or a garage sale. However, the cleaned out garage is NOT a new place to store more clutter. It's simply a holding area for the items awaiting the charity truck or your garage sale. Once the garage sale is over, donate the items that didn't sell to a charity.

Step 4. Do a little bit each day.

Set aside at least an hour per day to keep the process moving. Don't move on to the next area until the first area is completely cleaned out.

If you feel too overwhelmed or uncertain about the process of de-cluttering your home, seek out professional help by hiring a professional organizer. Check the Internet for organizers in your area. Not only will they assist you in purging your things, they'll also help you stay organized so you don't collect too much stuff all over again.

Start a habit of getting rid of something every time you buy something new. Something coming into the home means that something goes out. If your bookshelves are too full, don't buy another bookshelf. Instead, donate your old books to the library. It's a great tax write-off, and the library will be delighted to have them.

By the way, renting a storage unit is NOT the solution to the clutter problem! Even though things are stored away from your home, you are still energetically "tied" to them. If you have to pay for additional storage away from home, then you have *too* much stuff!

Once you've conquered your clutter, you will have prepared your home for the feng shui enhancements found in the following chapters. Remember that the results you receive from your feng shui enhancements are directly proportional to the effort you put in. Clearing clutter sets the stage for welcoming the excellence to come.

Chapter 5
Feng Shui Tips for Every Room

*The architect should strive continually to simplify; the
ensemble of the rooms should then be carefully considered that
comfort and utility may go hand in hand with beauty.*
— *Frank Lloyd Wright*

Feng shui can be applied to any living space, from studio apartments to grand mansions. Whether you rent or own your place, live alone or share with others, can make minor or major changes, the goal of feng shui is always the same: *to create a space that **feels** as good as it looks.* With some of the basics of interior feng shui already covered, let's take the scenic route through your home and consider feng shui tips for each room.

Entryways

Call it what you like—foyer, mudroom, entryway, or vestibule—many homes have a transition area just inside the front door. This area is significant not only because it forms your first impression of the interior of a home but also because it's where an important shift occurs. As with so much of feng shui, this shift has to do with your survival instincts.

When you're outdoors, whether in a city or a rural area, your survival instincts are constantly on alert, scanning the surroundings for potential dangers or threats to your safety.[1] Your "outdoor" awareness is subtly different than your "indoor"

---

[1] Grant Hildebrand, *Origins of Architectural Pleasure* (Berkeley: University of California Press, 1999), 58-59.

awareness. Therefore, as you enter a building, you need a few seconds to decompress and acclimate to the new surroundings and the new sensory experience. Your survival instincts relax once you sense that an environment is safe. The advantage of a well-defined entryway is that it gives your survival mechanism a moment or two to shift focus from the outside world to the inside world. It also allows time for guests to adjust to their new surroundings, rather than stepping immediately into the interior of a home, which may be an unfamiliar setting.

For a home's occupants, the entryway serves as a buffer zone of safety between the public world outside and the private world inside. In feng shui, the safer we feel, the more comfortable and relaxed we feel. A home with a clearly defined entryway will feel more secure and more comforting to guests and occupants alike. The following diagrams illustrate this concept:

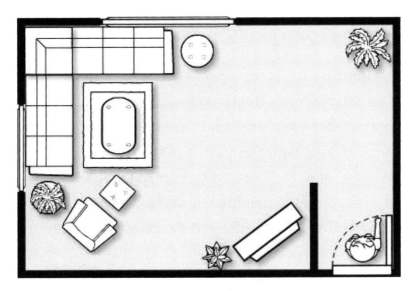

Figure 5.1

Figure 5.1 shows an ideal entry configuration because the person entering the space is protected on both sides by the walls of the entryway. In this scenario, the person's survival instincts will remain relatively relaxed. Because there's no threat from either side, the person's focus will be on what's directly in front of him/her. The people living in the home also experience a sense of safety because this small area limits the access that newcomers have to the rest of the dwelling.

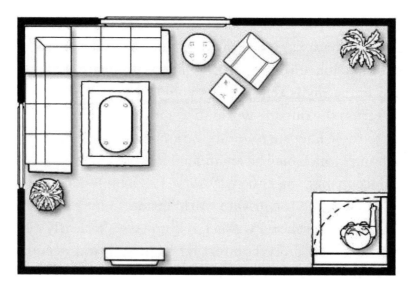

Figure 5.2

The entryway in figure 5.2 is less optimal than the entryway pictured in figure 5.1. Although this entryway has flooring that differs visually from the rest of the room, it offers protection on just one side. The side without the wall opens directly into the living area, making both the guest and the residents feel more vulnerable. Because the area that must be assessed by survival instincts is larger (i.e., in the front *and* to the side), there's a heightened sense of vulnerability. For residents, a newcomer entering the home has easier access to the home's interior.

In order to create a well-defined entryway, add a small barrier just inside the door on the side without the wall. Figure 5.3 shows a plant positioned behind the chair closest to the door. Providing a buffer between the door and the open room makes the space feel better for residents and guests alike.

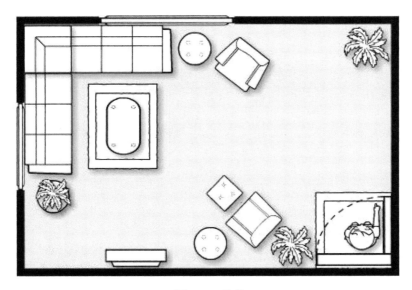

Figure 5.3

The least desirable configuration of all is shown in figure 5.4. The person walking into this home has no protection on either side when the door is allowed to swing all the way open. It will take longer to relax and feel comfortable when entering a home like this, and occupants may find themselves feeling unsafe in a home with no protective buffers in the entryway.

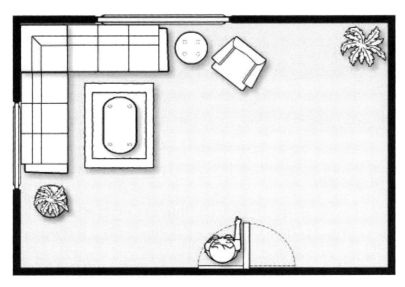

Figure 5.4

In figure 5.5, we've remedied this situation by placing buffers on both sides of the door. An area rug helps to define the space, while a low bookcase on the right and a tall plant on the left work to create a feeling of protection for those entering the home.

Figure 5.5

When adding a buffer, make sure that it's not too heavy, too close to the door, too oppressive, too tall, or too large; otherwise, it may feel threatening. If the object you choose doesn't feel right, you may create an even worse situation than if you had done nothing at all. Experiment with different objects that you already own such as plants, low bookcases, small tables with lamps, panel screens, or new arrangements of existing furniture before buying something, so you'll know what feels best in your home.

The Front Door (Revisited)

As you learned in chapter 3, the best front door is one that's solid and doesn't have glass or windows set into it. The common-sense reason for this is safety. With a solid front door, you feel more secure and able to relax. Safety and security are high priorities for feeling comfortable in your home.

If your front door includes glass and you can't or don't want to change it, ask yourself whether it makes you feel vulnerable or diminishes your feelings of privacy. If either answer is yes, consider blinds or curtains for the window. Anything that makes you feel safer will make you feel better in your home.

If you have a front door with a large window in it or with a window located to the side of the front door, an intruder may be able to break the window and gain access to your home by simply reaching in and unlocking the door. In this case, I highly recommend installing a double deadbolt, which requires a key to open the door from either side. I had this window configuration in a home that I rented many years ago, and I felt very vulnerable. After I installed a double deadbolt, I felt much safer. I kept the deadbolt's key in a drawer near the door (but not within reach of the window), so I could easily unlock it when I needed to.

Light and Bright

In order to make the entryway feel its feng shui best, the space should be clean, well-lit, and free of clutter. How do you brighten a windowless entryway? It's best if the light is brought in from above the door. A skylight or a window that sits above the front door is ideal. This is the preferred location for a light source because it brings in light without sacrificing security. In the evening, be sure that your home's entrance is well-lit both inside and outside to provide residents and guests with a sense of protection and comfort.

Reality Check

Myth: *Mirrors in your entryway push all the fortune out of your home.*

Many people place mirrors in entryways either to visually expand the space or to bring in more light. I've read in feng shui literature that placing a mirror opposite a door pushes the good energy out instead of welcoming it in. I don't know about pushing energy out the front door, but I do know that it's unpleasant to walk into a home when you sense that someone is walking toward you. This is what your reflection may look like, especially with the outdoor glare behind you before your eyes have adjusted to the indoor lighting.

If natural light isn't an option in your entryway, mirrors that are carefully placed may help draw in more light. Just remember that it's better to place a mirror on the side walls of the entrance rather than on the wall opposite the door.

Organizing "Dumping Areas"

Whether you enter through the main door of your house or through the garage, be sure to designate a place that's attractive and accessible for placing keys, sunglasses, mail, and other items that tend to be dumped by the main entrance. Choose a drawer, an attractive box, or a container with a lid to store loose items. This will keep the entryway calm and orderly, and never again will you have to search all over the house for your keys or sunglasses!

If you have children and would like to solve the problem of their things piling up near the main door, give them convenient storage options like cubbies, baskets, cupboards, or benches with storage. Attractive storage options keep things organized and out of sight, making the entryway feel calmer and more relaxing. By establishing a particular storage place for schoolwork, backpacks, library books, and homework, you'll be doing your child a huge favor by helping him/her get organized. When your child gets into the habit of placing items in his/her personal storage basket or cupboard and then checking it before leaving for school, important items may never be forgotten again! This is a terrific stress reliever for both parents and kids, and relieving stress is great feng shui!

Expanding the Feeling of a Small Entryway

If an entryway is small and cramped, you can make it feel more spacious by painting it in light colors. You can also place artwork on the wall opposite the front door. Choose a scene that portrays depth, such as a rolling landscape or mountains. If your budget allows for it, you may want to hire a muralist to paint a trompe l'oeil mural on the wall opposite the door with a scene that will fool the eye into thinking there's more space in the entryway than there actually is.

Entry Hallways

When there's a direct view from the front door straight down a hallway to the backyard and beyond, I call this the "Bowling Alley Effect." Without the benefit of architectural elements or décor to break up the view, the feeling of standing at the front door and seeing straight out the back of the house is not unlike looking down the straight lines of a bowling alley to the pins at the end. With this configuration, all the attention is directed toward the back of the home, reducing awareness of what else is going on inside the home.

Reality Check

Myth: If the front door aligns with the back door, money will fly in the front door and right out the back.

In some feng shui circles, it's said that being able to see out the back of the home from the front door will cause money to rush in the front door and right out the back. If you've read up to this point, you know that I don't agree with this explanation. I've met with plenty of clients living in homes with this arrangement who were doing quite well financially.

There are reasons, however, why this configuration is not optimal from a feng shui perspective, though they don't have anything to do with the accumulation or loss of money. As you may expect, the explanation involves survival instincts and attunement with the natural world. Next, we'll examine what's really going on in a home with an entry hallway like this and realize, once again, that feng shui actually does *make sense.*

The Bowling Alley Effect can reduce our sense of comfort and safety. Most of the time, the public rooms (like living rooms and foyers) are located toward the front of the home, and the private rooms (bedrooms, bathrooms, family rooms, and kitchens) are located toward the back of the home. A view straight through the home, from front to back, allows easy access to the private areas of the home, which increases our feelings of vulnerability.

In chapter 2, you read that scientific studies indicate a human preference for meandering pathways. A view directly to the back of the home from the front door eliminates the feeling of mystery and doesn't invite discovery of the home itself. Remember that a straight path increases speed, and a meandering path slows down the pace (a concept that traffic engineers understand very well). Therefore, when you enter a home that has a clear, straight pathway through it to the backyard, you feel drawn to the back of the home. In doing so, you often avoid exploring and appreciating the other rooms of the home at a leisurely pace.

I frequently encounter the Bowling Alley Effect while staging model homes in housing developments. Many times, I'm called in because the builder has one or two models that aren't selling as well as the others. The sales and marketing personnel are often perplexed as to what makes these homes less desirable.

Time and time again, I find that the model lagging in sales has a long hallway leading from the front door straight through the home and ending with a clear view of the backyard. The Bowling Alley Effect is especially strong if there's wood flooring with planks positioned vertically down the hallway from the front door.

When I report back to the builder's staff, I always begin by saying, "Let me guess. When prospective buyers walk in the door of this model, they go straight to the back of the house, check out what's there, and then go right back out without exploring all the wonderful features of the rest of the house." I watch as their eyes widen in amazement because what I'm describing is almost always what's occurring.

I then explain that the straight hallway removes all sense of mystery and causes people to speed up and zip through the house instead of taking time to explore it. Like a moth drawn to a flame, prospective buyers are pulled toward the back of the home and aren't inclined to explore further. If you live in a house like this, how can you rectify the Bowling Alley Effect? Fortunately, there are several easy solutions.

One solution that works, regardless of whether the hallway is narrow or not, is to add a runner with a horizontal pattern. The runner provides visual interest, and the horizontal pattern breaks up the long vertical line of the hallway. If the hallway is wide enough, you can place tall plants at intervals to distract from the view at the end of the hallway and focus attention on the rooms and artwork that may be placed along the way. Figure 5.6 indicates how placing plants in the hallway creates a meandering pathway of sorts, as discussed in chapter 3. Adding plants at intervals in the hallway also provides a prelude to the view outside.

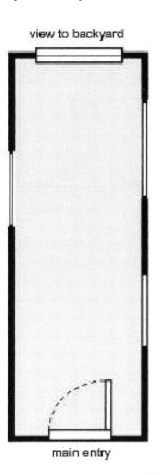
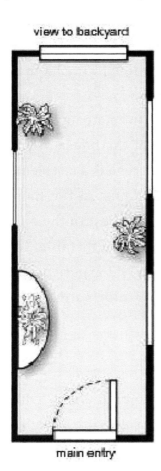

Figure 5.6

Three-dimensional artwork, relief sculptures, artifacts, or masks may also be displayed on both sides of the hallway if it's wide enough to accommodate them without feeling cramped or crowded. As with plants, these items draw attention and distract from the view out the back. In a narrow hallway, it's best to display artwork on just one side, since artwork on both sides can make a narrow hallway seem even narrower.

If the hallway is very wide, you can place tables, chairs, and benches along it to create more interest and slow down the view from traveling too quickly toward the back. I've used Japanese shoji screens to accomplish this effect in offices and homes with long, wide hallways or passages (see figure 5.7).

A shoji screen can create a more intimate foyer, while still letting in light from the back of the house. If your décor will accommodate it, a shoji screen is a simple and inexpensive solution to many dilemmas in the home. You will find that, by adding visual interest to the entry hallway, your home will feel more comfortable, less hurried, and more relaxed—and you will experience the effects of good feng shui. For more information about shoji screens, refer to the appendix.

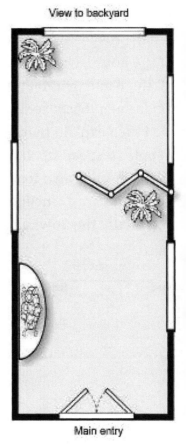

View to backyard

Main entry

Figure 5.7

Stairways

In most two-story houses, the personal and private rooms of the house—the bedrooms and bathrooms where we sleep, dress, bathe, make love, and retreat from the outside world—are located upstairs. These are the spaces where we feel the most vulnerable and need the most privacy. The first floor of a home, particularly the area around the front door, is usually the most public part.

Reality Check

---

*Myth: If the stairway faces the front door, then
all your money will roll out the door.*

You may have heard this before. It's been said by some feng shui enthusiasts that, if the stairway directly faces the front door (that is, if you walk in your front door and do not turn, you will go straight up the stairway), all of your luck and money will roll down the stairs and out the front door.

I don't think luck has anything to do with feng shui or that fortune is like a ball that can roll down the stairway and straight out the door. Having the stairway face the front door is undesirable for a much more common-sense reason. The explanation, once again, involves survival instincts as they relate to the public and private areas of a home. As you are about to learn, this understanding is much more practical and compelling than a silly story about your money rolling down the stairs and out the front door.

When you enter a home and the stairway is located directly across from the front door, your attention is pulled straight upstairs, exposing the most private area of the home to the public area of the home. This creates an awkward experience for guests and occupants alike. I like to say that having the stairway directly across from the front door is like meeting someone for the first time and having them pull their shirt up over their head—too much information a little too soon! Furthermore, a home with the stairway directly across from the front door doesn't feel as safe as a home with the stairway in another location. When you're upstairs sleeping, you may feel more vulnerable knowing that there's easy access to the bedrooms, should an intruder break in during the night. Homes almost always feel best when the public, formal rooms are located toward the front (yang) portion of the home and the more private, personal (yin) rooms are located toward the back, away from the main entrance. Think of it this way: the rooms that you frequent in your bathrobe or pajamas for part of the day—the bedroom, the bathroom, the kitchen, and the family room—feel best when out of view of the main door to the home. In the book *A Pattern Language,* the authors state, "Unless the spaces in a building are arranged in a sequence which corresponds to their degrees of privateness, the visits made by strangers, friends, guests, clients, family, will always be a little awkward."[1]

So, what do you do if your stairway faces the front door? The best thing to do is to distract the eye away from the stairway as much as possible. While it may not make you feel safer, it will lessen the strong statement that the stairway makes when you walk in the front door. Start at the front door, and take a look up to the view at the top of the stairway. The wall at the top of the stairway should be painted the same color as the walls leading up the stairway so that it blends in and doesn't draw your eye upward unnecessarily.

Next, remove any artwork, pictures, or objects at the top of the stairway. A focal point at the top of the stairway directs attention to the second floor. In order to turn the focus away from the stairway, there needs to be a focal point adjacent to the entryway. In figure 5.8, this has been accomplished by placing a patterned area rug on the floor between the stairway and the door and placing plants near the side of the stairway. Ideally, there would be some eye-catching artwork on the living room walls that could be seen from the entryway. These features keep the eye anchored on the downstairs rooms, rather than leading it up the stairway to the bedroom areas.

---

[1] Christopher Alexander and others, *A Pattern Language* (New York: Oxford University Press, 1977), 610.

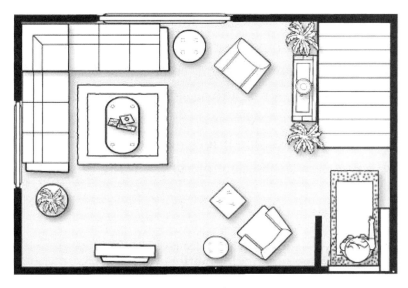

Figure 5.8

Living in an "Upside-Down House"

Once in a while, the second story of a home is actually the main living area, and the first floor is where the bedrooms are. My grandmother's house was designed like this to capitalize on the ocean view. As children, we use to call it an "upside-down house." If this is the case in your home, then you *do* want to pull the eye up the stairway toward the more active living areas, rather than keeping it focused on the private areas downstairs. Reverse the instructions above by placing your focal points and contrasting paint choices on the upper levels and removing any décor that would entice visitors to linger at the entry-level floor.

Decorating the Stairway

The stairway should be easy to navigate and well-lit, both during the day and at night. The area should be free of clutter or other items that obstruct the top or bottom of the stairway or its landings. Keep the stairway clean and clear so that this very busy area of your home remains safe and flows smoothly.

It's best to leave the walls of the stairway empty and display artwork in other areas of the home. Keep in mind that placing artwork and photos on the walls along the stairway can be distracting for some people, especially older people or people who have trouble climbing stairs. Artwork on the walls obstructs passage and requires people to navigate around it, so as not to bump the artwork as they go up and down the stairway. A cascade of pictures down the walls of the stairway accentuates the slant of the staircase, making it appear steeper than it actually is. The steeper it appears, the less safe it feels. If you really want to display artwork on the stairway walls, then choose one picture that can be hung horizontally, and secure it well.

Stairs with Open Risers

Stairs with open risers have no backing between the stairs, so you can see through them to the floor below. These types of stairs are discouraged because the visible drop to the ground below can make people feel unsafe. Usually, open risers are used in areas that need more light, but if there's a way around the lighting issue, I recommend having some kind of backing attached to the rear of each stair.

Spiral Staircases

Spiral staircases exemplify almost all of the no-no's associated with stairs. Most spiral staircases have open risers. The twisting of each stair forces steps to be wedge-shaped and generally smaller than usual. Due to their difficult-to-navigate shape, extra care must be taken going up and down spiral staircases, causing a heightened level of anxiety, possibly leading to accidents.

If you already have a spiral staircase in your home, there is little you can do to remedy the situation, short of replacing the staircase with a more traditional one. However, filling in the open risers with some sort of sturdy backing will visually connect the stairs and make the staircase feel a bit safer. Also, adding a non-slip surface to each step is essential to increasing safety.

Storage Areas under Stairways

If you have children and there's a closet, storage area, or crawl space under your stairway, consider turning it into a whimsical play area. Children delight in having secret spaces to call their own. The area under the stairway offers a wonderful opportunity for a little reading nook, a playhouse, a hideaway, or a toy room. Children love the feeling of privacy that these small areas afford.

If space allows, a cushy blanket, a light, a beanbag chair, and some books and toys can make this tiny area cozy and fun. The area under the stairway is a great option for toy storage on the main floor of the home. When it's time for clean-up, children's toys are likely to be cleaned up more easily if storage options are easy to access and easy to use. Not only will your children love their under-the-stairway sanctuary, it also helps to keep this area of the home from collecting clutter or accumulating items that sit, sometimes for years at a time, without being moved. Storage areas under stairways that lie undisturbed for long periods of time can increase feelings of lethargy and stagnation in the home and need to be attended to.

If you have a home without children, consider creative uses for the space under the stairway. It might be suitable as a wine cellar, a small office, a pet retreat, a storage area for sports equipment that's used regularly, or as a pantry for items that are too large for the kitchen. These are great ways to keep this area from becoming a receptacle for forgotten and unused items.

Ceilings

Ceiling height can impact the way you experience the feng shui of a particular room. For a room to feel comfortable, the ceiling height should be proportionate to the length and width of the room. If a foyer has a dramatically high ceiling, it may not feel welcoming. Most people feel comfortable in a room where the ceiling height is between seven and ten feet—any higher than that and survival instincts begin to go on alert. Comfort and relaxation come from being able to keep your gaze at eye level while still being able to see the line of the ceiling without tilting your head. When a ceiling is taller than ten feet, you can't easily see what's going on above you without moving your eyes or your head. Survival instincts are pretty basic, and even though you know intellectually that there's nothing dangerous going on when you can't see the ceiling, your instincts may tell you otherwise and make it harder to relax.

Ceiling height also affects social interaction and feelings of intimacy in a room. The higher the ceiling, the less personal the room feels. In the book *A Pattern Language,* the authors write, "In particular, make ceilings high in rooms which are public or meant for large gatherings (10 to 12 feet), lower in rooms for smaller gatherings (7 to 9 feet), and very low in rooms or alcoves for one or two people (6 to 7 feet)."[2]

Cathedral ceilings in modern homes are designed to make a bold, sweeping statement but are not designed to provide the occupants with a feeling of comfort or protection. The term "cathedral ceiling" refers to the great churches built during the middle ages. The purpose of the grand cathedral was to make the average person feel small in the eyes of God. It is an awe-inspiring experience to enter a cathedral today and must have been even more so during times when most people lived in dark, damp hovels. The cathedral, with its soaring ceilings, provided an other-worldly experience of majesty and wonder.

The dramatic impression of a cathedral ceiling may entice you to buy a home, but once you're living in the home, the rooms with the tall ceilings often become neglected and seldom used. You'll notice that family and friends prefer to spend time in rooms with lower ceilings (between seven and ten feet).

How to Remedy Tall Ceilings

If you have a room with very high ceilings, remove any sources of visual interest that draw the eye up toward the ceiling. Placing artwork up high on the walls or hanging long, vertical pieces, such as drapes on very tall windows, should be avoided. Consider the following ideas to make the space feel more intimate and relaxing:

- Paint the ceiling in a tone that's slightly darker than the walls to give the impression that the ceiling is lower than it is.

- Create visual interest at the lower level of the room with plants, patterned area rugs, colorful pillows, vases, and attractive items displayed on tables.

---

[2] Christopher Alexander and others, *A Pattern Language* (New York: Oxford University Press, 1977), 881.

- Choose artwork with horizontal lines, such as seascapes and landscapes.

- Select accent pieces and accessories in bold or dark colors
  to keep the focus in the room at floor level.

Low Ceilings

Conversely, if a room has ceilings that are too low, you may feel stifled and claustrophobic, which survival instincts often register as feeling confined. Rooms with very low ceilings benefit from natural light—the more, the better. Consider adding skylights. Use light paint colors on the walls and ceiling. Vertical lines will also make the room feel taller. Add wallpaper with vertical stripes, long drapes, or artwork with long, vertical lines (such as trees) to visually heighten the room.

Open-Beam Ceilings

Many people feel that open-beam ceilings lend rustic charm to a room. Lodges and large hotels often feature open-beam ceilings in their lobbies to create a certain ambience. The higher the ceiling, the less oppressive the exposed beams will seem. If the ceiling is very high, exposed beams can visually lower the ceiling, making the room feel more intimate. On the other hand, if a ceiling is low, exposed beams will only make it appear lower, and the room will likely feel oppressive and uncomfortable.

Reality Check

Myth: Open-beam ceilings bring bad luck.

Are open-beam ceilings bad luck? I get asked this question a lot when I consult with clients. Often, they've read or heard that open-beam ceilings bring all sorts of negative experiences—from headaches and joint problems to divorce.

Once again, the "bad luck" associated with open-beam ceilings stems from common-sense advice, which has been replaced by superstition over time. In order to understand why open-beam ceilings were considered bad feng shui, we need to go back to the time and place where feng shui began.

China is a land prone to seismic activity. When structures were built (by hand) in earthquake-prone China hundreds of years ago, it was sound advice to avoid sleeping or sitting for long periods under load-bearing beams. However, it's important to note that open-beam ceilings are not inherently bad. In fact, almost all buildings require ceiling beams to hold up the roof. Therefore, it's simply how you feel when sitting or sleeping in a room with open-beam ceilings that determines your experience. This is entirely subjective and differs from person to person. Some people like the feeling and ambience that beams provide, while others find them oppressive and threatening.

Remember, if it feels good, it's good feng shui. If the exposed beams in your home don't feel good to you, then read on for some solutions.

Open-Beam Ceilings in the Main Rooms

When ceiling beams are exposed in rooms where there's a great deal of movement, for example in living rooms, family rooms, and kitchens, the beams can add charm and architectural interest. Open-beam ceilings in these rooms may not feel threatening because you're not spending extended periods of time directly under them. However, sleeping under an open-beam ceiling can, for some people, feel threatening and impact restful sleep. Open-beam ceilings can activate survival instincts in that there's something heavy looming overhead while you're sleeping and vulnerable for hours at a time.

For other people, having an open-beam ceiling in the bedroom may be interesting or attractive and not threatening at all. I once lived in a charming, little beach cottage with whitewashed walls and open-beam ceilings throughout. Instead of feeling vulnerable, I loved lying in bed and looking up at my ceiling. I never felt unsafe or threatened by the beams, and I actually missed them after I moved.

On the other hand, I once slept in a mountain lodge with very heavy exposed beams over the bed, and I never slept a wink because they felt so oppressive. Ultimately, you have to be the one who decides whether or not the beams feel good to you. If you're bothered by an open-beam ceiling in your bedroom, consider the following changes:

- Paint the beams the same color as the ceiling and walls to lessen their impact.

- Sleep under a canopy bed, which may help you feel more secure.

- Remove the beams, if it's possible to do so.

- Cover them by "dropping the ceiling" and creating a false ceiling.

Of course, if you sleep in a bedroom with open-beam ceilings and they don't disturb your sleep or the way you feel, then you have nothing to worry about. Having beams on the ceiling of a bedroom is an individual choice and needs to be considered on a case-by-case basis.

The Amount and Size of Ceiling Beams

Some rooms have only one ceiling beam running the entire length of the room. Usually, this is a load-bearing beam, meaning that it's structural and is holding up the roof. Most likely, the architect left this beam exposed to bring architectural interest to the room. This type of beam is common in rooms with pitched ceilings. Generally, this kind of a beam isn't a problem because it's the only exposed beam, giving you some flexibility in whether to sleep or sit directly under it by where you place the furniture.

If the ceiling beams are small, they tend to have less of an impact than larger, heavier beams. Then again, a ceiling with many small beams can feel too busy and will draw attention up to the ceiling. A room with lots of exposed ceiling beams can decrease feelings of relaxation because you have no choice but to sit or sleep under them. This effect can be minimized by painting the beams the same color as the walls and ceiling.

Color

When ceiling beams are stained or painted in dark colors, they appear larger and lower than if they're painted in light colors or in the same color as the ceiling. In my current home, I have a large sunroom with an open-beam ceiling. The previous occupants had painted the walls in white and the ceiling beams in black. The black beams not only looked ugly, but they significantly lowered the visual height of the 8-1/2-foot ceiling and were the main thing that you noticed when looking at the room. The heavy-looking black beams totally ruined the atmosphere in this sunny and cheerful room.

To solve the problem, I had the ceiling and beams painted in the same white as the walls, and the effect was dramatic. Not only did the room feel incredibly lighter and brighter, but the beams now made the sunroom feel more interesting and charming than it had before.

Social Rooms (Family Rooms, Living Rooms, Great Rooms)

Family rooms, living rooms, and great rooms—what I call "social rooms"—all have the same basic purpose: a place where people can gather for conversation, entertainment, and relaxation. In this section, you will learn how to create social rooms that encourage positive interactions and experiences for yourself, your family, and your guests.

Reality Check

Myth: *By arranging furniture in specific patterns, the occupants will experience better luck and greater fortune.*

Feng shui is sometimes called "the art of placement," perpetuating a misguided notion that by arranging furniture in specific patterns, people can somehow increase their luck and fortune. While this concept is tossed around carelessly by laymen and feng shui practitioners alike, I've met very few people who actually understand the reasoning or meaning behind it.

While moving furniture around may not increase your luck, I do know that arranging furniture properly can increase feelings of comfort and relaxation. Incidentally, one of my favorite things to do with clients is to rearrange furniture in rooms that don't feel right. It's so much fun to see their faces light up when they first experience the improvement in the way a room feels after it has been rearranged using their existing furnishings and décor.

The main goal of feng shui is to create a place that nurtures and inspires you—a place where you and your friends and family can relax, rest, and enjoy yourselves and your lives. When your home feels like a positive, supportive place, you'll most likely find that your life in general is happier and more successful. *This* is the fortune of feng shui!

Furniture Choices and Arrangements

When arranging furniture in social rooms, seating arrangements should be relaxed and not too formal. Be sure that the furniture you choose feels good when you sit on it. Think twice about shopping for seating on the Internet. There are many sofas, chairs, and sectionals that look great in pictures but are miserable to sit on. Be sure to try your seating choices in person before you buy them.

Seating areas should be located within eight feet of each other, or the room loses a feeling of intimacy, making conversation more difficult. Seating areas need adequate tables nearby to accommodate drinks, food, books, magazines, the remote control, or whatever else you need within reach while relaxing. Blankets and extra pillows can make the room more comfortable, but be sure to have convenient storage options such as a trunk or a cupboard for these items when not in use.

Inconsiderate Friends or Bad Feng Shui?

I once did a consultation for a couple who lived in a very small, one-bedroom house. The husband was against having a coffee table in the living room. He felt it would crowd the room, so he dissuaded his wife from putting a table in front of the sofa. In spite of the small size of their home, this couple entertained a lot. In fact, I don't think I've ever met two people who entertain more than this couple. Still, they complained constantly about how their clumsy guests would spill food and drinks on the carpet. They wondered why their friends "couldn't be more careful" when visiting.

It's not difficult to understand what the source of the problem was. By eliminating the coffee table, they didn't provide enough surfaces where guests could place their food or drinks. As a consequence, there were likely to be more spills. I pointed this out, and the husband adamantly declared that he wasn't going to change his opinion on adding a coffee table. His stance was that he needed more considerate friends, rather than a coffee table! There was no sense in trying to reason with his logic, so I dropped the subject. When I drove past their house recently, the carpet-cleaning van was parked out front—again.

Choosing Furniture

By now, you understand that softening hard angles and sharp corners is important to making a space feel better. When deciding what shape the furnishings should be, avoid sharp angles and points as much as possible. Instead, opt for soft, rounded edges. Choosing softer lines will make the entire room feel more welcoming.

If you already have a piece of furniture with sharp corners, such as an end table, consider placing the piece on the diagonal in a corner. This placement makes the room feel better than placing the table at a right angle to the corner. Chairs also feel better when arranged on an angle in a seating area. Figures 5.9 and 5.10 illustrate how placing furniture on angles can create a less formal, more comfortable seating arrangement.

Figure 5.9

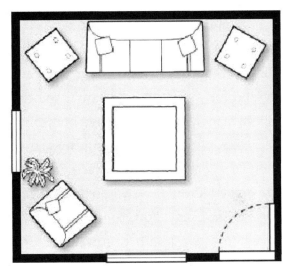
Figure 5.10

When placing furniture, don't be afraid to *think outside the box* with your arrangements. Have a friend help you place your sofa, television, or bookcase at an angle. Then, step back and see if that arrangement makes the room feel any better. It may, and it may not. If an idea doesn't work, the worst thing that can happen is that you put the furniture back to where it was. Try moving furniture away from the walls, or place different groupings together. Add rugs, pillows, and tables, or subtract the same. If you have too much furniture, either get rid of it or add it to another room that needs more. If you have too little furniture in a room but you don't want to add more, an area rug will do wonders to take up empty space.

Survival Instincts and Furniture Arrangements

To make the most of seating arrangements, you must consider the effect of improperly placed furniture. Safe, comfortable, and relaxing surroundings increase positive feelings and interactions. The first thing to consider in a seating arrangement is how the larger pieces relate to each other. Feng shui advises against seating arrangements where people sit directly across from each another. This arrangement is known as "Confrontation Position."

To better understand the effect of this arrangement, try the following experiment with a friend: Ask your friend to stand up and face you in a relaxed position, as if the two of you are going to have a friendly face-to-face conversation. (Don't tell your friend what you're trying to do just yet.) Stand there with your friend for a second, and you'll see that each of you has a shoulder turned, ever so slightly, away from the other person.

Now, without advancing toward your friend, gently pivot your shoulder so that you're *directly facing* your friend. You'll notice that your friend will either step back or pivot a shoulder away from you again. Your friend may even react in a surprised or startled way. You, too, will feel the shift from relaxation to tension. This shift in energy is a result of how our survival instincts respond when we feel directly confronted by someone.

The way that Confrontation Position works is simple. Your most vital, vulnerable organs are located toward the front of your body. There's a strong instinct to protect these vital organs, and that instinct carries over into interactions with others—even with people you know well and with whom you are completely comfortable. When you stand with your shoulders directly facing another person, you're sending a non-verbal message that's confrontational, causing survival mechanisms to go on alert and creating a heightened sense of tension. Normally, when you're talking with another person, you stand with your shoulders and body weight shifted slightly away from that person. This stance gives each person a subliminal advantage in easily turning to flee (and protecting the vital organs), if there's suddenly a threat.

The previous exercise is a great example of what *not* to do when arranging seating. When people are forced to sit directly across from one another, the same dynamic occurs as if they were standing directly across from each other. People will feel tense and less relaxed when seated this way, and these feelings are the opposite of good feng shui.

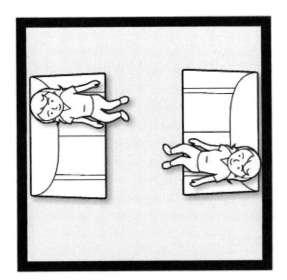

Figure 5.11 shows what happens when two love seats are placed directly across from one another and two people sit down. Most of the time, one person will sit at one end of one love seat, and the other person will sit at the opposite end of the other love seat. This allows them to have a relaxed conversation without feeling confrontational.

Figure 5.11

Figure 5.12 shows what happens when three people sit down. Two must sit side by side, and the third person will most likely choose to sit in the middle on the other seat rather than sit directly across from one of the other people.

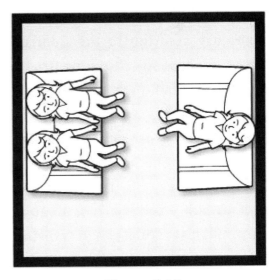

Figure 5.12

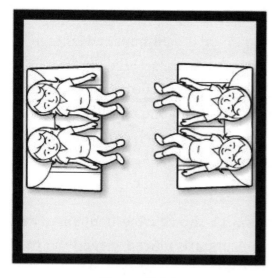

Figure 5.13

In figure 5.13, there's a fourth person. Now all the available seats are taken, and everyone must face each other directly. When there's no choice but to sit directly across from someone else, people will tend to sit with their legs crossed or their bodies turned slightly sideways. By sitting this way, people are unconsciously trying to protect their vital organs. Their survival instincts are trying to make a less-than-optimal seating arrangement feel more comfortable.

The only time when seating people directly across from each other works is when there's a large table that's high enough to cover most of the vital organs (think of a dining table versus a coffee table). A large piece of furniture, like a dining table, feels as though it's protecting the abdomen and chest, allowing people to relax even though they're sitting directly across from each other.

A Word about Sectionals

One easy solution to the Confrontation Position seating dilemma is to place furniture in an L-position, as seen in figure 5.14. This is why a sectional sofa is such a great piece of furniture. It allows people to easily see one another without having to strain their necks (as they would sitting side by side), and it avoids Confrontation Position. A sectional can also divide a very large room into smaller, friendlier areas.

Figure 5.14

If you're thinking about buying a sectional, keep a couple of things in mind: First, a sectional sofa can look deceptively small in a showroom. Carefully measure your room and the sectional before you buy. Bring these measurements home, and place newspaper on the floor of the room to represent the dimensions of the sectional. This will give you a good idea of the actual footprint of the sectional and help you determine whether this large piece of furniture will work in your house.

Also, avoid choosing the chaise lounge piece that's attached to many sectionals (see figure 5.15). This piece creates an obstacle in the traffic pattern through a room because it sticks out, which can also make furniture placement tricky. The chaise also disrupts the flow of energy between people because only one person is able to stretch out and recline, while the others must sit upright, creating a feeling of imbalance within the group.

Figure 5.15

Figure 5.16

A wonderful alternative to the chaise lounge is a large ottoman coffee table, as shown in figure 5.16. An ottoman coffee table is a very versatile piece of furniture. It can be pushed up against the sofa as a footrest or used with a tray for drinks and food. It can also provide extra seating. Some ottoman coffee tables even have lids that open, providing storage for toys, throw pillows, and blankets. Because they're made of cloth or leather, ottomans have soft edges, which add good feng shui, especially in homes with small children.

Colors for Furnishings

A large piece of furniture can be a substantial financial investment. You may get more longevity out of a piece if you opt for neutral fabrics and colors. This will ensure that you won't get tired of the piece before it wears out. A strong pattern and/or color statement may become tiresome as your mood and taste change over time. A neutral color can always be jazzed up with bright throw pillows. Keep in mind that furnishings upholstered in dark fabrics will appear larger than pieces upholstered in light colors, so they are not ideal for small rooms.

Furniture with Arms

It always feels best when chairs and sofas have arms rather than open sides. In feng shui, the ideal configuration for a home on a lot is known as Armchair Position, meaning that the home has protection from behind and from both sides. Chairs, sofas, and love seats with arms feel more secure than those without, as long as the arms aren't so high that one feels trapped when seated. Dining chairs are an exception to this, due to space constraints.

Furniture That's Too Large for a Room

As a feng shui consultant, I'm often confronted either with rooms having too much furniture or with furniture that's too large for the room. Both conditions can make a room feel claustrophobic and uncomfortable. I once worked in a home where an average-sized living room had so much furniture in it that one of the sofas completely covered the fireplace, and a gigantic 72-inch television completely covered the main window. To make matters worse, the sofa was upholstered in a large, busy floral pattern, which made it seem even larger. My client admitted that even though the television was in this room, no one liked to sit in there. When I explained that the furniture was too large for the room, my client said simply that her husband wouldn't let her change it, and she didn't know what to do.

This scenario happens often during consultations. In an ideal world, the client would get rid of the huge, overstuffed furniture, replace the monster television with a smaller-sized one, and consider solid fabric choices over loud patterns. In this case, however, the family's budget didn't allow for these expensive changes. So, we agreed to move one of the large sofas upstairs to a loft area and relocate the television to the wall next to the (now exposed) fireplace. While the remaining sofa with the loud pattern still screamed for attention, the room was starting to feel better; there was more light, and it felt good to see the fireplace.

The next improvement I suggested was to slipcover the remaining sofa with a solid neutral color in order to make it less obtrusive. To show my client what I was aiming for, I had her grab a large, plain bed sheet. We covered the sofa with the bed sheet, and the transformation was remarkable. My client was amazed when she saw and felt how much better the room looked with just these simple adjustments. Her family commented positively on the difference, and they started to use the room on a daily basis.

Focal Points and Furniture

The focal points in a room need to be considered when arranging furniture. A focal point can be a large window with a view, a fireplace, a television, a spectacular piece of art, or a large and commanding piece of furniture. When arranging furniture, it's best if the focal points are either on the same wall or adjacent walls. When focal points are on opposing walls, a room becomes awkward, and furniture arrangement is difficult.

I had a client named Nancy who needed help with her family room arrangement. She told me that she hated the room, and try as she might, she couldn't make the layout work. Like a child frustrated over a puzzle, Nancy was at wit's end when she called me. She couldn't figure out how to arrange the furniture comfortably in this long and somewhat narrow room (see figure 5.17). Adding to her frustration was the fact that this room had three focal points: a fireplace on one wall, a large window with a beautiful view on the longest wall, and a television on the wall opposite the fireplace.

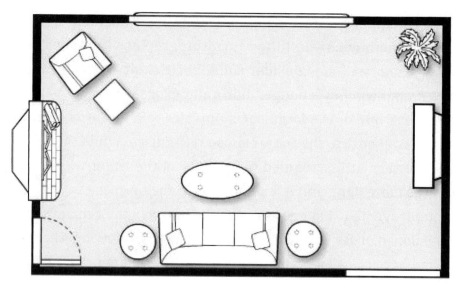

Figure 5.17

Nancy had placed the sofa on the wall opposite the large window. The main problem with the room was that two of the main focal points (the fireplace and the television) were on opposite walls, which made it challenging and uncomfortable to watch television, socialize, and enjoy the fireplace all at the same time.

I explained to Nancy that the solution to the seating dilemma in this room was to move one of the focal points (the television) and, in turn, the furniture. We placed the television diagonally in the corner between the fireplace and the large window. This way, all the focal points were next to each other on two adjacent walls rather than on three. We then placed the sofa at an angle across from the television, moved the chair and coffee table, and added a sofa table and a rug from another room. Now, anyone sitting on the sofa could easily see the fireplace, the television, and the view out the window. We also placed a mirror above the fireplace so anyone seated could see what was going on behind them. Figure 5.18 shows the changes we made in order to get the seating arrangement to function better. The room went from being Nancy's most frustrating room to her favorite room in just a matter of minutes, all without spending a penny!

Figure 5.18

Bookcases

Bookcases can add sophistication and elegance to a room or confusion and chaos. In feng shui, we are always striving for balance and harmony. A bookcase should add to the balance of a room rather than detract from it. If you enjoy displaying books in bookcases, here are a few tips.

First, conduct a thorough inventory of your books, getting rid of any tattered or used paperbacks. Keep books that you'll read or use as references, and donate the rest to charities, schools, or libraries.

Next, remove the dust jackets on hardcover books. Eyes are drawn to the bright colors and shiny textures of dust jackets. To maintain a feeling of calm and elegance in a room, remove the dust jackets and store them inside the book, opting to display the cloth spines and matte textures of the hard covers.

Finally, organize books by color on the shelves. Grouping books together by spine color can calm the visual stimulation created by the variety of books displayed in a bookcase. Position books at the front of the shelf so that the spines sit even with each other at the edge of the shelf. Books that are pushed to the back of a bookcase create a jagged, uneven line.

Bookcases that extend from floor to ceiling can seem oppressive, almost as if they're leaning over you—which they might be! Always aim for a feeling of safety with furniture placement. If a piece of furniture feels like it's leaning toward you or you imagine that it might fall on you, this is definitely not good feng shui. To minimize the effect of a towering bookcase, place the largest, heaviest books on the lower shelves, and place the smaller, thinner books on the upper shelves. If you wish to display objects on the shelves, follow the same advice: Heavy items are displayed on lower shelves, and more delicate items are displayed on upper shelves. Be sure to place fewer items on upper shelves and leave some open spaces. Whatever your eye sees, your brain automatically processes as information. The more things there are in a room, the more information that your brain has to process, and the busier the room will feel. Even a bookcase that's a beautiful and stately piece of furniture can become an eyesore if it's filled with a colorful hodgepodge of books and objects, making the room feel messy and disorganized. To store miscellaneous items, select cabinets with solid (not glass) doors to keep the room feeling relaxed and orderly.

Televisions

There's a lot of conflicting information regarding televisions that's perpetuated in feng shui circles. No matter what, the choice of whether or not to have a television and whether to leave it exposed or hidden are ultimately personal preferences. I personally enjoy watching television. It relaxes me at the end of the day, and I like to watch a good movie from time to time in the comfort of my home. My perception of the television is positive, and I don't view it as a disruption to my home life. Other people, however, strongly dislike the television as a focal point in a room.

If you prefer to hide the television, there are many creative ways to do so using sliding doors, paintings, or panels. Prior to the popularity of flat-screen televisions, people who chose to hide the television in an armoire or an entertainment center were actually doing more harm than good. It takes a large room with a high ceiling to accommodate a big piece of furniture like an armoire, and such a heavy piece of furniture needs to be balanced on the other side of the room with an equally large object or image; otherwise, the room will feel lopsided. All of this often creates a bigger eyesore than the television ever did. I've always thought of an armoire hiding a television much like an elephant wearing a dress. You can dress it up all you want, but by placing something large inside of something larger, all you've done is drawn more attention to it. Fortunately, the bulky television is a thing of the past, and the dilemma of the towering armoire has almost been eliminated.

Mounted Televisions: A Matter of Perspective

I often see televisions that are mounted much too high on the wall or above a fireplace. Although the television might seem like it's at a good height from a standing position, it's when you sit down that you notice how much you have to crane your neck to see it. A television should be placed so that the center of the screen is at eye level when you're seated.

Large Windows and Views

Few things make a room more spectacular than a beautiful, commanding view. However, very large windows also can make you feel exposed and diminish your ability to relax in a room. Large windows, especially floor-to-ceiling ones, can make you feel vulnerable—almost as though they might suck you right out of the room. In some feng shui literature, you may read that large windows "suck the chi right out of a room." In reality, a very large window can cause survival instincts to go on alert, and you may find yourself seeking out other places in the house where you feel more protected. How can you solve this problem without covering up the view? Fortunately, as my client Rosalee learned, the solution is fairly simple.

A Room with a View

Rosalee lived high on a hill in a beautiful home with sweeping, unobstructed ocean views. Her large and beautifully decorated living room featured floor-to-ceiling windows looking out onto the California coastline. The view was awe-inspiring. Yet, for some unknown reason, no one in Rosalee's family enjoyed sitting in this room. Instead, the family chose to hang out in other rooms, leaving this room and its beautiful view unused and neglected. Rosalee hoped that I could help her discover what was wrong and what could be done to make the room more welcoming. After all, it was this very room and its spectacular view that had inspired her to buy the house in the first place.

Rosalee had tastefully decorated the living room in shades of blue, chocolate, and cream. I asked her if she had a long scarf or shawl in a nice, chocolate color. She did, and when she brought it to me, I held it up along the edge of the window. Rosalee's expression spoke louder than words. She said she couldn't believe how different the room felt.

Of course, it was feng shui at its finest—the cloth and the darker color around the window provided the illusion of a buffer zone between the interior of the home and the exterior view. Much like adding a mat around a painting, the cloth framed the view and gave the eye something to rest on in the safety of the room before looking out the window. You can see the difference that the curtains made in figure 5.19. The panels gave the view depth, contrast, and interest, while providing a visual feeling of protection. They also added a sense of coziness and warmth that the room had previously lacked.

Figure 5.19

After Rosalee had drapery panels made and hung in her living room, she told me that her family had begun to spend as much time as possible in this room. The drapes remain open, so the view is just as commanding as before, but the secure feeling that the drapes provide remedied the uncomfortable feelings that the bare window used to promote.

When adding drapes or curtains to a large window, remember that they don't necessarily need to span the entire window. Often, they can be just panels on either side of a window. Sometimes a valance can help, too, as long as it doesn't detract from the view or feel oppressive. When adding cloth panels, curtains, or drapes along the edge of a window, you'll also be activating the Goldilocks Principle by balancing a very large, cold, smooth surface (the window) with the texture of the cloth (the drape), which in turn will make the room feel even better.

Kitchens

For many people, the kitchen is an important part of the home. For some, it's so important that it's one of the biggest considerations in choosing a new home. Frequently the hub of activity, a kitchen that's well-designed also functions smoothly and easily. Conversely, a kitchen that's poorly designed can result in frustration and irritation, two emotions that we try to minimize or eliminate in feng shui.

The ancient Chinese placed great importance on the preparation of food and created several feng shui criteria for making the process as safe and efficient as possible. When applying feng shui guidelines to a kitchen, it's important to remember that many of the guidelines originated at a time when people cooked over an open fire, and starting the fire was a laborious and sometimes dangerous undertaking.

With the advent of natural gas, indoor plumbing, and electricity, the function and efficiency of modern cooking areas differ vastly from the kitchens of long ago. As such, some of the original feng shui guidelines for the kitchen no longer apply to modern homes. However, when these outdated guidelines are mistakenly applied to modern kitchens, they no longer make sense and end up sounding like silly superstitions. As you can imagine, the kitchen has become fertile ground for many feng shui myths and misunderstandings. Let's take a look at a few of them to see if we can separate fact from fiction.

Reality Check

Myth: To avoid misfortune, make sure the kitchen sink is never located directly across from the stove.

Some feng shui lore attributes a host of negative repercussions to a kitchen with an "incorrect" layout. Often, it mentions that the sink should never be placed opposite the stove or next to it because water and fire are conflicting elements.

It's very important to remember that the system of feng shui began thousands of years ago, ages before indoor heating, plumbing, electricity, gas ranges, or matches. In order to cook a meal, people in ancient China had to start a fire, maintain it, and take care that it didn't go out. In the days before matches, making a fire was an arduous task, so discouraging the placement of water near an open flame made perfect sense back then. While it's true that water is the destructive element to fire (see chapter 6), it's perfectly fine to place the sink next to or across from the stove. This is another feng shui myth with practical origins that has lost its meaning in modern culture.

As you'll learn in more detail in chapter 6, every element in the five element cycle—water, wood, fire, earth, and metal—has a corresponding element that destroys it. Yes, water is destructive to fire, but you don't hear other statements like, "Never put a plant in soil." (Wood absorbs earth.) Or, "Never cook in a metal pot." (Fire melts metal.) Every element has a destructive element, but the element cycle is *not* why the Chinese originally discouraged water near the open flame where food was being cooked. It was simply that having water too near the cooking fire was impractical.

These days, we cook on electric and gas stoves with heat that is easily accessible. Granted, you wouldn't want water poured over your stove while you're cooking, but nothing "bad" will happen if your sink is opposite or next to your stove. In fact, mine has been this way for the entire twelve years I've lived in my home, and nothing bad has ever happened as a result!

A Mirror under the Range Hood

If you have a very dark space under the hood that hangs over your stove, a mirror placed on the wall above the stove can lighten up the dark space. A mirror is also an easy surface to clean after cooking. If you can find a mirror made of Mylar® (some home improvement centers sell them), even better. Mylar® is a reflective material that's lighter than glass and won't shatter like glass does. You don't need to drill holes in the granite or tile backsplash to place a mirror behind the stove. Simply rest the mirror on the back of the stove if there's room, or use museum putty to stick it to the wall. You'll be amazed at how it opens up the space. If the mirror reflects a window, it will seem as if you added another window to the room. Hanging a mirror under a range hood can really transform the way your kitchen feels. Just be sure to place the mirror safely away from heat and open flames.

Reality Check

Myth: *Kitchen mirrors bring good fortune.*

While placing a mirror under an oppressive range hood is a great way to lighten up a dark space, there are also misunderstandings in feng shui over why placing a mirror above the stove is a good idea. A common feng shui myth states that having a mirror behind your stove "doubles the wealth" by reflecting the image of the food cooking on the stove. Another kitchen myth states that a mirror behind your stove prevents people from sneaking up behind you and startling you.

Gee, how many times in all the years that you've been cooking has someone startled you at your stove? I can remember it happening to me only once, and it was when my boyfriend at the time slid his arms around my waist and kissed me on the back of my neck while I was cooking dinner—certainly not bad feng shui!

Feel free to add a mirror behind your stove to brighten up a dark area, but don't expect your wealth or "luck" to double just because you did this! With all the superstition out of the way, let's examine some common-sense ways to give your kitchen good feng shui.

As with all rooms in the home, the kitchen must be a space that's relaxed, comfortable, and easy to use. If you're remodeling your kitchen, be sure to consult with a kitchen design expert in addition to a contractor. It's important that traffic patterns and ergonomic issues be addressed in the early stages of your kitchen design. A kitchen expert will know the proper dimensions and arrangements for lighting, appliances, and countertops to make your kitchen efficient and pleasing.

The kitchen should be a safe, happy, clean, and well-organized space where meals are prepared easily and efficiently. Even if you don't love to cook, the kitchen's long-term association with family, health, and a happy home is long-lived. Creating a kitchen that feels positive and welcoming goes a long way toward enhancing the overall feeling of the entire home. Below are some key points to keep in mind regarding the feng shui of your kitchen.

Lighting

Lighting greatly influences the way you experience your kitchen. After leaving the privacy of your bedroom and bathroom in the morning, the kitchen is usually the first room that you spend time in during the day. Studies indicate that most people rate a sunny kitchen in the morning as "highly preferable" over kitchens that don't receive direct morning sunlight. Exposure to sunlight stimulates the production of serotonin and melatonin, which directly affect mood and attitude. Exposure to natural sunlight in the morning helps regulate circadian rhythms and internal body clocks to set the tone for the day to come.

If it's impossible to receive sunlight through your kitchen windows in the morning, installing a skylight or a solar tube may be an option. A simple way to make the kitchen feel better is to replace all of the partial-spectrum light bulbs with full-spectrum bulbs. Full-spectrum lighting mimics the natural light of the sun. The room will be illuminated with a clear, bright light instead of a dingy, yellow light. Changing the kitchen light bulbs to full-spectrum bulbs is an easy and relatively inexpensive enhancement that renters and homeowners alike can implement. It's especially beneficial for those living in apartments or condos with windowless kitchens.

Colors

Paint choices impact the feng shui of a kitchen because color influences attitude and emotion. While paint choices are highly subjective, there are basic guidelines on choosing paint for your kitchen. As always, the most important thing in feng shui is that your space feels good to you. If it feels good, it's good feng shui, so ultimately you'll have to decide for yourself which color scheme will make you happy.

Red and Orange

These colors stimulate the appetite and can be associated with eating and over-eating. Notice that many fast-food restaurants use red and orange in their logos and décor. That's no accident—they're hoping that you'll buy more and eat more! With obesity at record levels, the strategy seems to be working. So, while these colors are associated with food, think twice before putting them in your kitchen if you're trying to watch your weight.

Blue

Blue is the opposite of orange on a color wheel. Blue makes people feel less hungry because blue food is rarely found in nature. If you use a lot of red and orange in your kitchen, blue is a great balancer. Too much blue, however, and your meals may not seem as appetizing—an unfortunate side effect for those who love to cook and entertain.

Black

Black is not a good color to use in a kitchen. Black can make a room feel smaller, and the kitchen is a room where space is often at a premium. Many people choose to complement black countertops and appliances with bright white walls, flooring, or cabinetry. The result can be dramatic but can also feel very cold—certainly not a nurturing place where people will want to relax and hang out.

If you like the crisp look of a black and white kitchen, you may want to add small accents in red to make the room visually "pop." A red teakettle on the stove, a white bowl filled with red apples, a red accent rug, or red tea towels are small bursts of color that will balance the extreme of black and white.

If you really want to use black in your kitchen, either on countertops or with appliances, consider adding light earth tones—mocha, taupe, or tan—rather than white on the walls, the cabinets, or the floor. Earth tones will balance the heaviness of black, making the kitchen feel warmer and more inviting.

Earth Tones, Soft Yellows, and Gold

Earth tones, soft yellows, and gold work well in kitchens. Browns and tans add a relaxed, cozy feeling, while soft yellows and gold can evoke feelings of security and happiness. These colors encourage people to gather together, to laugh, to share, and to enjoy a meal. However, be sure to avoid painting the kitchen walls in a bold shade of yellow. This color can be over-stimulating and make people prone to arguments.

White

White is associated with cleanliness, which is a desirable trait for any kitchen. However, a completely white palette can make a kitchen feel cold and unfriendly, not to mention that white shows every spill and smudge. If you enjoy the crispness of a white kitchen, be sure to balance it with red accents to warm up a potentially "chilly" room.

Safety

Creating a feeling of safety in the kitchen is very important to good feng shui. The kitchen provides many opportunities for household accidents. The stove, sharp utensils, and hard, slippery surfaces make it a hazardous area.

Knives

One easy and important way to create better feng shui in your kitchen is to store your knives in a drawer. Displaying knives in a block or, worse, on a wall-mounted magnetic strip creates a safety hazard and is not good feng shui. Knives make people feel threatened and vulnerable. Knives that are displayed on countertops are the sharpest ones we own; therefore, it's even more important that they are not displayed.

I was talking to a group of my feng shui students when we got on the subject of knife blocks in kitchens. I was telling them about the preference in feng shui for keeping knives hidden away in drawers and cupboards, since they're threatening objects that can make us feel unsafe.

A student named Marie shared an important story that demonstrated the practicality of this feng shui suggestion. She told the group that three years earlier, she was burglarized. She was upstairs in her bedroom when she heard the intruder downstairs. Panicking, she called 911.

The emergency dispatcher asked Marie if she had any weapons in her home. Marie said, "No." The operator then asked Marie if she had a knife block in her kitchen. She said, "Yes."

The operator responded, "Then you have weapons in your home." After the police arrived and caught the intruder, Marie asked about the knife block. The officer explained that when an unarmed burglar breaks into a home and is startled, the knife block provides an easily accessible weapon leading to a potentially dangerous situation. They, too, recommended that Marie keep her knife block in a cupboard and out of reach of intruders (and children).

Heavy Objects Overhead

Avoid hanging pots and pans from ceiling-mounted racks. Not only does this add to the appearance of clutter, it poses a threat to your safety. You don't need to live in earthquake country to know that something stored above your head can fall and hurt you. It's best to store pots and pans in cupboards out of sight.

Many times, kitchen cupboards are installed below ceiling height, leaving a decent-sized space between the top of the cupboard and the ceiling. While it may be tempting to display or store objects up there to fill the space, don't do it. In addition to the potential and perceived dangers of objects overhead, these items also draw attention to the ceiling, rather than keeping your attention at eye level where it's more relaxed. If you really want to decorate the top of your cabinets, keep the area free of heavy, decorative items and consider putting a few (not too many) light and airy silk plants instead. Keep in mind that objects placed above the cabinets also become hard-to-reach dust collectors. Over the years as a feng shui consultant, I've seen some pretty unappetizing, filthy objects pulled from their perches above kitchen cabinets. If you choose to put silk plants up there, be sure to take them outside and hose them off regularly.

Microwave Ovens

In feng shui, we are always trying to live as harmoniously and happily as possible. An integral part of being happy is being healthy. While not conclusive, there is a significant amount of scientific data warning that the use of microwave ovens may be harmful to health. Some studies question the impact of microwaves on the nutritional value of food, and there's a growing body of evidence suggesting that the electromagnetic fields (EMFs) emitted by microwave ovens may be harmful.

If you must cook food or boil water in your microwave oven, please stand at least six feet away from it while it's on; this distance helps to reduce your exposure to EMFs. Never stand in front of the microwave oven while it's running. You're exposing your head, specifically your brain, to a lot of electromagnetic radiation that may jeopardize your health. I encourage you to research this issue and decide for yourself whether using a microwave oven is a health risk that you're willing to take. When it comes to health and well-being, I feel it's better to be safe than sorry.

Clutter

Too often, I see kitchens that are overcrowded, cluttered, and messy. The counters overflow with gadgets, spices, boxes, dishes, and knickknacks. In order for your kitchen to have good feng shui, you must minimize the clutter. When you minimize clutter, you maximize efficiency.

A good rule of thumb for removing clutter from kitchen counters is this: If you don't use something at least three days per week, it should be stored in a cupboard, not on the counter. If you haven't used your food processor since last Thanksgiving and it's now May, it should be stored in a cupboard or a large drawer. Rarely used appliances and gadgets can be stored in the garage or in other closets in the house. Items kept in kitchen cupboards should be items that you use regularly.

Pantry drawers or cupboards are also targets for mess and clutter. Clean them out regularly! Every time I clean out my own pantry, I discover items that I've bought over and over again—thinking I needed more—only to discover that I had two or three already in my cupboard. Make a habit of using up stored staples before buying new ones. You'll be delighted with both the extra cupboard space and the money you'll save on grocery bills. If space is an issue, add shelves or racks to the inside of cupboards to make the space function more efficiently. Get rid of things that you don't use regularly, or store them neatly in the garage or in clearly labeled bins.

Dining Rooms

Dining rooms are designed to be spaces where people can gather to share a meal. The operative word here is "share." When you dine with others, you share a common experience that binds people together. When considering the feng shui of your dining room, the most important feature is the dining room table.

The Dining Table

From a feng shui perspective, a round table in the dining room is highly preferred to a rectangular one. When people are seated at a round dining table, everyone is seated more or less equally. Since there's no head of the table, as with a long rectangular table, everyone can make eye contact and converse easily with everyone else.

Families share the events of their day more readily when seated at a round table rather than at a rectangular table. If you want to know what's going on with your kids, seat the family at a round table (and of course, turn off the television) during the evening meal. Many of my clients have told me how shocked they were that this actually worked. Instead of hurrying through their meals, the children spent more time at the table, eating and sharing the events of their day with parents and other family members.

When entertaining, guests will relax much more at a round table. There's a feeling of camaraderie that occurs, and they tend to linger over their meal, share conversations, and remain seated at the table for coffee, dessert, and perhaps an after-dinner game. I have a round table in my dining room, and it's so relaxing and conducive to entertaining that sometimes it takes a real effort to get people to leave the table and either go into the other room or go home!

If you're considering a perfectly square table, the eye contact and equality are almost the same as a round table. However, the sharp corners of a square table do not feel as relaxed and comfortable as the safety of rounded edges. Many round tables have leaves that can be added or removed to accommodate more guests. If your dining room is long and narrow and won't allow for a round table, an oval one is a better choice than a rectangular one because the edges are softer. However, an oval shape will not promote the same feeling of unity that a round table will.

Colors

Colors for dining rooms are similar to the colors discussed for kitchens. Warm colors are generally more comfortable and inviting than cool colors, and reds and oranges stimulate the appetite. If you're going to paint the dining room in red, I suggest doing so on just one accent wall. While red is associated with hunger and food, it can also lead to heated discussions and arguments—definitely not good feng shui!

More Ideas for Dining Rooms

When the dining room is optimized from a feng shui perspective, it can serve as the setting for experiences that are pleasing, relaxing, and fulfilling for you and your guests. Here are some tips on creating a positive dining atmosphere:

- Vary the lighting in the dining room by installing dimmer switches, which can be adjusted to the occasion and the mood.

- Make sure that dining room chairs are comfortable and provide adequate back support to encourage a relaxing and pleasant experience.

- Consider that most people look better in soft candlelight. A large mirror on a dining room wall can reflect candlelight from the table and make a small room seem larger.

- Drapes, made of luxurious fabrics that cascade to the floor, can add to the sensuality of a meal.

- Elegant colors such as gold, deep red, burgundy, forest green, and chocolate brown used in curtains, chair cushions, or table decorations bring a rich, sumptuous feeling to the dining experience.

Bedrooms

I know someone who can fall asleep anywhere, anytime. She could curl up near a train track and keep snoozing as the trains roll by. I, on the other hand, have been an insomniac all of my life. My mother used to say that I was like the princess in *The Princess and the Pea* because it was so difficult for me to sleep. Those who've had periodic or chronic bouts of sleeplessness know all too well how a lack of sleep can impact your whole day and how frustrating it is to spend night after night eluded by restful sleep.

Throughout my life, I've spent a great deal of time and money trying to find the perfect bed and the perfect bedroom environment. I've owned waterbeds, air beds, canopy beds, magnetic mattresses, pillow top mattresses, memory foam mattresses, and just about every other type of bed you can imagine. I've tried audiotapes, herbal remedies, acupuncture, medications, and countless other sleep aids. Nothing has ever worked consistently enough to cure my insomnia. However, the one thing that *has* helped is feng shui.

The bedroom is one of the most important rooms in the home because sleep is a vital component to health and well-being. By considering feng shui principles when designing and arranging a bedroom, a great deal can be done to create an environment that's beautiful and conducive to a good night's sleep.

Location, Location, Location

I once had a client named Judy who lived in a beautifully restored, Spanish-style mansion. Judy and her husband had purchased the property when it was in a state of disrepair and had spent years and a great deal of money lovingly returning it to its original grandeur.

The one thing that bothered Judy about the home was that she and her husband slept in a quiet, modest bedroom in the back of the home, rather than in the cavernous master bedroom that overlooked the front of the home. Since the home had a very grand master suite, Judy felt as though she and her husband should be using this as their bedroom, but try as they might, neither one of them ever slept well in there. Judy wanted to know what could be done to fix the problem and whether it made any difference, from a feng shui perspective, that they didn't use the designated master suite as their bedroom.

I assured her that the most important thing was whether or not they were sleeping well. The fact that they slept better in the other room made it clear that this was the best bedroom for them to use. She was very relieved to learn that not sleeping in the huge master suite was just fine. Judy and her husband proceeded to convert it into a home theater.

When you have a choice of bedrooms, it's crucial to choose the bedroom that feels best, whether or not it's the designated master bedroom. You're the most vulnerable when asleep, so bedrooms need to be safe and private. The most important consideration is that the room feels restful.

Usually, the front of the house is the more active side. It generally faces the street and has less privacy and more noise than the back of the house. The active, stimulating side of the house is known as the yang side. Ideally, a bedroom, especially an adult's bedroom, should be located on the yin side—typically located at the rear of the home, where it's quieter, more private, more restful, and more protected from the street.

The master bedroom in Judy's home faced a very busy street. The noise from the street could be heard in the bedroom at all hours. Even if Judy had gone to the expense of reducing the noise by installing soundproof windows and heavy drapes, the feeling of being exposed on the more active side of the house would always be unsettling.

Frequently, children are not as bothered by being located in bedrooms toward the front of the house as adults are—perhaps because they know that their parents are home to protect them or perhaps because they sleep more deeply than most adults. Whatever the reason, locating a child's room toward the front of the home is usually preferred to having the adults sleep there.

Don't Give the Master Bedroom to Your Child!

If you choose not to use the master bedroom as your bedroom, think twice about giving it to your child or teenager. There's a subliminal message that will be sent to a child that may give him or her the feeling of having more power in the household than the parents may be comfortable with.

Similar to a junior employee being given a better office than the boss, when adults give the master bedroom to a child, they're creating a subtle imbalance of power in the family structure. When occupying the master bedroom, the child may begin to see himself/herself as the most important member of the family. This is something that parents should guard against, or they may experience power struggles with their child. Instead of using an unoccupied master bedroom as a child's room, it can be a great location for a common room—a game room, an office, a home theater, or a workout area. All of these uses are acceptable as long as a child isn't given the room solely as his/her own bedroom.

Large Bedrooms

The scenario that I just mentioned regarding Judy and her overly large master suite illustrates another important consideration when determining the feng shui of a bedroom. In recent years, many master suites have been designed to be so large (in order to make a dramatic statement when buyers are touring the model homes) that they've lost the intimacy and privacy needed for restful sleep. Clients with larger bedrooms are consistently at a loss for what to do with all that space. The bedroom needs to feel restful, private, and intimate. What may seem like a fantastic feature in a model home is often not practical for day-to-day living. If you have a very large bedroom and wish to make it feel more comfortable, here are a few ideas:

- Create a sitting area with cushy, luxurious fabrics and pillows.

- Paint the walls in rich, warm colors. Browns, tans, taupes, rich hunter greens, and warm purples help a room feel cozier and more welcoming. One of my clients painted the wall behind her bed in a beautiful chocolate brown, adding warmth and drama to the room.

- Add drapes on the windows in similar rich colors.

- Add a patterned area rug to take up visual space without cluttering the room with more furniture.

Floor Choices in Bedrooms

I am often asked by clients which type of flooring they should have in their bedrooms. There's no hard and fast rule about flooring in the bedroom—it comes down to choosing what *you* love—but there are some things to consider. Many people love the look of tile or hardwood but not always the feel. Unless you live in a very warm climate, tile often feels too cold for a bedroom. Hardwood floors can also feel hard and unfriendly, and bedrooms need to feel soft and cozy in order for us to rest well. If you're considering carpet for any room in your home, consider it for the bedroom. It feels great on bare feet, makes the room quieter, and creates a gentler feeling in the room. If your bedroom floor is already tile or wood, consider investing in a large, cushy area rug with a thick pad underneath. The room will feel much more relaxing, and you may sleep better as a result.

Beds and Bedroom Furniture

Choose furnishings that fit the size and scale of the room by applying the Goldilocks Principle: anything that's too big, too small, too hard, too soft, too hot, or too cold may keep you from relaxing, thus preventing restful sleep. A bedroom that's stuffed with too much furniture or oversized furniture feels claustrophobic, and a room with too little furniture may feel cold and uninviting.

Choosing a Bed

Since the bed is usually the largest piece of furniture in a bedroom, it becomes the focal point and should be something that feels and looks beautiful. The ideal bed frame, from a feng shui perspective, is made of wood and has a prominent headboard with no holes or slats in the headboard. Wooden headboards that have been upholstered are also acceptable. Metal beds, such as brass beds, don't feel or look as warm and secure as wood. Furthermore, metal actually conducts electricity, and for some very sensitive people, sleeping near a lot of metal can keep them from sleeping peacefully.

Just as an animal usually sleeps with its back bolstered up against something, having a wood bed frame with a significant headboard gives a feeling of protection from behind while sleeping. Even if your bed is pushed up against a wall, having a solid headboard feels more secure than having just a wall as the headboard. The headboard needs to be securely attached to the bed frame, as opposed to something decorative that simply rests on the wall behind the bed. The goal is to create a feeling of being surrounded and protected by something substantial.

As with all furniture, measure the bed frame carefully before you make your purchase. Before you buy, bring the measurements home, and place newspapers on the floor of the bedroom to represent the dimensions of the bed. By doing so, you'll be able to visualize how much floor space the bed will take up and whether it's going to fit well in the room.

If your bed is placed diagonally across a corner of the room, the space between the corner and the headboard can sometimes feel empty. Consider filling it with a Japanese shoji screen or a tall silk plant, such as a ficus tree trimmed with strands of small, clear lights.

To give the bedroom a finished look, add matching nightstands and lamps on either side of the bed. The symmetry will balance the way the room feels and make it appear more restful.

Bedding

Your choice of bedding depends on your taste in colors and textures as well as the feeling that you want to create. Warm tones, such as tans, browns, creams, and soft neutrals, are more conducive to relaxation, rather than cool, bright, or vibrant colors. No matter what your style, I always recommend buying sheets with the highest thread count you can afford. Sheets with a thread count of 350 or more are soft and feel good against your skin during rest. It's usually worth paying a bit more for better sheets. You "wear" sheets for more hours than any set of clothes you own, so it's important to choose something that's comfortable.

Up until a few years ago, high thread-count sheets were expensive and considered a luxury. Now, you can find them just about anywhere at reasonable or even reduced prices. Try looking for sheets and linens at stores that sell name-brand items at discount prices. Sometimes the markdowns are as high as 75 percent! I always buy my sheets from these stores. The quality is excellent, and the savings are incredible.

Window Coverings

If your bedroom lacks privacy during the day due to neighboring houses that are too close, add soft sheer curtains for daytime, and pull luxurious fabric drapes over them at night. Sheer curtains bring softness and elegance, making the bedroom feel warmer. Floor-length drapes and curtains in sensual colors promote feelings of romance and relaxation.

Out With the Old

If your bedroom is filled with furnishings and décor from a previous relationship, it's possible that this is impacting your current relationship or your desire to manifest a new one. Living with items that remind you of the past, particularly if the memories are negative, are items that need to be eliminated, especially from the bedroom. If you're still living with bedroom furnishings from a previous marriage or relationship, do yourself a favor and replace them with fresh new pieces, including a new mattress. You may be reluctant to replace something that works well with something new, but the fresh perspective and energy you'll gain will be well worth your investment.

Artwork

Frequently, the bedroom isn't treated with as much care as other rooms of the house when it comes to décor. This is unfortunate because how your bedroom makes you feel can directly affect how well you sleep and how you feel about your life and your relationships. Artwork in the bedroom should be considered very carefully—it's the last thing you see at night and the first thing you see in the morning. Science has proven that the brain waves and subconscious mind are most susceptible to suggestion right before we go to sleep and right after we wake up. The artwork you choose for your bedroom can make or break the overall feelings in the room.

Catastrophic Artwork

A few years ago, a young woman named Leah called to schedule a consultation. She was very upset and in a hurry to meet with me right away. She told me that since moving into a new condo with her husband and young son, her marriage had become a war zone. Her husband, Mike, had become angry, combative, and sullen since the move, and Leah was at a loss for an explanation. Her friend was a client of mine and suggested that perhaps a feng shui consultation could help Leah discover and remedy the source of her marital problems.

I met with Leah a few days later. She was an attractive, petite, young woman with sparkling eyes and a beautiful smile. However, I could sense the strain that she was under as she told me about the past few months of her life. Leah told me that she and Mike had purchased the condo six months ago, after Mike's father had passed away. They were able to purchase the condo with the money that Mike had inherited, and they were very excited about being first-time homeowners.

Since moving into the condo, however, Leah's once loving husband had become combative and irritable. Leah told me that she didn't like sleeping in the master bedroom anymore and chose to sleep on the sofa or in her son's room. She said, "Mike goes to bed angry and wakes up angry, and I have no idea what's causing this." Leah told me about the volatile relationship that Mike had with his father. Mike's father was in his late 60s when Mike was born. His father was a Holocaust survivor, a famous artist, and a schizophrenic. Leah told me that, growing up, Mike had both feared and respected his father and that their relationship had always been strained. Along with money, Mike had also inherited a few paintings by his father. The paintings were huge canvases of abstract art, all depicting the violence of the Holocaust. Mike insisted on placing the largest of the paintings, a six-by-eight-foot piece, in the master bedroom on a wall that faced the foot of their bed. It was the only wall in the condo that was large enough to display this dramatic painting. The blood reds and images of death filled the room, and I recoiled when I saw it.

Even though it was very obvious to me, neither Leah nor Mike realized how much this painting in their bedroom was impacting their marriage. Leah even confided to me that she was considering a divorce. I told her that the painting had to be removed as soon as possible. She told me that Mike would never go for the idea and was almost in tears when Mike suddenly came home from work. When he walked in the door, he was abrupt and not thrilled to see a stranger in his home, especially after working all day. When Leah told him who I was and what I was doing there, he reacted with cautious curiosity.

I complimented Mike on his home and family and asked him to tell me more about his father and the artwork. Mike talked about how famous his father had become in the art world, how honored he was to have inherited some of his father's paintings, and how difficult it had been to have this mentally ill, eccentric, and creative older man as a father. I got a strong sense of Mike's mixed feelings and confusion over his father since his passing.

When I pointed out that having the large Holocaust painting in the bedroom was most likely impacting his own emotions and, in turn, his marriage, Mike let out a heavy sigh and softly agreed. He explained that he was really torn over what to do with the paintings because, although he wanted to honor his father, he found the artwork unsettling. I suggested that Mike donate the paintings to a Holocaust museum. That way, his father's work would be honored, many people could see it, and it would be out of the house. Both Leah and Mike were thrilled at this suggestion.

A week later, Leah called to say that the paintings were on their way to a museum and that Mike had almost immediately turned back into the loving man she married. She was now sleeping in their bedroom again, and there was peace in their lives. Leah went on to say that she'd found some framed garden scenes to put in the bedroom and that the effect was calming and peaceful. Mike and Leah's experience shows that what you choose to display in your home affects you on deep, emotional levels and can greatly impact your relationships and your life. When you understand the deep relationship you have with your surroundings, you can really begin to fully appreciate the power of feng shui.

Guidelines for Choosing Art for the Bedroom

When choosing artwork for the master bedroom, choose serene, positive images. To strengthen partnerships, it's best to choose artwork that depicts people or objects in pairs. The image can be of any pair: two cats, two trees, two flowers, or a pair of paintings that go together and are displayed next to each other. I had one client who found a painting of a two pears (a pair of pears), and he thought this was quite clever. Because artwork conveys an emotional message, it can become an external affirmation of what you have or would like to have in your life.

In the master bedroom, try to avoid pictures with strong religious overtones or familiar people—friends, children, or parents. For some, items like these displayed in the bedroom are "mood breakers" and may reduce intimacy. If you wish to display religious images or photographs of familiar people in your home, it may be best to place them in rooms other than the master bedroom.

I have a rather lighthearted story to share with you regarding artwork in the bedroom. I had a consultation with a lovely, middle-aged client from Mexico named Patricia. Prior to our appointment, Patricia mentioned on the phone that her biggest concern was the intimacy in her marriage, which had suffered since she and her husband had moved into their new home. Patricia wanted a feng shui consultation with a special emphasis on creating love and romance with her husband.

Patricia and her husband, Filipe, had built an incredible custom home to their exact specifications, and it was truly breathtaking. The craftsmanship and attention to detail were incredible. From a feng shui perspective, I couldn't see anything in the home that might be negatively affecting their love life—until we got to the master bedroom. In her attempt to make the home as beautiful and as blessed as possible, Patricia had hired a muralist to paint a *life-sized* image of Our Lady of Guadalupe on the wall facing the foot of the bed. I had to suppress a giggle when I saw it because there was no mystery as to why the intimacy in Patricia's marriage had suffered after moving into her dream home. I would think that many people might have trouble feeling sexy with the Virgin Mary watching over them!

I gently suggested that they consider painting over the mural, but Patricia was strongly against that idea. At the same time, she also missed the romance that she once shared with her husband and knew something had to be done to improve the situation. After some thought, I suggested that perhaps they could hang a beautiful curtain on the wall framing the image, and when romance was in the air, they could close the curtain and have the privacy they felt they needed. It was a solution that worked wonders for Patricia. Within a week of hanging a new curtain, she called happily to tell me that her romantic life was back on track.

Safety

As with other rooms in the home, placing heavy objects overhead in the bedroom can make you feel oppressed and vulnerable. It's best to avoid placing heavy items, including large mirrors, pictures, and shelves, on the wall behind your bed. Sleeping with something heavy overhead alerts your survival instincts to possible danger and may inhibit restful sleep. This can include sleeping under ceiling fans. For some people, sleeping directly under a ceiling fan inhibits restful sleep. If this applies to you, consider removing the ceiling fan and purchasing an oscillating floor model or a tabletop fan for the bedroom.

If you have a beautiful large headboard, that alone is enough decoration for most bedroom walls. However, if you feel like there's still too much empty space on the wall behind the bed, consider batiks, fabrics, very lightweight artwork, or even painting the wall in a darker color, design, or texture to add visual interest. Whether or not you live in an earthquake-prone area, you'll rest easier knowing that nothing can fall on you while you're sleeping.

Lighting

I like to be creative with lighting, especially in the bedroom, and it's fairly easy to create good mood lighting. Here are some simple, inexpensive ways to bring mood lighting and restful energy into your bedroom:

- Place overhead lights on dimmer switches.

- Place a Japanese shoji screen in a corner with a light behind it. The rice paper filters the light, creating a beautiful, Zen-like ambience in the room.

- Add a tall silk plant, such as a ficus tree, and attach strands of small, clear lights to the branches for a creative and romantic touch.

- Add a salt lamp for soft, ambient lighting.

I love including salt lamps in bedrooms, especially children's rooms. (Refer to the appendix for details.) The gentle glow from inside the rock reminds me of the softness of candlelight. Additionally, salt lamp enthusiasts claim that the lamp emits negative ions that help clean the air and neutralize the electromagnetic energy in a room.

Candles are, of course, the old standby for mood lighting, but there's a risk of fire. I recommend either placing a candle in a dish with some water or using battery-operated "candles" that mimic the look of candles without the fire danger. By the way, if you favor scented candles, be sure to use candles made with natural wax and pure essential oils. When you burn a candle, you also inhale whatever the candle is made of; therefore, it's important to avoid toxic chemicals or harmful ingredients. Health food stores are usually good sources for candles made from natural ingredients.

No-No's in the Bedroom

The bedroom is for rest, relaxation, and connecting with your partner. It is not the place for exercise equipment, computers, or televisions.

Exercise Equipment

I've seen more treadmills, stair climbers, and rowing machines used as clothing racks than I can count. Having exercise equipment in the bedroom can add up to a nightly guilt trip and amplify negative body-image issues. If you get into bed every night thinking, "Oh, I really should have exercised today. I'm so fat. I didn't exercise again. I'm so lazy. Well, maybe tomorrow," then you're setting yourself up for a restless night's sleep. If there's no place other than the bedroom to house the exercise equipment, then consider setting up a panel screen to hide it when it isn't being used.

Work-Related Items

Keeping work-related items out of the bedroom is essential to rest. If you keep items from your career or job in your bedroom, you may find it difficult to turn off from work in the evenings and to wake up relaxed in the morning. School-related items may have the same effect.

If there's absolutely no other place for work-related items other than in the bedroom, then stow them in a cabinet or closet or set up a panel screen to hide them. Even covering them with a cloth (such as a bed sheet) at night is better than doing nothing. It's very important that you disengage from work and study in the evenings, so you can rest and have the energy to tackle whatever you need to accomplish the next day.

Electrical Items

Be mindful of electrical appliances in the bedroom. The issue is that all electrical appliances generate electromagnetic fields (EMFs), even when they're turned off. Too much electromagnetic energy can impact sleep patterns. It's best to have as few electrical items as possible in the bedroom. To minimize the amount of EMFs that you're exposed to nightly, keep electric clock radios and other electronics at least three feet away from your head while you sleep. The National Institute for Occupational Safety and Health writes, "Since magnetic fields often drop off dramatically within about 3 feet of the source, workers can stand back from electrical equipment, and work stations can be moved out of the 3-ft range of stronger EMF sources."[1]

If your headboard shares a wall with a large electrical appliance, such as a refrigerator on the other side, it's important to know that most appliances emit more EMFs from the back, rather than the front. If your headboard shares the same wall as the back of a large appliance, you are likely being exposed to more EMFs than you realize. You can always test the EMF reading in your house by purchasing an EMF meter. See the appendix for more information.

If you use an electric blanket at night, you are sleeping in an electromagnetic field of energy that may be harmful to your health, not to mention the fire hazard that it creates. If you really love getting into a warm bed, then turn the blanket on for a few minutes before you get into bed. When it's time to get into bed, *unplug* (that's right, unplug) the blanket to make sure that you aren't sleeping under a field of electricity all night. You may find that you sleep better and wake up more refreshed that you did before.

Televisions and computers tend to demand attention, so keeping them out of the bedroom not only reduces the EMFs but also focuses your attention on rest, sleep, and romance with your partner. If you enjoy watching television in bed, then find a television that's not too large or too commanding for the intimacy of your bedroom. The television should blend in with the furnishings, rather than dominate the room.

Bed Position

Security and safety needs are instinctual and active twenty-four hours a day. Even when asleep, your survival instincts are working to protect you. The primary component that determines restful sleep is whether or not you feel safe. In order

---

[1] National Institute for Occupational Safety and Health, "Fact Sheet: EMFs in the Workplace," no. 96-129; http://www.cdc.gov/niosh/emf2.html.

to feel safe in your bedroom, your bed should be positioned so that you can see the bedroom door without being in direct line with it. When you can easily see the bedroom door, your survival mechanism relaxes because you're able to see who's entering the room, giving you time to protect yourself from potential danger.

Reality Check

Myth: Sleeping with your feet pointing toward the bedroom door brings bad luck and even death!

Feng shui advises against positioning your bed so that your feet point directly toward the door. Some people mistakenly call this placement the "Coffin Position," suggesting that something unfortunate might happen as a result. This notion harkens back to a time in China when people died at home in their beds. Customarily, the body was carried out of the room feet first. This practice was incorrectly attributed to feng shui as the rationale for not placing your bed in this position.

While it *is* true that you don't want your feet lined up directly with the door when you're lying down, it isn't because something terrible will happen. It's because, when your feet are facing toward the door, your body is exposed to anyone who may come to the door. This position creates feelings of vulnerability because you're more accessible to someone who may enter the room. Such an exposed position means that you have less time to protect yourself against possible harm. Although these feelings are often subliminal, they can affect your ability to sleep well. That's the real reason to avoid this bed position.

The Command Position in a Bedroom

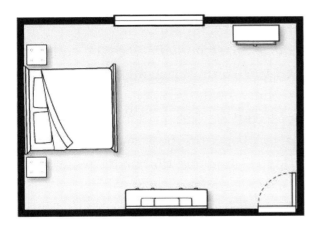

Figure 5.20

Figure 5.20 shows the optimal position for a bed within a room. This is known as the "Command Position." Similar to the Command Position for seating in a room, the Command Position for a bed is when the headboard sits against a solid wall and there's a clear view of the door without being directly in line with it. This bed position allows survival instincts to relax a bit more because you can see who's entering the room, giving you an extra second or two to respond if necessary.

In figure 5.21, the bed is located directly in line with the door. With this layout, you're likely to feel less secure because, even though you can see the door, you're too close to it to feel safe. Your survival instincts will be on higher alert because, with the bed positioned so closely to the door, you may feel that there's not enough time to react and protect yourself if someone enters the room.

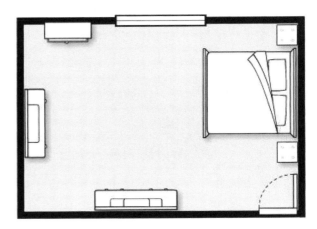

Figure 5.21

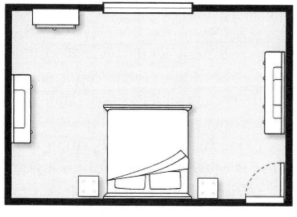

Figure 5.22

Figure 5.22 shows the least desirable bed position of all. With the headboard on the same wall as the door, you're unable to see the entrance to the room, creating a heightened feeling of vulnerability and, in turn, less rest and relaxation. This bed position also places the bed very close to the door. I often find that people who place their bed on the same wall as the door have difficulty sleeping well.

If possible, it's best to avoid this arrangement, but if you absolutely cannot avoid it, try placing a mirror on the wall directly opposite the door. This way, you'll be able to see the door in the mirror's reflection, and it may help you feel less vulnerable. Remember, the more secure you feel in your bed and in your bedroom, the better and more deeply you will sleep.

Reality Check

Myth: *Never have a mirror in the bedroom.*

Mirrors in the bedroom are often given a bad rap in feng shui. I've heard many ridiculous reasons why one shouldn't have a mirror in the bedroom. My favorite one is, "You don't want a mirror in your bedroom because you could wake up and startle yourself." I've also heard that having a mirror in your bedroom will cause infidelity in your relationship. There are circumstances, however, when a large mirror in the bedroom *may* impact restful sleep. Logically, what does a large mirror do to a room? It visually doubles the size of a room and reflects light. In a small living room or dining room, a large mirror is a wonderful enhancement, making the room feel more spacious than it actually is. However, a bedroom doesn't feel as good when it's excessively large. For some people, a room with large mirrors—such as mirrored closet doors—can feel too spacious to be comfortable. Large mirrors reflect more light, and for light-sensitive people, that can be a problem if they prefer a very dark room. Additionally, some people feel more restless in rooms that don't feel cozy. A large mirror is a cold shiny surface that can definitely make a room feel less comfy than it would feel without a large mirror.

If you like large mirrors in your bedroom and they don't seem to interfere with sleep, then they aren't a problem. On the other hand, if large mirrors or mirrored closet doors bother you but you don't want to replace them, then treat them like large windows by hanging soft curtains in front of them. During the day, the curtains can be left open to make the room feel more spacious, and at night, you can close them before going to bed for a more intimate feeling in the room. Not only will your room feel more restful, the curtains will add warmth and texture, making the room cozier and more comfortable.

Beds Placed under Windows

For many people, particularly children, sleeping directly under a window can increase feelings of vulnerability. For safety and a good night's sleep, the headboard should not be placed under a window. If this arrangement cannot be avoided due to the architecture of the room, be sure to have a good lock on the window as well as shutters or drapes to block out any drafts or light that may interfere with sleep.

Bathrooms Open to Bedrooms

Some newer homes have master suites featuring large, door-less openings that connect the master bedroom with the master bathroom. This is undesirable for several reasons: First, these two rooms serve very different functions and are very different environments. The bedroom is a dry, cozy room used primarily for rest and relaxation. The bathroom is a cold, wet room used for washing, grooming, and well, you know. Most people want privacy in the bathroom, and this open configuration reduces privacy. Also, couples with different work or sleep schedules have trouble getting enough sleep when one partner is going to bed later or getting up earlier than the other partner.

If your home has a large, door-less opening between a bedroom and a bathroom and it's impossible to install a door, try hanging a curtain across the opening. You can tie it back during the day and keep it closed at night. The curtain will give you and your partner more privacy and make the bedroom feel cozier. If hanging a curtain doesn't appeal to you, you can also place a decorative screen across part of the opening to create a feeling of separation between the two rooms. You'll be amazed at how much better it feels to not "sleep in the bathroom" anymore!

Children's Bedrooms and Playrooms

Many of the same rules apply to children's bedrooms as to adult rooms, but there are some unique considerations. Claire Cooper Marcus, professor emerita in the departments of Architecture and Landscape Architecture and Environmental Planning at the University of California, Berkeley writes, "Children need to have the freedom to express their emerging identities—separate from parents or siblings—through the personalization of space. This might be as simple as letting them pin up favorite pictures and photos or as elaborate as letting them choose the colors of their bedroom walls and drapes."[1] Children's rooms are their first step toward

---

[1] Clare Cooper Marcus, *House as a Mirror of Self: Exploring the Deeper Meaning of Home* (Berkeley: Conari Press, 1992), 45.

autonomy, so it's important that they have some say in the décor of their bedrooms (within good taste of course).

"But It's My Room!"

I recently worked with a mother named Caroline and her daughter, Molly. Caroline was good at decorating, and she had the color scheme and furniture all picked out for Molly's room. Caroline's choices were attractive, but Molly hated them. Caroline and Molly were fighting almost daily over the way the room should be decorated. At wit's end, Caroline made an appointment with me to ask for my help in convincing Molly to accept the colors and room design that she had selected for her.

The funny thing was, I ended up convincing Caroline that Molly needed more say in the matter, since she would be spending the most time in the bedroom. To illustrate my point, I asked Caroline to name a color that she didn't like. She answered, "Navy blue." I then asked how she might feel if forced to spend most of her time in a room that was painted in navy blue. She said that it would probably make her feel frustrated and angry; then she understood.

Forcing Molly to sleep and study in a room that was decorated in a way that she didn't like and had no control over was making her feel frustrated and irritable. These feelings were spilling over into other parts of her life, including her interactions with her mother and other family members. After discussing their respective likes and dislikes, Caroline, Molly, and I spent the afternoon compromising on colors, furnishings, and décor for Molly's room. By the time I left their house that day, both mother and daughter were happy with the new decorating scheme, and the peace between them had been restored.

Bed Position in a Child's Room

Just as with adult beds, a child's bed should be positioned so that he/she can see the door but not be directly in line with it. I'm frequently surprised at how often parents place children's beds in vulnerable positions and then wonder why the children don't sleep well or won't sleep in their beds at night. When this happens, I ask the parents where they would put the bed if this was their bedroom. It's always fun to see their look when they understand that they've placed their child's bed in a position that they would never have chosen for themselves. Keep in mind that, when placing a child's bed in the Command Position, most children under the age of ten will sleep better when one side of the bed is pushed up against a wall for an added feeling of security.

Children's Beds

Some toddler beds are made of brightly colored plastic in the shape of cars, trucks, and animals. As cute as these may be, the potential health repercussions are not worth the risk. Plastic is a petroleum product that continuously emits toxins into the air. This occurrence is known as off-gassing, and it's very unhealthy, especially when a child is inhaling these toxins all night long. As with adult beds, make sure that the child's bed has a solid wood headboard (no holes or slats) that's attached to a bed frame. When possible, avoid headboards and bed frames made mostly of metal.

Bunk Beds: Good or Bad Feng Shui?

There's some disagreement over whether or not bunk beds create bad feng shui. The thinking is that sleeping on the bottom bunk isn't good because there's something heavy and oppressive over you, while sleeping on the top bunk is unsafe because you're so high off the floor.

Sometimes, there's not enough room in a child's bedroom to accommodate two separate beds, so a bunk bed is a space-saving alternative. Additionally, many children enjoy sleeping in bunk beds. However, please be aware that every year hospital emergency rooms see many seriously injured children that have fallen off the top bunk or off the ladder of a bunk bed. If you choose a bunk bed for your child, be sure that it has sturdy rails around the top bunk for safety and a non-slip ladder that's securely attached. To have good feng shui, you must feel safe in order to feel comfortable. It's ultimately up to you and your child to decide whether or not a bunk bed feels safe enough to be the best feng shui choice for the bedroom.

Mirrors in a Child's Room

As with adult bedrooms, avoid large mirrors in a child's room for two reasons: First, mirrors can make a room less restful. Second, children might accidentally run into it and break the mirror, seriously injuring themselves.

Artwork for Kids

It almost goes without saying that the artwork displayed in a child's room should be positive and upbeat. If your child is a prolific artist, you may want to create a specific area to display his or her masterpieces. Instead of tacking up the latest creation on the wall or the refrigerator, consider purchasing a bulletin board to easily add and remove the latest artwork.

A wonderful place to display children's artwork without cluttering up your home is the garage. When displayed properly, children's artwork provides color in the garage and makes children feel proud that their work is being displayed so that everyone can see it as they come and go in the car.

You can also use easy-to-change picture frames to display a child's artwork in a specific area of the home. Have your child choose a piece of artwork to go in the frame, and then find a place where the artwork can be tastefully displayed. Having a picture frame to display the "Picture of the Week" will keep the colorful chaos in your child's artwork from competing with your home's décor, while still contributing to your child's self-esteem.

Do not hang anything heavy above a child's bed including shelves, heavy pictures, large mobiles, or toy hammocks. Just as in adult bedrooms, having things hanging overhead while children are sleeping contributes to feelings of vulnerability.

Electronics in a Child's Room

Keep electronic items at least three feet away from a child's bed to reduce the influence of electromagnetic fields on sleeping children.

Storage for Stuff

Feng shui isn't just for adults; it's for kids, too. In order to keep your child focused and organized, it's important to have an easy-to-access storage system for toys and books. Children's books and toys are brightly colored, and even when arranged in a tidy fashion, they can make a room feel overwhelming and messy. One of the best things you can provide is a storage cupboard with doors. This way, all of the toys can be easily put away and stored out of sight.

If your child's room already has a bookcase or if you're concerned about small fingers getting shut in cupboard doors, you can also cover the bookcase with a cloth. Tack or nail a cloth over the open side, or better yet, install a tension rod with a pocket curtain that hangs in front of the bookcase to hide the items underneath. A tension rod will fit easily inside the top shelf. Select a cloth or curtain in a solid color rather than a pattern. A pattern will only make the room seem busier, while a solid color will calm it down.

Another attractive storage option is a large wicker trunk or a sea grass basket with a lid. If you live in a small space and storage is at a premium, you'll find that large baskets and trunks blend easily with most décor styles. The easier you make it for children to clean up after themselves by providing convenient storage, the more organized they will learn to be.

Locations for a Child's Bedroom

If there's a choice of bedrooms, children usually tolerate bedrooms at the front of a home better than adults do. The front of the home is usually the more active, yang side. Since children tend to sleep better than adults, the yang energy at the front of the home is usually not as disruptive to children as it can be to adults.

If your child doesn't sleep well due to noise, either from inside or outside the house, consider an air purifier with an ionizer for the bedroom. Make sure that the air purifier is not a silent model but instead has an internal fan. Air purifiers with fans provide gentle whooshing sounds or white noise that can drown out unwanted sounds. Air purifiers with ionizers emit negative ions that make a room feel more relaxed and restful. (Have you ever felt sleepy on a rainy day? It's due to the negative ions that are released during rainfall.) Children with allergies often benefit from the use of air purifiers with HEPA filters. These types of filters reduce airborne particles that can cause allergies. As with all electrical appliances, keep the air purifier as far away from the bed as possible to minimize exposure to electromagnetic energy, and keep it out of reach of children for safety reasons.

Sharing a Bedroom

Everybody needs a space of their own, no matter how small that space may be. When children share a bedroom, it's best that each child has his or her own bed, unless they really want to sleep together. It's also important to demarcate the boundaries of each child's space so that each feels a sense of autonomy and privacy. If children share a bunk bed, the upper and lower bunks can serve as somewhat private, individual areas. If children have separate beds, it's nice to have some kind of small partition between the beds. A screen, a curtain, or even a low bookshelf can serve this purpose. The barrier doesn't have to be high to create a feeling of privacy. Also, decorative gauze or netting can be hung over each child's bed like a tent. Kids love it, and it's a fun and inexpensive way to decorate the room and give each child a special place to be.

Colors and Decorations for Kids

Parents often use bright, primary colors to decorate a child's room. Reds, yellows, and blues are easy for children's eyes to discern, and these colors are associated with fun and play. While these are great colors for toys and playrooms, they're not good colors for bedrooms. A child's bedroom is primarily used for rest and sleep, and soothing colors are more conducive to this than bright colors. In fact, one study of the effect of color on emotions demonstrated that babies who occupied rooms painted in bright yellow cried more often and longer than those occupying rooms painted in other colors. The study also showed that adults became angry more quickly and stayed angry longer in bright yellow rooms than in any other color of room.[2] Soft colors in shades of blue, green, purple, pink, and tan will feel more soothing and calming for your child than bold stimulating colors such as red, orange, or yellow.

Children enjoy soft fabrics and textures. Their skin is much more sensitive than adult skin, so soft textures can be especially soothing to them. Include fluffy area rugs, squishy pillows, and bedding in satin, silk, corduroy, velvet, or velour. Eliminate anything that's scratchy, rough, prickly, or spiked.

Decorate your child's room with images that encourage the imagination. Fairies, angels, and outer space themes promote thought and creativity far more than cartoons and other mass-produced commercial images. Most children have an affinity for animals and nature, and if done right, these images can provide calming features to the room. One theme that I discourage in a child's room is an undersea theme. I once worked with a client who had gone to great lengths to create an underwater world in her child's room. The walls and ceilings were painted like the ocean, which was teeming with sea images and animals. She told me, however, that her son had breathing problems and nightmares. The room, while interesting and creative, felt claustrophobic. It was no surprise to me that her son reacted to his space with breathing problems. A bedroom is a warm, dry space that should be soothing and calming. The theme of a wet, cold undersea world is incompatible with these qualities.

It's important that children have input into how their bedrooms will be decorated. Involve children in the discussions regarding paint choices and design themes for their rooms. Ultimately, they'll be the ones spending all their time there. If they like what they see, they'll be more comfortable and better able to sleep well.

Playrooms

If your house is large enough to have a playroom, be sure to equip the playroom with ample shelves behind cupboard doors and toy boxes with lids to make it easy for children to clean up the room. I've met many parents who complain that their children never pick up after themselves, and in many cases, the parents haven't provided any convenient places for children to store their things. When

---

[2] Rebecca Jones, "The Color of Love," *Rocky Mountain News*, March 9, 1997.

this happens, you're setting up your child for failure and setting up yourself for irritation and frustration. Avoid this whole drama by having adequate and attractive storage options for your children's possessions, and reward them for keeping their toys and games put away and out of sight when not in use.

Regularly purge toys, clothing, and books that are no longer used. It's easy to accumulate stuff as children grow out of it and get bored with things so quickly. Many parents make a rule that something new cannot be acquired until something old has been given away or gotten rid of. This is a wonderful habit for children and adults alike. If you'd like a playroom but your home is just too small to accommodate one, consider converting your garage. If you're willing to park your car elsewhere, the garage can be turned into a great playroom with a coat of paint, a large carpet remnant, and some full-spectrum lighting.

I once had a client who lived in a very small house with three young children. She was overjoyed when I suggested the option of the garage as a playroom. The tension from a family of five living in such close quarters was mounting. The garage conversion solved the problem of overcrowding and gave her children a large space in which to store their toys and to play safely. If you decide to convert your garage into a playroom, be sure to find another location to store paints, fertilizers, cleaning products, and other toxic or hazardous items.

As I mentioned earlier, the closet or storage area under the stairway is also a fun place for a child's hideaway. Children love to feel cozy and protected in a place of their own. Most of us can remember creating forts and hideaways when we were young. Using this area as a little hideaway provides not only a safe place for children to play but also a terrific location for storing toys downstairs. This is a much better use of the space than allowing stored items to stagnate under the stairway for long periods of time.

Rooms for Teens

It comes as no surprise to parents that teenagers are unique in their outlook toward their lives and their environments. Feng shui can certainly help teens and parents navigate these challenging years. In order to create good feng shui for teens, we need to look at what children in this age group need in order to feel comfortable in their surroundings.

Around age nine, children begin to distance themselves from their parents and seek social support and approval from their peers. As they move through their teens, children become more and more concerned with the image that they portray to their friends and to the world at large.[3] Most of us recall our teen years as a time of turmoil and self-doubt. Both teens and tweens need private spaces where they can retreat from stress and spend time alone.

Just as a home represents the qualities and personalities of the people who live there, a bedroom is where older children should be allowed to express their individuality through color and décor choices. The design statement that a teen makes in his or her personal space reflects what the teen is experiencing at the present time. Sometimes, these design statements can tune parents into special problems that a teen may be experiencing but not otherwise expressing.

Teens and Décor Choices: Carly's Story

Feng shui is an effective tool to help children, teens, and adults create more positive and productive living spaces. By changing aspects of your surroundings, you can change aspects of yourself.

One particularly memorable consultation came when I worked with a family who had a very unhappy, almost suicidal, teenage daughter named Carly. Carly's mother, Barbara, was at her wit's end and called me to find out if feng shui could help her daughter. When I saw this young lady's room, it was clear that her surroundings were contributing to her depression. Carly's room was decorated with pictures of skulls, heavy metal groups, and posters relating to death and destruction. Furthermore, she kept the drapes in her room closed, so it was always dark and gloomy. A room like this symbolizes a dilemma in feng shui. It's like the chicken-or- the-egg story: Was Carly depressed because her room was decorated

---

[3] DAK Kopec, *Environmental Psychology for Design* (New York: Fairchild Books, 2006), 159.

this way, or was her room decorated this way because she was depressed? Probably a little of both.

Fortunately, Carly thought it was "cool" that her mom had hired a feng shui consultant to help with the house. As part of our time together, I had the opportunity to sit down and talk with Carly about her bedroom and her feelings. As I interviewed Carly about her room, she revealed that she felt a scary "presence" in her closet that was giving her a creepy feeling. I suggested that the creepy feeling in her closet was a result of all the negative imagery in her room, and I shared with her that feng shui helps us understand how our surroundings deeply influence our inner life and emotions. I asked Carly about her dreams and ambitions for the future. She shared with me that she really wanted to go to fashion design school and become a clothing designer. I explained to Carly how feng shui can help us create a space that supports our goals and desires and can actually help us realize them. I suggested that, in order to reach her goals, her bedroom needed to reflect what it was she wanted to manifest in her life. I shared that the way she had chosen to decorate her room was actually increasing her fears, rather than supporting her ambitions.

A bit later, Barbara joined our conversation. Together, we discussed colors that Carly would like in her room, and we looked online for artwork that would reflect her goals and dreams. I proposed designating one wall that would work as a large bulletin board for Carly to post her fashion ideas. In order to help with her depression, I reminded Carly to keep her curtains open during the day.

After we had the ideas all set for Carly's room, I did a space clearing and a blessing to bring fresh energy into the room (see chapter 8). Before my eyes, I watched a sullen teenager turn into an enthusiastic young lady. Many wonderful things came out of this consultation. Even before I had left that day, Carly had begun to take down all of the negative images in her room. Just five days later, she had made *all* of the changes in her room. Barbara called to tell me that she felt like she finally had her daughter back. Carly was cheerful and bubbly again, busily sketching in her design book, and chatting with her friends. It was as if an ominous, dark cloud had been lifted from their home. The last time I heard from

Barbara, it was to tell me that Carly had graduated from high school with honors and had been accepted to a prestigious design school. Barbara attributed part of Carly's success and transformation to the feng shui work that we had done in her bedroom that day.

Carly's story demonstrates an important point for teens and feng shui. While teens need to have autonomy and freedom to express their interests and personalities in their environment, it's also important to pay attention to the effect that their spaces have on them. The teen years are an important time for establishing independence. The challenge here can be deciding how far a parent is willing to let their child go with this expression, particularly if it's overly negative.

Most adults remember going through a rebellious stage in their youth, and most came out of this phase unscathed. But for some children, especially those who are more sensitive, this stage needs gentle guidance. In Carly's case, this guidance came in the form of a feng shui consultant with a new set of eyes and another perspective to get things on track.

Décor for Teens: Choices within Reason

Sometimes parents can work with their teens on making positive choices about their bedrooms by offering to purchase new bedroom furniture. Working cooperatively with your teen is the key to this process. Approach the project with a willingness to help your teen create a great space. If you need ideas or help, there are plenty of sites online with great decorating ideas for teens. Internet sites that sell posters are good resources for artwork that you can both agree on. In short, keep the images positive and focused on the healthy things that interest your teen, such as sports or hobbies.

Working together to choose paint colors for the room, even if the colors are a bit "out there," is another way you can encourage your teen's self-expression. After all, it's only paint and can always be changed later. To introduce paint choices, have your teen choose several colors from a paint fan. Ultimately, you will pick the paint color from the samples that your teen has chosen. It's a nice way to give your teen some autonomy and for you to have some say in the matter as well. If the color is too strong or shocking for an entire room, then compromise by painting just one wall in the strong color and painting the remaining walls in a neutral shade.

Furniture for Teens

As with all family members, a teen needs a bed with a solid headboard (no holes or slats) securely attached to a bed frame. Likewise, the bed should be positioned with a clear view of the door but not in direct line with it. Teens also need a place to entertain their friends. The more comfortable the space is, the more the kids will want to hang out there. Many parents prefer knowing what their kids are doing, and one way to encourage them to spend time at home is to help them create an environment that's suitable and "cool."

Depending on the size of the room, it's best to have more than just the bed as a seating option for friends. Consider adding an armchair, a futon, or a beanbag chair as comfortable places for their friends to sit. Adding a small table, perhaps a folding one that can be put away, for drinks and snacks will help keep spills and messes off the floor.

I've had clients turn garages, attics, extra rooms, and basements into "teen rooms" where teens and their friends can hang out, watch television, play video games, and listen to music. By creating a designated entertainment space for teens, these parents are able to keep closer tabs on their teens and their activities, while also providing a space for them to be with their friends and have fun.

Electronic Equipment in Teen Rooms

Teen bedrooms are filled with all sorts of electronic gadgets: phones, computers, televisions, and video games. When deciding where to place all of this equipment, the first thing to remember is that electronics should be placed at least three feet away from the bed. Most harmful electromagnetic fields fall to safer levels when electronics are at least this distance away from the body.

The next thing to focus on is how the electronic equipment is being used. Since teens use the computer to do at least a portion of their homework, the computer is no longer a toy but more of a work-related item. In feng shui, having equipment in a bedroom that symbolizes work can become a source of stress. Therefore, if a computer is necessary for your teen, you may want to consider placing it in another room of the house. Many parents prefer to have a family computer located in a more public area in the home, where they can monitor what their children are exploring online. If the computer is left in the bedroom, it should not be in direct view of the bed—meaning that it should not be the first thing that the teen sees upon waking and the last thing that the teen sees before going to bed.

Video games and televisions are also active, busy pieces of equipment. To lend a more peaceful feeling to the room, provide a place where electronic equipment can be hidden while not in use. This can be as simple as placing the items in a closet or storing them inside cabinets with doors.

Study Areas

Teens need established study areas. The trick here is to allow your child to find the space in the home that feels best to him/her. Too often, parents spend valuable time and money on a desk and study area in their teen's bedroom only to find out that the teen prefers to do homework on the bed or at the kitchen table. Before you set out to design a study area for your children, be sure to ask questions about where they prefer to do their homework. Just like adults, children and teens should have a clear view of the door when they are studying. If you are purchasing a desk for your child's room, avoid desks with hutches.

These desks are undesirable for three reasons: (1) the hutch forces a person to face a wall, often with his/her back to the door; (2) the hutch provides too many places for clutter to gather, leading to disorganization and feelings of being overwhelmed; and (3) taller hutches can feel unsafe, as there's a feeling of objects looming overhead.

Figure 5.23

Remember to also provide full-spectrum task lighting and ergonomically correct seating. Closed shelves are preferable to open shelves in order to keep clutter to a minimum. The more optimal the space is for studying, the more productive your teen will be.

Bathrooms

Over the past few years, there's been a trend toward larger, more elaborate bathrooms. Homebuilders know that beautiful bathrooms help to sell homes. In newer homes, bathrooms have evolved from purely functional spaces into areas of luxury and comfort. Master bathroom suites, as they're now called, often include separate dressing areas, large walk-in closets, whirlpool bathtubs, spacious showers, built-in saunas, and steam rooms. While the role of the bathroom has evolved, some of the feng shui superstitions associated with the bathroom have not. Let's clear up the misconceptions, so we can explore the wonderful role that the bathroom plays in feng shui.

Reality Check

Myth: You must keep all the drains in your bathroom closed, or your money will go down the drain.

Ah, the bathroom. It's frequently the most maligned, misunderstood area of the home from a feng shui perspective. If the bathroom could talk, I believe it would quote Rodney Dangerfield and say, "I get no respect." I can't count the number of homes I've entered where the client proudly proclaims, "I always keep my bathroom door shut, the toilet lid down, and all the drains closed." Then, they look at me with that hopeful expression of child waiting to be praised for a job well-done.

Often, these clients have "read in a book" that the bathroom is a terrible, evil place because toilets and drains will suck money and energy right out of the house unless they're kept closed at all times. I had one client who even placed rocks on top of each closed drain and on the back of the toilet to make sure that her money and "good luck" would stay in the home. She had read this ludicrous idea in a feng shui book and had diligently done this to every drain in her house. As ridiculous as this sounds, it persists as one of the most popular and silliest myths in feng shui today.

When we examine the cultural context in which feng shui was first developed, it's easy to understand where the bathroom earned its malevolent reputation. In ancient China (as in much of the underdeveloped parts of the world today), indoor plumbing did not exist, and outdoor facilities were rudimentary at best. Bathing was not done in the same area as elimination, and the outhouse was often nothing more than a fetid hole in the ground. It's easy to understand why this area was associated with less-than-desirable energies.

Fortunately in modern societies, our bathrooms are clean, often beautiful rooms with attributes vastly different from their primitive counterparts. As long as the bathroom is clean and in perfect working order, it attracts no more negativity than any other room in the house. It's no more a vortex of escaping energy than opening a door or a window. In truth, the only way to lose money down the toilet or the drain is to empty your wallet into the toilet and give it a good flush! For most of us, the bathroom is *not* an evil, horrible place, but if you keep the door shut all the time, mold and mildew will grow, no doubt turning it into one! Rest assured that as long as your plumbing and fixtures are in good working order, it's not necessary to go to great (and preposterous) lengths to assure that money doesn't flow out of bathroom drains.

Creating a Spa Experience at Home

As a direct result of the increasing demands of everyday life, spas have become incredibly popular. Spas offer relaxation and pampering to those who are overworked or excessively stressed, restoring peace and harmony in their lives. Feng shui strives to do the same. I've been involved with the design of many world-class spas and will share some feng shui secrets so that you can enjoy a spa experience at home.

Color and Décor

Bathrooms are cold, wet places with a lot of hard, shiny surfaces. When we get out of the shower or bath, we're cold, wet, and naked. Frequently, people make bathrooms feel even colder and wetter by decorating with cool colors such as blue, white, and shades of aqua.

To make a bathroom feel relaxing and restful, it's best to choose colors that provide feelings of warmth and comfort. These colors include earth tones ranging from rich chocolate to tan to cream. Accenting with these nurturing colors relaxes us and makes us feel safe. Paint, tile, towels, rugs, shower curtains, and artwork can be used to bring warm colors into the bathroom.

Try this: Close your eyes for a minute, and picture yourself getting out of the tub or shower in a light blue bathroom. Then, picture yourself getting out of the tub or shower in an earth tone bathroom. Most people say they feel warmer and more relaxed when they think of the earth tone bathroom. A powder room can be painted any color that suits your fancy, but a bathroom where bathing and showering take place usually feels better in an earth tone color scheme.

Sea Life and Water-Themed Bathrooms

Because the bathroom is associated with water, people often decorate it with sea life and ocean themes, especially in bathrooms used by children. The problem here is that this cool, wet theme can make the room feel very cold and uncomfortable.

If you wish to decorate your bathroom in a sea life motif, I suggest using earth tones rather than shades of blue. I've seen some beautiful bathrooms that integrate sea shells into the décor by choosing colors for walls and towels in shades of salmon, gold, soft yellow, and tan, while using the textures of sea shells to create interest. Try to avoid cold, watery colors such as blue. Minimize artwork of fish and sea life, and avoid images of lakes or oceans in the bathroom for a more relaxing experience.

Images of Nature

As with all areas of the home, adding images and materials from nature (excluding water themes) enhances feelings of ease and relaxation. Baskets, plants (real and silk), stones, pebbles, and artwork depicting peaceful nature scenes can help make the bathroom feel like a comfortable retreat.

Texture

The bathroom is one place where the Goldilocks Principle really comes in handy. A bathroom is full of smooth, cold, hard surfaces that can be balanced by adding more softness and texture. Fluffy bath rugs and luxurious towels are easy ways to integrate warmth and texture into the bathroom. Many stores that sell overstocked items also sell luxurious towels at a fraction of the price found in most department stores.

On the walls, grass cloth wallpaper can be used for a dramatic effect, as can tiles and trim that contain smooth pebbles, tumbled stone, or even fossils for a really unique flair. Choosing natural wood cabinetry and woven accents, such as wicker baskets, also creates interest by bringing a variety of textures into the bathroom.

Many bathrooms have sliding glass shower doors atop the edge of the bathtub. While practical, the visual result is another large, cold, shiny surface in the bathroom. A quick trick that I've used in many homes, including my own, is to hang a beautiful cloth shower curtain, using a shower-curtain tension rod, in front of the shower doors. The glass doors are still used to keep water out of the bathroom when showering, but hanging a cloth shower curtain across them when not in use brings a feeling of warmth into the room.

For added sophistication and glamour, remove the flat, generic bathroom mirror and replace it with a beautiful formal mirror in a carved frame. Some home improvement and online stores sell beautiful mirror-frame kits that are very pretty and easy to install on your existing bathroom mirror. Framing the mirror adds interest and elegance to the bathroom, along with much-needed texture.

Floors

Clients often ask me what type of flooring is best for bathrooms. The answer depends on personal taste and budget. However, the one thing that I never recommend in a bathroom is carpet. Carpet absorbs moisture and can become a serious breeding ground for germs, mildew, and mold—not to mention odors. Cold tiles on a bathroom floor can be warmed up with area rugs designed for use in the bathroom. These rugs have non-slip backings and can be machine-washed as needed.

Privacy

Privacy is an important aspect of good feng shui in the bathroom. As I mentioned in the previous section on bedrooms, many master suites in newer homes have large, door-less openings connecting the bedroom with the bathroom. If there's no door separating the bedroom and the bathroom, consider adding one for the sake of privacy. If a door is too expensive or architecturally difficult, a curtain can perform this function as well. Proper window coverings, door locks, and fans that are in good working order also ensure privacy and relaxation in the bathroom.

Lighting

Bathrooms are where many people get dressed and do their hair or make-up before going out. In order to look your best, it's very important to have good lighting. As with other rooms in the home, I highly recommend full-spectrum lighting. Because full-spectrum lighting provides a more realistic color range, it can help prevent you from making color choices that might look great in the bathroom but horrible in natural light.

For a relaxing and restful bath or shower, candles go a long way toward setting the mood. If you want to avoid candles for safety reasons, you can use battery-operated lights that are made to look like flickering candles or install dimmer switches in the bathroom to create a similar ambience.

The Commode

I mentioned earlier that there are a lot of myths and misconceptions regarding the bathroom, particularly the toilet. While money won't be lost down the toilet when you flush, the room does look and feel better when the toilet lid is kept closed.

In feng shui, we try to surround ourselves with only pleasant images, and looking at the inside of a toilet bowl isn't one of them. Likewise, if you're designing the layout of a bathroom, it's preferable to place the toilet so that it's not the first thing you see when you open the door. Not only does this create a more pleasant view from the adjoining room, it also provides a greater sense of privacy.

Scent and Air Circulation

Many spas use scent to create a soothing ambience for clients. If you use any kind of scented product in your bathroom, be sure that it's natural, such as pure essential oils. (See the appendix.) Scents of citrus and eucalyptus are cleansing and rejuvenating, while lavender and sandalwood can be relaxing and soothing. Additionally, many pure essential oils are anti-microbial, helping to kill germs and bacteria that can multiply in damp places like the bathroom.

Bathrooms need excellent ventilation to keep them free of mold and mildew. If you suspect that your bathroom isn't receiving the air circulation that it needs, be sure to remedy the situation as soon as possible. Keep the bathroom door open to increase air circulation. It's a myth that you need to keep the door shut, and health hazards abound when air circulation is poor, giving rise to mold and mildew.

Plumbing

Water is the most corrosive substance on earth. Given enough time, water will dissolve anything on the planet (just look at the Grand Canyon). Water damage is one of the most destructive types of damage to a home. Over time, leaks can destroy the foundation and structure, attract deadly mold, and seriously impair the health and well-being of a family. Ignoring or postponing plumbing issues will add up to big problems later. Therefore, it's very important that all plumbing is kept in excellent condition and that bathrooms are kept as clean and attractive as possible.

Home Offices

According to the U.S. Department of Labor, almost a quarter of the working population of the United States works from home at least part-time, and the numbers are steadily growing.[1] Given how common home offices are, it's surprising how many dismal ones I've come across in my years of consulting.

I've seen many home offices relegated to coat closets, laundry rooms, dining room tables, and even one in a bathroom! It's no wonder that these clients complain about how working from home hasn't been as satisfying or as pleasant as they once envisioned. In order for your home-based business to be successful, you must create an optimal work environment. If you don't like your office or workspace, that feeling carries over into the attitudes you have about your work, diminishing your effectiveness. Fortunately, feng shui has a lot of great suggestions to help you optimize your home office.

Location

First and foremost, your home office must be placed in an ideal location. I can't emphasize enough how important it is that you feel comfortable in the space that you have designated for your work.

A study by Dr. Sherry Ahrentzen, a social ecologist, found that "those who reported being most satisfied with working at home almost all had separate rooms where they could close the door and be cut off from the potential distractions of people using the kitchen, watching television, and so on."[2]

If your home or apartment has the luxury of an extra bedroom, the utilization of this space as an office becomes obvious. What surprises me is how many people don't consider this to be a viable location for an office. Too often, a client will keep this extra bedroom as a guest room and relegate the home office to a dingy corner

---

[1] U.S. Department of Labor, Bureau of Labor Statistics. *American Time Use Survey, 2009*. Washington, D.C.

[2] Sherry Ahrentzen, PhD, "A Place of Peace, Prospect, and ... a PC: The Home as Office," *Journal of Architectural and Planning Research* 6, No. 4 (Winter 1989): 271-288.

or the kitchen table. When I ask how often they have houseguests, many clients will reply, "Oh, I don't know—maybe two weeks out of every year."

That's when I do the math for them. "Let me get this straight: You use this room for guests 14 days a year, at the most, leaving 351 days a year when the room is sitting idle? Even if you had houseguests a whopping 100 days a year, that still leaves 265 days when the room isn't being used." When I point this out, clients often react as though they've just discovered a secret room in their home, even though it's been there all along. If you need a home office that can also serve as a guest room, there should be no ambiguity about the function and purpose of the room; it needs to reflect its primary function as an office. If the room is set up as anything other than an office (i.e. guest room, workout room, or sewing room), the psychological value of the space diminishes, and the results will be a lowered respect for your work and reduced productivity.

If the room is to double as a guest room, consider adding a Murphy bed, a sofa bed, a futon, or even an inflatable mattress for occasional overnight guests. Having a regular bed in the office isn't ideal because it's a large, dominating piece of furniture that not only takes up a great deal of space but also psychologically designates the room as a place of rest, rather than a place of work. The advantage of a sofa bed or a futon is that, when not in use, either can provide extra seating in the room while maintaining the integrity of an office atmosphere.

In choosing which room will become the home office, the primary considerations are whether or not the room feels comfortable and whether it's conducive to work. It's crucial that the office space be as aesthetically, psychologically, and ergonomically pleasing as possible. If you love the space that you're spending time in, this positive attitude will carry over into your work.

Usually, rooms situated toward the front of the house are more suitable than rooms located in the back. The front of the home is usually the more active, yang portion, and the rear of the home tends to be the quieter, sleepier, yin area. Choose an active, sunny space as your home office. If it's too quiet, too dark, or too shady, you may find yourself napping instead of working.

Wireless technology allows us great freedom in choosing where to locate workstations. You may set up your office in one part of the home but end up using your laptop computer somewhere else. There are no hard and fast rules about where to do your best work. You need to decide that for yourself.

Get Creative

If you don't have the luxury of designating a separate room as an office, then consider other under-utilized areas of the home. One of my clients never used her formal dining room and desperately needed a space for her home office. This is something she had never considered, and it ended up being a wonderful solution to a big problem.

If your home office space is in one of the more public rooms of the home, like the dining room, living room, or family room, then it's important to put away your work so that it's not in view while you're relaxing. Decorative panel screens are an easy and inexpensive solution for dividing a room and creating the feeling of an extra space. Using a screen in a mixed-purpose room to demarcate the office area is an effective way to help you detach from work when it's time to take a break. You can also use furniture, such as credenzas and attractive cabinets, to store office supplies and to keep other work items out of sight in these rooms when not in use.

A Space of Her Own

A client of mine named Cheryl called just after she had started a home-based fashion design business. She and her husband, Mark, had two home offices crammed into a small, upstairs bedroom where tensions were mounting.

I suggested that, if they didn't mind parking their cars in the driveway, the garage might be a viable option for her workspace. Cheryl and Mark both loved this idea. She cleaned up the garage, bought a large remnant of indoor-outdoor carpet, painted the walls, and put up curtains to hide some of the storage shelves. She furnished it with a comfortable chair, a drafting table, her sewing machine, and other business necessities. She added a large mural of a beach scene on one wall, placed some silk plants in the corners, and changed the lighting to full-spectrum bulbs to give the garage the feeling of having a skylight. The once mundane garage was magically transformed into a fun, creative studio for Cheryl's design work. She had all the space that she needed, and this solution eliminated the tension over sharing the small, upstairs bedroom.

Not in the Master!

Of all the places to consider for the home office, there's one place that is strictly off-limits: the master bedroom. As I pointed out earlier, the bedroom is a place of rest and rejuvenation, not a place of work. By locating a home office in your bedroom, you never really get a psychological break from work. It's difficult to rest when the last thing you see upon retiring and the first thing you see upon awakening is your work area. It almost goes without saying that having an office in your bedroom is a great way to kill any feelings of romance. When selecting a place for your home office, choose anywhere in the home that feels good to you, as long as it isn't your bedroom.

Lighting

I mention lighting often throughout the book because lighting is an important consideration in any setting. With the amount of hours we spend working every day, lighting is a special consideration in work environments. Sitting under fluorescent or partial-spectrum lighting for long periods of time can cause eyestrain, an inability to concentrate, and depression, which all affect productivity.[3]

If your work area doesn't have good natural lighting, replace the lights with full-spectrum bulbs. They are available is sizes to fit almost any light fixture and can be found at your neighborhood hardware or building supply store. Full-spectrum bulbs for desk lamps and task lighting are available at most office supply stores. When the lighting in your environment is optimized, the result will be a more positive attitude and an improved sense of well-being.

---

[3] Fritz Hollwich, PhD, *The Influence of Ocular Light Perception on Metabolism in Man and in Animal*, Hunter and Hildegarde Hannum, trans. (New York: Springer-Verlag, 1979).

Layout and Desk Arrangement: Finding the Command Position

Once you've located your workspace, the decision on where to place your desk (if you use a desk) becomes the next important consideration. If space allows, you should place your desk in the Command Position within the room. As shown in figure 5.24, the Command Position in any room is the corner located diagonally across from the main door. The Command Position is sometimes called the Power Position in feng shui. Both descriptions are correct and hinge on Basic Principle #1: Protect your back.

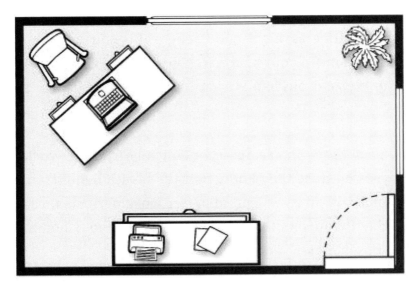

Figure 5.24

By sitting in the far corner with a clear view of the door, you'll be able to keep an eye on the door without being directly in line with it. When seated in this position, your survival instincts will calm down because you'll feel more in control of your surroundings. The Command Position allows you to relax and concentrate on your work. To test which area of your home office feels best for your desk position, take a chair and sit in various locations around the room—looking into the room, looking out a window, or facing a wall. Consider how each position makes you feel. Most people find that, while trying this activity, the Command Position feels the best.

Occasionally, it's impossible to sit in the Command Position. In this case, a mirror strategically placed on your desk can provide a view of the door to let you know what's going on behind you. Even if you live alone, you'll feel more relaxed at your desk with a view to the door.

Home Office Décor, Color, and Furniture

Décor and paint are vital to creating an optimal workspace. Choose artwork that's positive and motivating, and choose paint colors that you love. One of the luxuries of having a home office (other than avoiding a long commute and being able to work in your pajamas) is being able to decorate it any way you wish.

For your home office to have good feng shui, you need to minimize any distractions or irritations in your space. Needless to say, a home office should be a "kid-free zone," to keep curious hands away from important papers and equipment.

Furniture

Businesses spend millions to create ergonomically friendly work environments for their employees because they know that the health benefits and comfort that workers experience will, in turn, lead to better work performance, higher morale, and fewer sick days.[4] You should approach furnishing your home office with the same considerations in mind.

It's difficult to get things done when your back or shoulders ache or your wrist is bothering you while working on the computer. An ergonomically correct desk, chair, and computer station are important to the success of your home office, especially if you spend several hours sitting in one spot.

As I mentioned in the section on teen bedrooms, avoid desks with tall hutches. Hutches force people to sit facing the wall, create too many spaces for clutter, and increase tension due to something looming overhead. Built-in desks can also be undesirable since many built-ins face the wall instead of out into the room. Built-in desks also limit furniture configurations, which may change over time as your needs

---

[4] DAK Kopec, *Environmental Psychology for Design* (New York: Fairchild Books, 2006), 252-253.

change. Instead, opt for a traditional desk or table that will allow you the freedom to change things around.

Organization

Organization is a key component of a successful work environment. For storage, select cabinets with solid doors instead of open shelves or cabinets with glass doors. Open shelves, even if well-organized, can make a room feel messy and cluttered. The calmer a room is visually, the calmer its work environment will be. Storing items in cupboards or closets with solid doors makes the room feel more restful, more organized, and more efficient.

Many people enjoy having tall bookcases in a home office. With tall bookcases, it's important to avoid placing them either behind you or very close to your desk. A tall, bulky bookcase placed too close to the desk can create feelings of uneasiness and vulnerability. It's difficult to feel safe and to concentrate on work when something tall and heavy is looming overhead. Similarly, avoid placing cabinets, cupboards, or shelves above head level (while seated) to keep the room feeling safe and comfortable. Within bookcases, organize books by placing heavier ones on the bottom shelves and lighter ones on the top shelves to make the bookcase feel lighter and less oppressive.

Sharing a Home Office

I frequently consult with couples who share home office space. As with the fashion designer mentioned earlier, this arrangement can create stress and tension in the relationship to the point of frequent arguments over territory issues. Not all couples who share home offices experience conflict, but it is common.

Often, tension arises out of different work styles: One person is tidy; the other is messy. One person is quiet; the other is loud. This is when my role feels more like that of a marriage counselor than a feng shui consultant! If two people must share a home office, the first thing to consider is desk placement. Avoid placing the desks in Confrontation Position (directly across from and facing each other). It's also important that both people are seated in such a way that they can see the door from their respective workstations, if possible.

It's beneficial to demarcate space for each person. Separate spaces can be established by using plants, shoji screens (see figure 5.25), or bookcases to create a feeling of privacy and of autonomy for each person. Consider setting up complementary work schedules so that each person can use the home office alone, while the other person works elsewhere.

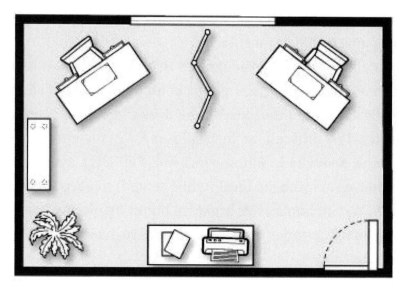

Figure 5.25

Working from home can be liberating and satisfying. Feng shui can help create an optimal working environment. While it may take some creativity, forethought, and even negotiation, the positive benefits and successes will be well worth the effort!

Hallways and Transition Areas

Hallways are transitional spaces necessary for getting from one part of the house to another. They are often neglected opportunities for improving the feng shui of a home.

Narrow Hallways

A narrow hallway can feel uncomfortable and claustrophobic. The illusion of a wider passage can be created by painting the wall at the end of the hallway a darker shade than the sides of the hallway. One combination that I saw recently featured a long hallway with cream-colored paint on the sides and a beautiful chocolate brown paint on the wall at the end of the hallway. The homeowners had hung a simple but beautiful painting on the end wall and installed a light to emphasize the painting. The effect was attractive and elegant, and the hallway didn't feel as cramped or monotonous as it would have if painted in one color. Another creative client of mine painted the walls of a long hallway in a soft yellow and chose eggplant purple for the end wall of the hallway. The result was a fun, whimsical look that worked well in her home and with her taste.

Mirrors

Avoid placing a mirror at the end of a long hallway. A mirror visually doubles the length of the hallway, making it seem even longer. Also, as you walk down a hallway toward a mirror, it can feel as if someone is approaching you, and that can feel strange. To create a focal point at the end of a hallway, consider a well-lit piece of artwork rather than a mirror. If the hallway needs even more light, artwork that is framed under glass will reflect light, especially if the main colors in the artwork are light and bright.

Artwork

Many people use hallway walls to display artwork or family photos. While both might seem suitable for this space, displaying too many items on the walls of a narrow hallway can make it feel cluttered and disorganized. As people walk down the hallway, tensions increase because they're afraid of bumping pictures off of the wall. Generally, narrow hallways don't provide enough space for people to step back and admire artwork or photos, so these items often go unappreciated in such a location. If a hallway is too narrow to display artwork or photos on the walls, consider adding a runner on the floor to break up the monotony. In a standard hallway, it's best to display artwork or photos on one side only. In wider hallways—those that can accommodate furniture without creating an obstacle—displaying artwork or photos on both walls can make the hallway appear narrower.

Rarely Used Rooms

In the past few years, there's been a U.S. trend of filling housing developments with very large homes. These homes range from 3,000 to 6,000 square feet and frequently have many more rooms than a family needs or uses. One problem with having a large home is that unused rooms often feel neglected or stagnant. The listless energy from unused rooms can affect the chi of the entire house, creating an atmosphere of lethargy.

To get the energy moving in these rooms, place things in them that need periodic attention: an answering machine to check, a plant or tabletop fountain that needs water, or an aquarium that requires care. Each of these necessitates that you enter the room every few days, which keeps the energy circulating. When a room is used regularly, the energy in the room feels better.

Guest Rooms

If your home has a furnished guest room, set it up according to the same feng shui principles used for other bedrooms. Consider bed placement, mirrors, colors, and décor as though you will be sleeping in this room. Extra touches will make it even more comfortable for your guests. Consider these:

- Provide coat hangers in the closet and at least one or two drawers in a dresser so that guests can unpack their clothing.
- Set up a suitcase stand or make room in the closet to store suitcases.
- Include a comfortable chair, a good reading light, and possibly a television.
- Offer an easy-to-use alarm clock on the nightstand.
- Add extras like bottled water and a box of tissue.
- Place a set of towels on the bed or in the bathroom for your guest.

If your guest room is used infrequently, consider placing a sheet or other cloth over the bedspread when the room isn't being used. While guest rooms are often dusted and vacuumed along with the rest of the house, the bedspread in a guest room can remain untouched for months. I once visited a friend who had a lovely guest room with a comfortable bed. However, when I got into bed that first night, I could barely breathe from all the dust covering the bedspread. A sheet or other cloth placed over the bed in the guest room can protect the bedspread and pillows from dust.

When considering how to make your guests feel more comfortable, think about the amenities that a fine hotel would offer, and try to incorporate some of these into your guest room. By creating a relaxing and comfortable environment for your guests, you're extending the good feng shui of your home to them.

Garages

In most suburban neighborhoods, the garage dominates the front of the house—sometimes even dwarfing the size of the house itself. Americans place a great deal of emphasis on their cars, and many people spend hours a day commuting. Technically, the garage was never designed to be a main entrance. Over time, however, the garage has become the primary entrance for many people. My clients often tell me that they don't remember the last time they entered the house through the front door.

When the garage is used as the primary entrance, basic feng shui guidelines for main entrances should be applied. The garage should be clean, well-lit, clutter-free, safe, organized, and always provide a positive first impression. Feng shui is about bringing peace and happiness into your surroundings and into your life. What you experience when you first arrive home affects the way you feel and the interactions you have with others.

Consider the garage as you would any other room in your home. Remember, however, that the garage is the only room where one entire wall is periodically lifted, exposing the whole room for the world to see. When you think of the garage in this way, do you really want it to be a room that embarrasses you?

Many homebuilders scrimp on costs when it comes to the garage, leaving this area with exposed studs, insulation, pipes, concrete, and wires. If your garage is in this condition, finish the interior walls with drywall, and paint them in a light, welcoming color. As a finishing touch, paint the garage floor using non-toxic, eco-friendly paint to create a clean, attractive surface.

Consider adding art to your garage. Artwork that doesn't fit the décor of your home might be perfect in the garage. The garage is ideal for fun murals, posters, children's paintings, and other art that you love but might not feel comfortable displaying elsewhere in the home. Hang pictures that make you smile, lift your spirits, and give you a positive feeling as you drive in.

Clutter and Storage

Clutter and storage in the garage deserve special mention. Organization is very important here, especially when the garage is serving as a main entrance to your home. If you see nothing but chaos when your garage door opens, you'll most likely feel irritated and exhausted. When you enter your home through a cluttered and disorganized space, you're also setting the stage for some tense exchanges between you and your partner, your children, or your housemates. If possible, use cabinets with doors rather than open shelving for storage. Keeping items behind closed doors will provide a calm, rather than chaotic, first impression. If your garage is orderly and organized, you'll feel more positive and relaxed when you arrive home.

The garage shouldn't be a dumping ground for everything that doesn't fit in the house. I once did a feng shui consultation for a client who had so much stuff in her garage that she actually had a sofa hanging from the ceiling! How it was hoisted up there is still a mystery to me, but if you're hanging large pieces of furniture from the ceiling because there's no room left on the ground, then you have way too much stuff!

If you tend to procrastinate about getting things done (most people with clutter issues fall into this category), then call a local charity to schedule a donation pick-up. Once you get rid of all the clutter in your garage and organize the space, you'll be amazed at how much more positive and uplifted you'll feel when you arrive home. You simply can't go wrong with upgrading your garage. Finishing the garage not only creates a wonderful, pleasing, and calm first impression, it greatly adds to the resale value of your home.

Laundry Rooms and Utility Rooms

Often, the interior door to the garage leads right into a laundry or utility room. This configuration is unfortunate because the laundry room is a place where you do chores. After working all day, the last thing you want to be reminded of is the work you have waiting at home. Entering your home daily through a laundry room can result in feelings of exhaustion and a sense that your work is never done. Here are some feng shui ideas to make this area more welcoming:

- Keep the laundry room or utility room clean, organized, and pleasing.

- Ensure that everything is in excellent working order.

- Add full-spectrum lighting if there are no windows to the outside.

- Paint the room a soothing color, and add pleasant artwork if the space allows.

- Pay careful attention to storage. All storage in this area should be organized, and items should be kept in closed cabinets and drawers.

- Have a hamper system for laundry, so it doesn't wind up strewn all over the floor or counter.

While entering your home through your laundry room isn't ideal, if you must do so, make it as peaceful and as pleasing as possible.

Attics, Basements, and Storerooms

Many homes have attics, basements, crawl spaces, or other designated storage areas where it's tempting to allow unwanted and unused items to fill up the space. As with garages, I encourage clients to become more creative when considering the purpose of these areas and their potential as expanded living space. If you need a home gym, home office, playroom, teen hangout, or something that the regular rooms in the house cannot accommodate, consider these storage areas. It's amazing how a can of paint, good lighting, and an area rug can transform a storage space into useful square footage that you didn't realize you had.

First and foremost before transforming any space into a living area, be sure to check for radon gas, asbestos, mold, or mildew of any sort. It would be awful to go to the trouble of remodeling a space only to find that it's loaded with health dangers. A specialist can come to your home and assess an area, particularly the basement, for any health or safety hazards before you invest in making changes.

Moving On

Now that we've concluded the tour through your home and learned how to enhance the feng shui of your home from a Form School perspective, let's move on to the more energetic aspects of feng shui. In the next chapter, you'll learn how to enhance the chi of your home through the age-old method of Compass School feng shui.

PART III

ENERGETIC ASPECTS OF FENG SHUI

Chapter 6

Energizing Your Home with Compass School Feng Shui

The most beautiful thing we can experience is the mysterious.
It is the source of all true art and all science.

— *Albert Einstein*

Up to this point, you've learned about the physical aspects of feng shui, known as Form School feng shui. Form School feng shui helps you examine and then adjust your physical surroundings in order to optimize the way you feel in your home. If you apply the information presented in the previous chapters, you will have gone a long way toward achieving excellent feng shui in your home. If you've carefully integrated those concepts into your environment, you may be amazed at how much more positive your home feels and how much happier you are as a result of these changes. For those who wish to take the exploration of feng shui a step further, please read on.

Along with Form School, Compass School feng shui is one of the oldest systems of feng shui and is still widely practiced. It ranges from simple applications to complex formulas. This chapter presents the basic foundation of Compass School feng shui so that you may develop a working understanding of its principles. Without this grasp of the basic principles, the more complex aspects of Compass School feng shui can easily overwhelm and confuse a beginning student. Too often, this frustration becomes a stumbling block that results in people giving up on feng shui entirely. This is unfortunate because you don't need to implement *all* of the advanced formulas in feng shui in order experience its benefits.

Compass School feng shui is an energetic aspect of feng shui that's not easily explained from a scientific perspective. However, researchers in the fields of physics and quantum mechanics are rapidly making new discoveries that describe many previously unexplained phenomena.[1] Perhaps at some point, scientific information will verify the energetic aspects of feng shui. For now, I'm going to begin with the basics of Compass School feng shui so that you can begin the process of energizing your home.

The Five Elements

The Chinese have studied human energy for hundreds, if not thousands, of years. The ancient Chinese suggested that, in addition to its veins and nervous system, the human body also has pathways of energy known as "meridians." These meridians carry chi—or life force energy—throughout the body. When chi flows smoothly along the meridians, the body is in a state of good health. However, if the energy becomes blocked or if there's too much or too little energy in one area, chi becomes unbalanced, which may lead to disease. These imbalances are referred to as excesses of either yin or yang energy in the body. Acupuncture and acupressure were developed in ancient China to stimulate and unblock energy along the meridians. Practitioners of Chinese medicine employ these and other techniques to bring yin and yang energies into equilibrium. Through the skilled use of these practices, the body is brought into harmony and returns to an optimally healthy state.[2,3]

---

[1] Bruce Rosenblum and Fred Kuttner, *Quantum Enigma: Physics Encounters in Consciousness*, (New York: Oxford University Press, 2006).

[2] Giovanni Maciocia, *The Foundations of Chinese Medicine: A Comprehensive Text for Acupuncturists and Herbalists* (London: Churchill Livingstone, 2005).

[3] Alex Holland, *Voices of Qi: An Introductory Guide to Traditional Chinese Medicine* (Berkeley: North Atlantic Books, 1999)

Compass School feng shui is like acupuncture for a building. Similar to the energy meridians in the body, Compass School feng shui postulates that there are energy meridians running through the earth as well as through homes and buildings. These meridians create energy points where compass lines intersect with the walls of a building. When the energy is running smoothly along the meridian lines of a building, the people who live or work there may enjoy more positive experiences. When the energy is blocked or hampered in some way, people can experience this blockage as unhappiness, confusion, irritability, illness, or a feeling of being stuck.

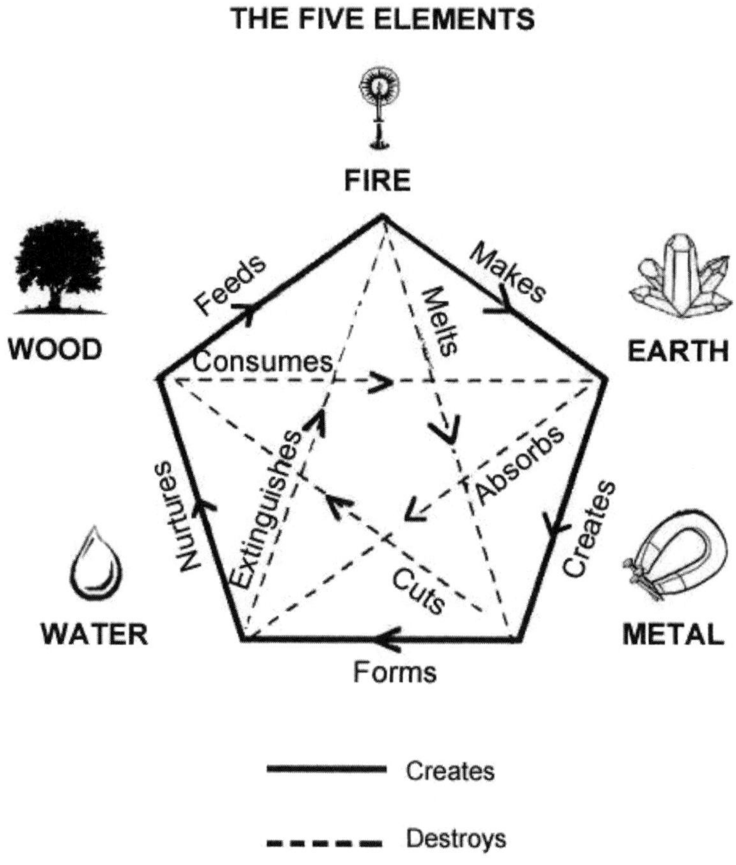

THE FIVE ELEMENTS

Figure 6.1

Figure 6.1 illustrates the properties and cycles associated with the five elements. Each element has unique materials, shapes, and colors associated with it. Based on the compass directions that relate to your home, there are certain elements to either add or avoid in particular areas. Below, you'll find the characteristics and qualities of each of the five elements. After we review them in depth, I'll show you how they're used and where to place them.

Water

Material: any body of water, such as oceans, streams, rivers, ponds, pools, birdbaths, aquariums, and fountains

Shape: free-form, non-geometric shapes like the shape of a puddle

Colors: blues and very dark colors, including black

Symbols: items made of glass, images of waterscapes, and shiny, reflective surfaces

When using water to activate an area, circulating water is best (i.e., fountains and water features with pumps, such as pools and aquariums). Circulating water stimulates energy, keeping it from becoming stagnant. If an area needs to be energized by water, it will *not* work to just add a picture of water or anything else that *symbolizes* water. Actual moving water is necessary to activate a space where water is needed.

Wood

Material: anything made of wood or derived from a plant, such as trees, bushes, flowers, cotton, and wood furniture

Shape: tall, vertical shapes like stripes, columns, or poles to symbolize a tree trunk

Color: green

Symbols: artwork featuring flowers, plants, or forests as well as silk plants and floral fabrics

When using wood to activate an area, living plants are best. However, avoid using Bonsai trees or anything that's purposely dwarfed or stunted. The energy here should be growing and expanding, not restricted.

Reality Check

---

*Myth: Dried plants and flowers bring bad luck
and should be avoided.*

Much has been written in feng shui literature that associates dried plants with negative energy. Some of this information goes to the extreme by crediting dried plants with all sorts of calamities. This, of course, is untrue.

This myth is based on the concept that dried flowers and plants were once living and are now dead. Hence, displaying these "dead" items in your home will attract negative energy. Think about it. If this were true, then you'd have to get rid of all your wood furniture too or risk being surrounded by dead energy all the time. Nonsense!

While dried flowers may not evoke the same vitality and energy that living plants do, they are by no means bearers of negative events and catastrophes. In fact, under certain circumstances, dried plants can have very positive associations for people—as mementos of weddings, proms, and other happy occasions. When displaying mementos of dried flowers, make sure that they don't get too dusty or brittle, as they may become an eyesore rather than reminders of a pleasant event.

If you're using dried flowers for décor purposes only, you may want to consider realistic silk alternatives. Silk plants can be used to symbolize a healthy plant in an area that needs the look of foliage but cannot support a healthy living plant. Keep in mind that a silk plant, no matter how realistic it may look, is a replica of a living plant and should only be used to improve the décor of a room. Silk plants may not be substituted for real plants when an area needs to be activated by the wood element.

Fire

Material: anything with an actual flame, such as a fire in the fireplace, a lit candle, or a gas stove. Fire can also include the electricity that produces light in lamps, computers, and televisions as well as solar-powered and battery-operated items.

Shapes: cones, pyramids, and triangles. Think of how a flame is shaped—a wide base that comes to a point on top.

Color: red

Symbols: artwork of sunrises and sunsets or strong red design statements

Remember that a candle, a stove, or a fireplace is only a fire element when it's lit, and an electrical item is only a fire element when it's turned on. When using fire to activate an area, an easy option is to set a lamp timer for three hours a day (enough time to allow the energy to be present to activate this area). Also, a table lamp or a floor lamp is more specific and effective than overhead lights for this purpose.

Earth

Material: anything that comes from the earth, such as sand, rocks, stones, pebbles, minerals, tile, clay, granite, brick, and cement

Shapes: squares, cubes, and rectangles

Colors: gold, yellow, tan, and brown

Symbols: mountain or desert scenes

To bring the earth element into your home, don't overlook things like countertops and floors. If you have granite countertops or tile or stone floors in an area, you definitely have plenty of the earth element in that location. Porcelain sinks, toilets, and bathtubs also fall into the earth category because porcelain is made from clay, which of course, comes from the earth.

Metal

Material: anything made of metal, such as gold, silver, bronze, steel, brass, and copper

Shapes: circles, arches, and ovals

Colors: silver, gray, white, and very light (pastel) colors

Symbols: gongs, metal furniture, or items made from metal such as bowls, coins, sculptures, and wind chimes

Wind chimes may also be hung indoors to bring the metal element into an area. When searching for decorative items made of metal, be sure to browse arts and crafts shows, home décor stores, and online retailers.

Elemental Cycles

The diagram of the five elements (figure 6.1) may be read either clockwise or counter-clockwise, with the five elements always appearing in the same order: water, wood, fire, earth, and metal. This order reflects the natural cycle of these elements. Much like a game of Rock-Paper-Scissors, the elements either support or destroy one another based upon their natural relationships. In your home, these energetic interactions help to determine which elements are needed to strengthen or activate a particular area and which elements need to be avoided.

The Productive Cycle

Figure 6.2 shows the clockwise order of the five elements as water, wood, fire, earth, and metal. The clockwise cycle is known as the Productive Cycle or the Creative Cycle, meaning that each element increases or energizes the element that comes next in the cycle.

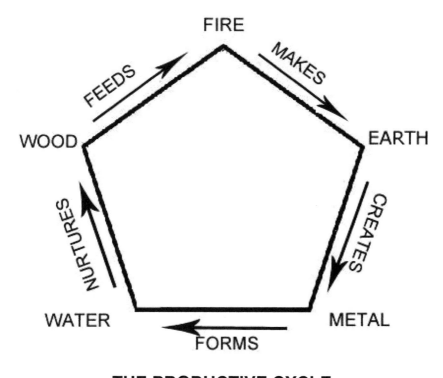

THE PRODUCTIVE CYCLE

Figure 6.2

To more fully understand the Productive Cycle, consider these interactions found in nature:

- Water nurtures wood: adding water to a plant makes it grow.

- Wood feeds fire: adding a log to a fire increases the fire.

- Fire makes earth: an erupting volcano creates more earth.

- Earth creates metal: metal is produced in the earth.

- Metal forms water: water forms on metal through condensation. (Think of a cold soda can on a hot day.)

The Destructive Cycle

While each element has another that supports or increases it, each element also has one that destroys or eliminates it. This cycle is known as the Destructive Cycle. In figure 6.3, the Destructive Cycle is identified by moving around the illustration in a counter-clockwise direction, and skipping one element, to arrive at the destructive element.

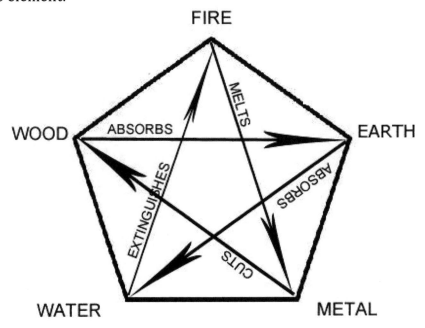

THE DESTRUCTIVE CYCLE

Figure 6.3

Again, look to nature for examples such as these:

- Water destroys fire: water puts out a fire.

- Wood destroys earth: plant roots (wood) absorb earth.

- Fire destroys metal: fire melts metal.

- Earth destroys water: sand and soil absorb water.

- Metal destroys wood: metal tools are used to cut trees.

Now that you've been introduced to the five elements and their cycles, you're ready to learn how to use them in your home.

The Life Aspiration Areas of the Pa Kua

One intriguing aspect of feng shui is how specific areas of a home correspond to specific areas of life and may be enhanced to bring about improvement in a particular area of life. Feng shui refers to these areas as "Life Aspiration Areas," and there are nine: Career, Knowledge, Family, Wealth & Prosperity, Fame, Love & Partnership, Creation, Synchronicity, and Health.

In a home, the Life Aspiration Areas are identified according to compass directions and are energized by the presence or absence of the five elements. To determine where each Life Aspiration Area is in your home, you'll need a compass. You can buy an inexpensive compass at a sporting goods shop or an automotive store. There may even be a compass feature available through your cell phone. If you don't know how to use a compass, don't worry—not everyone was a Scout! Ask someone for help, search online, or follow the instructions included with the compass. Some people have no trouble reading a compass, while others find it challenging.

You may also wish to purchase a feng shui compass known as a Lo Pan (see the appendix). Most Lo Pan compasses are in Chinese, however, the Lo Pan compass referred to in the appendix of this book is in English. This Lo Pan compass also comes with instructions, making it easier to read and apply to your floor plan than a regular compass or a traditional Chinese Lo Pan. As long as you can apply compass directions accurately to your floor plan, the choice of compass is up to you.

The Layout of the Life Aspiration Areas

The layout of the Life Aspiration Areas based upon compass directions is known as the Pa Kua. In some feng shui practices, this layout is also known as the Bagua; the terms are interchangeable and refer to the same thing.

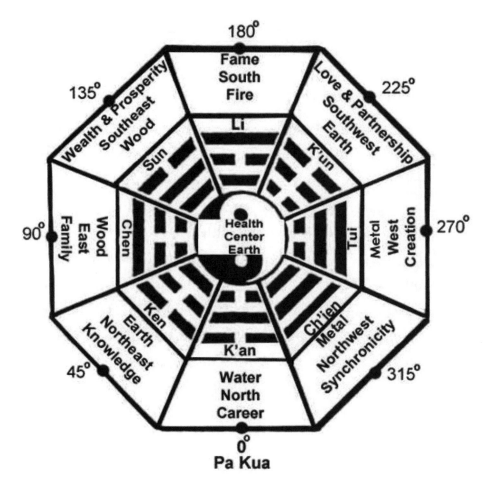

Figure 6.4

The Pa Kua has its origins in the ancient divination system of the I Ching.[1] The Pa Kua is divided into eight pie-shaped sections, known as trigrams, plus the center, making nine total Life Aspiration Areas. Each trigram corresponds to a compass point (see figure 6.4). When the Pa Kua is applied to the floor plan of a home, it can indicate *what* needs to be done and *where* it needs to be done in order to energize various aspects of your life.

---

[1] Tan Xiaochun, *The I Ching: An Illustrated Guide to the Chinese Classic of Changes* (Singapore: Asiapac Books, 1993).

The Pa Kua diagram is traditionally oriented with south at the top and north at the bottom, just as a Chinese Lo Pan is. It's thought that the reason for this is the importance that the ancient Chinese placed on the south as the direction of the most balanced light and temperatures throughout the day. But don't let this confuse you. North is still north, south is still south, and so on. You will use the directions in the same way you always have.

The Life Aspiration Areas in Detail

Each Life Aspiration Area or trigram is made up of the following characteristics:

- *Chinese name*: the Chinese name given to the trigram

- *Aspiration area*: the area of life that corresponds to this trigram

- *Main element*: the element that must be added to properly energize the space

- *Supporting element*: the element that directly precedes the main element in the Productive Cycle

- *Destructive element*: the element that is destructive to the main element and is best avoided

- *Depleting element*: the element that directly follows the main element in the Productive Cycle and should be minimized

- *Neutral element*: an element that doesn't exert an influence in the area

- *Colors*: the color(s) associated with each area[2]

- *Enhancements*: items that help to bring the proper element into each area

In addition to the elements for each Life Aspiration Area, you may wish to add artwork, mementos, affirmations, or other visual reminders and symbols of what it

---

[2] It is *not* necessary to paint or display the colors to activate the energy of each area. Adding the *actual element* is much more important to the energy of the space than the associated colors or symbols. The only exception is when the color red is added to the south. Red is a very intense color with a strong vibration and can add the fire element of the south. Remember that the *actual* element associated with each area is required to energize it.

is that you'd like to accomplish in these areas of your life. While these items cannot be used *instead* of the needed elements, they can be added to help you stay focused on what it is you'd like to manifest through your feng shui efforts.

South/Fame

South is associated with fame, reputation, and recognition. My clients sometimes misunderstand this area. They wonder why it's important to enhance this area of their home or yard if they don't want to be famous. While being famous is certainly a focus of this area, the south also corresponds to earning the respect of others. This area relates to positive acknowledgment, recognition, and promotion.

- *Chinese name*: Li

- *Aspiration areas*: fame, reputation, and recognition

- *Main element*: fire

- *Supporting element*: wood

- *Destructive element*: water

- *Depleting element*: earth

- *Neutral element*: metal

- *Color*: red

- *Enhancements*: (outdoors) fire pits, barbecues, fireplaces, tiki torches, solar-powered and electric lights; (indoors) stoves, ovens, fireplaces, candles, and electronics

Enhancements must be items that are used regularly in order to activate the fire element. The easiest and safest way to do this is to install either solar-powered lights that go on automatically or electric lights connected to a timer. In either case, the lights should come on for at least three hours a day (every twenty-four hours). This three-hour minimum allows the energy of fire to be present long enough to activate the area. Items such as stoves, ovens, fireplaces, candles, and frequently used electronic items, like televisions, also represent the fire element, but they must be on for at least three hours a day to be effective.

Since wood is the supporting element, consider adding healthy plants and flowers to this area. Because water is the destructive element, swimming pools, spas, or fountains should be avoided in the south area of your home or yard.

This area is also suitable for displaying trophies, diplomas, certificates, awards, and other accolades that you or your family members have earned. These can serve as reminders of the goals you've achieved relating to fame and reputation. Remember, however, that these items serve only as inspiration and not as substitutes for the element of fire in the south.

All the talent in the world. As any public figure who's been involved in a scandal can tell you, respect from others is something that you may not appreciate until you no longer have it. Advancing in your career, selling a product, or being nominated for an award are some of the benefits that can come from enhancing the Fame area of your home or business. While no one should be overly concerned about what others think, life is much easier when you're seen in a positive light. Following are two examples of the power of enhancing the Fame area.

I once had a client who was a talented photographer. Although his work was very good, he was having difficulty selling his photographs. While working with him, I noticed that he had a tabletop fountain running in the Fame area of his home. I explained that, in order to enhance his fame, he would need to remove the fountain from that area since water is the destructive element to fire. I suggested that he replace the fountain with a lamp connected to a timer that was programmed for three hours a day of light.

A month later, my client called to tell me that, shortly after our appointment, he met a couple who loved his work so much that they used their connections in the art world to arrange a showing of his photographs at an art gallery in New York. The gallery show was a huge success, and my client sold all of his photographs in one night! Needless to say, he became a huge proponent of feng shui after that experience.

Another client of mine was an aspiring jazz guitarist. Not only did he enhance the Fame area of his home with lighting, but he also painted the south wall in his home a beautiful, rich red. Within three months of making these changes, his first album held the number-one spot in the country for jazz music, and he has enjoyed great success ever since.

In both of these scenarios, my clients had great talent. The problem is, you can have all the talent in the world, but if no one knows about it, you'll never receive recognition for it or make a living with it. The photographer and the musician decided to go the extra step by using feng shui to boost the energy of their Fame areas, and in both cases, their efforts paid off in a big way.

Southwest/Love & Partnership

The southwest is associated with love and partnership. This is the place to enhance if you'd like to attract a love partner or enrich a relationship that you already have. Pay special attention to what's currently in place in this area of your home or yard that might not bode well for a healthy, happy, loving relationship.

- *Chinese name*: K'un

- *Aspiration areas*: love, romance, and cooperation

- *Main element*: earth

- *Supporting element*: fire

- *Destructive element*: wood

- *Depleting element*: metal

- *Neutral element*: water

- *Colors*: earth tones, yellow, brown, and tan

- *Enhancements*: (outdoors) river rock or pebbles as groundcover, garden statues or ornamentation made of ceramic, stone, tile, or cement; (indoors) statues, figurines, or tabletops made of ceramic, stone, or tile

Items made from earth are required in the southwest, and since this area corresponds to Love & Partnership, items in pairs are favored. Outdoors, consider placing a pair of large rocks or boulders in the southwest area of your yard. Pairs of cement or stone statuary may also be used. Indoors, display a bowl of pretty pebbles or a set of stones with inspirational sayings on them. Rose quartz is a mineral that's traditionally associated with love. A pair of hearts carved from rose quartz is a great addition to the southwest area of your home (see the appendix).

Most birds mate for life, so a pair of ceramic or stone birds in the southwest area of your home or yard would be ideal. Or, choose artwork depicting pairs: two people, two animals, two fish, two trees, two flowers, or two of just about any positive image will work here. Get creative! Include a picture of yourself and your sweetheart, if you have one.

A salt lamp is a wonderful addition to areas where the earth element is needed. A salt lamp brings the earth element and its supporting element, fire, easily into a space. It gives off beautiful light and has the added advantages of being a natural air purifier and stress reducer (see the appendix).

Often, single people will display items and artwork as single pieces in their homes, thus reinforcing the subliminal message that they are alone. If you're single and would like to be in a happy relationship, be especially diligent about how you display items and artwork in your environment. While it's important to display paired items in the southwest area of your home, you shouldn't limit the paired items to this area only. To enhance your love life, be sure to continue the theme of paired items and other partnership symbols throughout your home to enhance your love life.

Three's a crowd. Whatever you do, avoid placing items in groups of three, especially in the southwest. I once did a consultation for a single woman who had artwork all over her home that depicted three objects over and over again, including a very large painting of two women and a man in her living room, which happened to be in the southwest (Love & Partnership) area of the home. When I explained that this could potentially bring a partner who was already committed elsewhere, she became very self-conscious. She admitted that she was involved with a married man and had been ever since moving into her home, and she was extremely unhappy about it. After our consultation, she placed everything in pairs, and within two months, she met a wonderful *available* man and entered into a very happy, healthy relationship.

Stormy romances. A few years ago, the *New York Times* featured an article about a feng shui consultation that I'd done for a prominent client. The article highlighted a particularly interesting example of what *not* to display in the Love & Partnership area. My client was a single man who had pictures of shipwrecks hung on the wall in the Love & Partnership area of his home. I pointed out that this was not the best symbolism for manifesting a great relationship. Indeed, my client had spent the past few years going through a series of stormy, ill-fated romances and breakups. I suggested that he not only add the earth element to this area but that he also replace the shipwreck pictures with lovely old photographs of his grandparents on their wedding day—as they were happily married for many, many years. He did so, and within a short time, he entered into a new and wonderful relationship.

A child's room in the southwest. If a child's bedroom happens to fall in the southwest area of the home, it's especially important for parents to ensure that their relationship isn't focused primarily on their child. Having a child's room in this area of the home can make parents feel as if all their interaction revolves around their child, rather than each other. If this is the case, the room can be enhanced with a salt lamp or a child's rock collection. It's also nice to have a picture of Mom and Dad in the room (if Mom and Dad are still together). A fitting enhancement might also be Minnie and Mickey Mouse or Cinderella and the Prince, which wouldn't look out of place in a child's room.

The love of a lifetime. One of my favorite feng shui love stories happened early in my career. A woman in her late eighties, named Amy, called me to do a feng shui consultation on her home, with an emphasis on enhancing her love life. I'd done a consultation for her granddaughter, and it had worked so well that Amy wanted to try it herself. She told me that she had been a widow for twenty-five years. She was lonely and in need of companionship. I agreed to meet with her and do the best that I could, but I didn't want her to have any unrealistic expectations.

Amy and I had a delightful time during her appointment. Her wit and sense of humor were as sharp as ever. We had so much fun arranging items in pairs throughout her home and garden, and we ensured that there was plenty of the earth element represented in the southwest.

Two months after our appointment, Amy left me a voice mail sounding very distressed. "Cathleen," she said, "I am having a big problem and need to talk to you right away."

I thought, *Oh no! Nothing happened in her love life, and now she's upset with feng shui and with me.* With trepidation, I called her back.

"Cathleen!" she shouted into the phone when she heard my voice, "Cathleen, I have a big problem. My feng shui worked so well that I not only have one boyfriend, I now have TWO, and I can't decide which one I like the most." As you can imagine, this was a relief *and* rather amusing.

"Well Amy," I said. "Let's talk about the pros and cons of each one." After a lengthy conversation, Amy said that she felt so much better and that she would call me back with her decision. I heard from her about a month later. She told me she had chosen to marry the 92-year-old doctor and that they were about to embark on an around-the-world cruise for their honeymoon. I was delighted. The last time I heard from Amy, she and her husband were doing very well, and both felt that they'd finally found the love of a lifetime. Amy told me that she credits feng shui (and me) with bringing love back into her life.

West/Creation

Traditionally, the west is referred to as the area of Children & Creativity. At first glance, it might seem odd that these two are linked at all, but this area is associated with generating something new that hasn't existed before—whether that's a new idea, a new project, a piece of art, new music, or a child. I prefer to call this area

"Creation" because I think it better describes the concept associated with the west. If you're an artist, musician, writer, actor, or just a very creative person in general, you'll want to energize this area to support your creative endeavors. Likewise, if you're a parent or would like to become a parent, activating this area of your home helps to increase the positive energy associated with children.

- *Chinese name*: Tui

- *Aspiration areas*: children, creativity, and creation

- *Main element*: metal

- *Supporting element*: earth

- *Destructive element*: fire

- *Depleting element*: water

- *Neutral element*: wood

- *Colors*: white, silver, gray, metallic, and pastel

- *Enhancements*: (outdoors) wind chimes, metal patio furniture, sculptures, and metal lawn ornaments; (indoors) metal picture frames, metal sculptures, trays, tables and chairs with metal legs, home décor items made of metal, candlesticks, lamps, metal planters, pots, bowls, and vases

Over the years, I've been amazed at how often parent/child relationships improve once the west has been energized. To help your relationship with your children become more positive, consider placing photos of them in metal picture frames in the room that occupies the west portion of the home—unless that area falls in the master bedroom. (Having photographs of other people, including children, in a couple's bedroom may dampen feelings of intimacy and romance.)

Be careful what you wish for. One of my clients desperately wanted to have a baby. She and her husband had tried everything medically possible with no success. As a last-ditch effort, they called me to help with the feng shui of their home, hoping it would assist them in becoming pregnant. I explained that feng shui cannot solve all of our problems and that I couldn't promise them a pregnancy as a result of their feng shui consultation. They understood but wanted to try anyway, so we set about enhancing the Life Aspiration Areas of their home. I focused on activating the west (Creation), the east (Family), and the center (Health). My client was dedicated to doing everything that I suggested to energize her home.

Lo and behold, four months later she called to tell me that she was indeed pregnant ... with triplets! She joked that she probably should have placed only one large metal candlestick in the west rather than three! She was overjoyed with the news of her pregnancy, and five years later, my client and her triplets are doing well.

Northwest/Synchronicity

While this area is often referred to as Helpful People & Travel, it actually has more to do with synchronicity—being in the right place at the right time and connected with the right people. If you've moved recently and wish to meet new friends or liven up your social life, try enhancing this area. It's also a great area for anything connected with travel or movement.

- *Chinese name:* Ch'ien
- *Aspiration areas:* synchronicity, travel, friends, and networking
- *Main element:* metal
- *Supporting element:* earth
- *Destructive element:* fire
- *Depleting element:* water
- *Neutral element:* wood
- *Colors:* white, silver, gray, metallic, and pastel
- *Enhancements:* (outdoors) wind chimes, metal patio furniture, sculptures, and metal lawn ornaments; (indoors) metal picture frames featuring pictures

or photos of travel spots, vacations, or friends and family, metal chairs and tables, and items made from metal like vases, statues, and planters

If you want more activity in your life, be sure to avoid clutter in the northwest. While clutter should be avoided in all areas of the home, the northwest, with its emphasis on movement, is especially vulnerable. Clutter in this area may slow things down, causing your life to stagnate.

When a garage is located in the northwest area of a home, the residents often lead exceptionally busy lives. Many times, one of the people living in the household travels for a living, either as part of a job or with a longer-than-usual commute to work. This is because the northwest is associated with movement and travel. The main element for the northwest is metal, and with cars (very large metal objects) moving in and out of the garage regularly, the area is constantly being activated. My own home is set up like this, and that's certainly been my experience while living here!

North/Career

The word "career" is often associated with one's job, vocation, or place of employment. In feng shui, this term means so much more than just where you work or what you do for a living. On a deeper level, it pertains to the direction of your life. You or someone you know may be looking for meaning, direction, and purpose in life. Whether you want to energize your vocation and professional goals or need assistance with the direction of your life, you'll need to activate the north area of your home.

- *Chinese name*: K'an
- *Aspiration areas*: career and life path
- *Main element*: water
- *Supporting element*: metal
- *Destructive element*: earth

- *Depleting element*: wood

- *Neutral element*: fire

- *Colors*: black, blue, and very dark colors

- *Enhancements*: (outdoors) birdbaths, pools, and fountains;
  (indoors) fountains, fish tanks, and aquariums

Water in motion is the main element to place in the north. The movement of water helps stir the energy of this section. Stagnant water may slow down the energy in any area it occupies. In addition to a water feature, you may also want to display artwork, images, and items representing your desired career or life path. Some people choose to hang paintings of seascapes, lakes, and streams in the north. This is fine of course, but please keep in mind that an image of water is not a substitute for the actual element of flowing water.

For optimal energy flow, it's preferable to have the water flowing twenty-four hours a day, seven days a week (unless you're going to be away for more than a day or two). If you'd like to install an outdoor fountain but lack electricity outdoors, a solar-powered fountain is a great option. Check your local garden store or search online.

Most fountains bubble up from the center, spilling out in a 360-degree pattern, or they flow straight down. If your fountain has a spout, such as water coming out of an animal's mouth or another direction besides straight up or straight down, make sure that the flow of water is directed toward your home rather than away from it. The idea is to draw the energy *toward* the home, rather than to pull it away.

Avoid the use of harmful chemicals in any outdoor water feature. You don't want your fountain to be a source of illness or death for any animal that may stop by for a drink or a bath. Explore non-toxic alternatives instead.

When adding water to an indoor fountain, distilled water is preferable to tap water since mineral deposits from tap water are unsightly and can clog the flow of your fountain. Pet owners, take note: If you have a cat or dog who drinks out of your fountain regularly, *do not* use distilled water as it will deplete their bodies of necessary minerals. If your pet loves to drink out of the fountain, fill your fountain with filtered drinking water instead of distilled water. Yes, this will produce more mineral deposits and you'll need to clean the fountain more often (use vinegar to remove stubborn mineral deposits), but your furry companion will be much healthier as a result.

With any fountain, be sure to keep the water level above the motor. Running a fountain motor when it's dry will eventually break the motor. Make a habit of checking the water level daily. Some fountains need to be refilled every couple of days, while others may need refilling daily. From a feng shui standpoint, it's very important to keep the fountain and the motor clean and in good working order at all times.

On again, off again. Occasionally, a bedroom will be located in the north area of a home. While some people find the sound of a fountain soothing and relaxing, others find that it disturbs sleep. If you wish to enhance the Career area and it happens to be in your bedroom, find a fountain with a very quiet pump and keep it filled so that the falling water makes less noise. Although not optimal, you may have to run it during the day and turn it off at bedtime. You may want to connect the fountain to a lamp timer that's set to go on in the morning and off at night. While turning the fountain off and on isn't as ideal as having it running all the time, getting a good night's sleep is more important.

I once had a client who owned a hair salon. A month or so after her consultation with me, she called to say that something was wrong. Although she had followed my advice to place a fountain in the north area of her salon and another in the north area of her home, she said that her business would increase and then suddenly stop. It would increase again and then suddenly stop again. This was happening over and over. I asked whether she was turning her fountains on and off all the time, and she told me that she was. I reminded her to keep the fountains running twenty-four hours a day, seven days a week, unless she was going to be away for more than two days. Sure enough, after leaving her fountains running steadily, her business became steady, and she no longer experienced the dramatic ups and downs.

Northeast/Knowledge

The northeast area of the home is associated with inner awareness, knowledge, and spirituality. It relates to nurturing yourself, whether through study, meditation, or any type of self-improvement. Activate this area if you or anyone living in your home is going to school, studying, or learning something new. It's also a good place to enhance for spiritual development and inner growth.

- *Chinese name*: Ken

- *Aspiration areas*: knowledge, learning, spirituality, and self-improvement

- *Main element*: earth

- *Supporting element*: fire

- *Destructive element*: wood

- *Depleting element*: metal

- *Neutral element*: water

- *Colors*: earth tones, yellow, brown, and tan

- *Enhancements*: (outdoors) rock, brick, cement, tile, stone, pottery, and statuary made of rock or stone; (indoors) stone, tile, salt lamps, ceramic bowls, pottery, and statuary made of rock or stone

Because of the northeast's association with knowledge and wisdom, you may want to include statuary of wise or spiritual people or add rocks with inspiring words and messages etched or written on them. In addition to things made of earth, consider adding images of spiritual people, books, or other items that pertain to spirituality, learning, and education. It's a great place for a library or a study area. Depending upon its location in the home, it can be a place of quiet contemplation, prayer, or meditation.

Learning about love. A couple of years ago, a woman named Lisa called me because she was very confused about a feng shui issue in her home. She was single and longed for a relationship. She had read a feng shui book that advised enhancing the specific area of the home that was associated with the Love & Partnership trigram. However, the book oriented each trigram to the location of a home's front door, rather than to the trigram's compass direction. Lisa diligently applied all the suggestions in the book to this area of her home, yet nothing changed in her love life. She told me that a pair of doves had even made a nest outdoors in the area that she *thought* was the Love & Partnership area, but still no romance. Discouraged, she called me for help.

I asked Lisa to tell me what compass direction of her home she had been enhancing. She said, "The northeast. Why? What difference does that make?" I explained the differences between Compass School feng shui and the method she was using. Instead of enhancing her Love & Partnership area, Lisa had unknowingly been pouring all of her energy into the Knowledge area. When I told her this, she began to laugh. "You know," she said, "since I've been enhancing that part of my home, I've gone back to school, taken up yoga, and enrolled in a cooking class." Her Knowledge area had certainly been activated! I suggested that she direct her feng shui efforts to the southwest portion of her home to enhance her romantic life. Within two months, Lisa met a wonderful man, and a year later they were married.

East/Family

This area pertains not just to the family we've created for ourselves but also to our childhood family and our extended family.

- *Chinese name*: Chen
- *Aspiration area:* family, including childhood, extended, and current families
- *Main element*: wood
- *Supporting element*: water

- *Destructive element*: metal

- *Depleting element*: fire

- *Neutral element*: earth

- *Color*: green

- *Enhancements*: (outdoor) healthy plants, trees, flowers, bushes, wood fencing, and wood patio furniture; (indoors) healthy plants, wood furniture, wood picture frames, wood statuary and ornamentation, wood window blinds, and items made from wood, paper, or cotton

If your relationship with family members is positive, you may wish to display family photos in the Family section of your home (provided that this section is not located in the master bedroom or in a bathroom). While it's perfectly okay to exclude family photos in your home, healthy plants in the east are a must. If you don't have a green thumb, inquire at your local nursery or farmer's market for a hardy plant that will be forgiving if you forget to water it for a day.

When there are children in a family, I like to encourage my clients to designate a family altar. By this, I mean a place where family pictures can be displayed along with items that have special meaning for each family member—a favorite toy for a child, a golf ball for dad, flowers for mom, etc. Each person in the family chooses an item or two that they'd like to add to the altar. The items can be changed periodically as interests change. When you add photographs and personal items representing family to a designated space in the home, it promotes a feeling of solidarity and unity while honoring each person individually. The family altar doesn't have to be in the Family area of your home. It can be located anywhere that feels right. Just make sure to keep healthy plants in the east area of the home and to display the family photos or family altar anywhere that feels best to you.

Feng shui by "feel." People who are artistic, very sensitive, and/or very attuned to their surroundings frequently do what I call "intuitive feng shui." They place items in their homes according to what *feels* best, and from a feng shui point of view, they are often quite accurate. I've been amazed at the accuracy of some people, who will intuitively enhance areas of the Pa Kua without any prior knowledge of feng shui.

A client of mine, who's very artistic and sensitive, topped the charts when it came to intuitively enhancing her home. Joyce was an artist and an art professor at a nearby university. She had no prior knowledge of feng shui and was given a consultation by me as a birthday present from a friend. As I walked through Joyce's home, I marveled at how accurately she had arranged her home according to the Pa Kua, even though she knew nothing about it. Ceramic pottery was displayed in pairs in the southwest; a large metal sculpture that she had created stood in the west; and an assortment of candles that she used regularly was located in the south. As I walked through Joyce's home, I couldn't get over how she had arranged her home so perfectly from a feng shui perspective without any prior experience with feng shui.

We had toured almost all of her home when I suggested that there might be at least one area that she might not have succeeded in enhancing by intuition—the garage. When I told Joyce that her garage occupied the Family area of the home, she responded with a sly smile and said, "Well, let's take a look." Lo and behold, Joyce had hung pictures of family members in wood frames along the east wall of her garage. I was astonished. She told me that her husband disliked displaying family photos in the home, so she decided to hang them on "her" side of the garage so at least she could enjoy them as she came and went. I prodded Joyce. Surely she must have known about the Life Aspiration Areas in feng shui when she organized her home, but she swore up and down that she had no knowledge of feng shui before my visit. She had done it all by what felt right to her and was delighted to learn that she had intuitively done everything correctly, right down to hanging her family pictures in the garage!

Southeast/Wealth & Prosperity

Undoubtedly, the southeast area of Wealth & Prosperity is of great interest to most people. Everybody wants to know how to improve financial well-being. While feng shui cannot make millionaires overnight, it can help to activate the energy flow in this area.

- *Chinese name*: Sun

- *Aspiration areas*: wealth and prosperity

- *Main element*: wood

- *Supporting element*: water

- *Destructive element*: metal

- *Depleting element*: fire

- *Neutral element*: earth

- *Color*: green

- *Enhancements*: (outdoors) healthy plants, trees, flowers, bushes, wood fencing, and wood patio furniture; (indoors) healthy plants, wood furniture, wood picture frames, wood statuary and ornamentation, wood window blinds, and things made from wood, paper (such as books), and cotton

If you're interested in enhancing your wealth, place healthy plants in the southeast area of your home or yard. "Healthy" is the key word here. If a plant is dying or dead, it most certainly isn't going to increase the energy of the area where it's placed. If you need advice on keeping plants healthy or purchasing low-maintenance plants, talk to someone at your local garden center. Calculate the amount of hours that full sun or shade falls on the southeast part of your yard. Take this information to your local garden center and have an expert help you select a plant that will thrive in the available conditions. Remember to avoid plants that are spiked, very slow growing, or dwarfed.

Indoors, if the southeast part of your home doesn't offer access to plenty of natural light, then add full-spectrum light to help your plants grow. You may also wish to rotate plants throughout your home, so there are always healthy ones in this area. The southeast is no place for a plant infirmary, so don't try to nurse sick plants back to health here.

Clients sometimes think that, since the southeast is the Wealth & Prosperity area, they need to add coins to this area because coins represent wealth. The problem with this is that coins are made from metal, and metal is the destructive element for wood. (Metal cuts wood.) It's better to keep coins and any other metals out of the southeast area of the home. If you want to add money to represent abundance in the Wealth & Prosperity area, include paper money. Paper is made from wood and is the desired element for the southeast.

Fire is the depleting element in the southeast. (Fire burns wood.) Sometimes clients are concerned when a fireplace is located in this area. If this is the case in your home, here's something to consider: Most people use their fireplace only during the winter months—100 days a year, at most. That means that, for the majority of the time (265 days a year), there's no fire burning in this area. Most fireplaces are made from earth materials (such as brick or stone), and earth is neutral in the southeast, so the fireplace is actually representing the earth element at all times and only occasionally signifies the fire element.

If your fireplace is located in the southeast and you use it frequently, enjoy it, and be sure to have plenty of healthy, living plants in this area to offset the fire element. The same practice applies if your stove is located in the southeast: offset the fire element with plenty of healthy plants. Also, keep in mind that the Wealth & Prosperity area is no place for the stagnating energy of clutter or unwanted items.

Bathrooms in the Wealth & Prosperity area. Occasionally, clients are concerned when a bathroom falls in the Wealth & Prosperity area of their home. As I pointed out in chapter 5, it's a myth that money flows out through the drains of your home. There's no need to be concerned if a bathroom is located in the southeast. As long as the plumbing is in perfect working order, the bathroom can actually be a positive place for wealth due to the water element. Water is the element that increases wood, and wood is the main element of the southeast. Be sure to add a healthy plant in the bathroom, and you'll have nothing to worry about. If the bathroom has no windows for the plant to receive necessary light, then rotate plants from other rooms every few days so there's always a healthy plant in that room.

A garage in the southeast. When a garage is located in the southeast area of the home, finances can be a challenge. This isn't always the case, but I see it happen more often than not. Frequently, the occupants find that money comes in and goes out again just as quickly. Some are concerned about pulling their car (metal, the destructive element in the southeast) in and out of the garage and ask whether they should avoid this. By parking your car elsewhere, such as on the street or away from the southeast section, you can use the garage for another purpose—as a playroom, a studio, an office, or a game room (add a pool table or a ping pong table). Appreciate that your home at least has a southeast portion, even if it's a garage. Having a garage in the southeast is better than having the southeast portion missing entirely.

Remember that the garage is an "anything goes" area. I have clients with garages in the Career area who keep a fountain running in their garage. Others, with a garage in the Fame area, have connected their garage lights to a timer programmed for at least three hours a day of light. If your garage is in the southeast and receives natural light from windows or skylights, place some healthy plants in there, too.

Try to keep metal objects, like shelves or tools, out of the southeastern side of the garage, if at all possible. If you need storage, opt for bins or shelves made of plastic or wood, and store metal tools and other metal objects in a location that's conducive to metal. When it's time to replace the garage door, select a wood door rather than a metal door, if possible. Avoid filling the garage with clutter. Clutter increases stuck energy, and you don't want your finances to stagnate.

Be sure to plant healthy, growing plants outdoors in the southeast area of your property close to the garage. If you have a second story or rooms above the garage, add healthy plants to the southeast area of this room as well. To keep money flowing, strengthen other Life Aspiration Areas in the home, such as Career (north), Synchronicity (northwest), and Fame (south).

Center/Health

I became interested in feng shui when my own mother was diagnosed with terminal cancer. I wanted to do as much as I could to help her. While the changes that I made in her home didn't cure her (nor did I expect them to), she kept telling me how much happier and better her home made her feel. I honestly believe that the feng shui techniques that I implemented in her space extended the time she had with us. She lived much longer than any doctor thought she would, and during that time, she was happier and more positive.

- *Chinese name*: Tai Chi

- *Aspiration area*: health

- *Main element*: earth

- *Supporting element*: fire

- *Destructive element*: wood

- *Depleting element*: metal

- *Neutral element*: water

- *Colors*: earth tones, yellow, brown, and tan

- *Enhancements*: (outdoors) stone, cement, rock, tile, granite, a fireplace (combines earth and fire), or pottery; (indoors) granite, tile, salt lamps, and statuary made of rock or stone

Because of the way that the Life Aspiration Areas are mapped out, the Health area is almost always located indoors at the center of the home, meaning that there's no outdoor location to enhance—unless the home has a center courtyard. If you do have a courtyard or a missing piece in the center of your home, the Health area will be located outdoors, and you'll need to include the earth element here. Although plants are not a desired element in the Health area, since earth is the main element and wood absorbs earth, any plants here need to be as healthy as possible, and kept to a minimum. Amethyst is the stone that's traditionally associated with health and healing and can be a wonderful addition to the Health area of the home.

Chronic conditions. I've been a feng shui consultant for twenty years and have conducted well over a thousand consultations. I've seen too many situations where a long-term plumbing problem, such as a running toilet, a slow drain, or a leaking pipe in the Health area of the home, coincides with a member of the household having a chronic health condition in the chest or in the center area of the body. If you have a bathroom, kitchen, laundry room, or any other plumbing at the center of your home, it's crucial that this plumbing be kept in excellent condition at all times. If you suspect a leak or other plumbing problem in the center of your home, be sure to attend to it as soon as possible. It's better to be safe than sorry.

Stairway storage and health. Many homes have a stairway in the center of the house and a storage closet or crawl space under the stairway. If this is the case in your home, it's best to store items here that are regularly used, such as a vacuum cleaner, shoes, jackets, or keys, in order to keep the energy from stagnating. Having items that sit for long periods of time in the center of the home may lead to health issues for the home's occupants. If there are small children in the household, the storage area under the stairs can make a terrific playroom, hideaway, or toy closet. Children delight in this makeshift play area, and their use of it certainly keeps the energy in this space moving and active.

Many times, the center of the home ends up being a pass-through area or a hallway with no place to add the earth element. If this is the case in your home, keep the area clean and free of clutter. Hang artwork with healthy images, and be sure there's good lighting.

It would be incredible if feng shui could cure disease, solve our problems, and keep anything bad from ever happening to us again, but life doesn't work that way. However, one thing that I've found time and time again in my own life and in the lives of my clients is that feng shui is always leading us toward something better and more positive. It can make the challenges of life less challenging and more meaningful. I truly can't imagine my life without it.

Applying the Pa Kua and the Five Elements to Your Home

Now that you're more familiar with the Pa Kua and the five elements, it's time to put all that information into practice. The following steps will take you through the process of applying the Pa Kua and the five elements to your home:

Step 1

Draw a floor plan of your home.

Your first task is to draw a floor plan of your home. Try to be as accurate as possible with the dimensions. Many people find that using graph paper (where one square equals one square foot) makes it easier to draw the floor plan to scale. Make two or three copies of your floor plan before you begin writing on it, in case of any mistakes. You'll want the drawing to be a manageable size, so a blueprint of your home probably isn't the best option for this task unless you can have it reduced on a photocopier. Frequently, tract homes have floor plans available for their models. If you live in a tract home, you may wish to contact the developer and ask how you can receive a floor plan of your home.

If you live in a home with more than one level, draw just the main floor of the home. Usually, the main floor of a home is the first floor, but occasionally a home will have the main living area upstairs and the bedrooms downstairs. If this is the case, then the upstairs level should be considered as the main floor. You don't need to include the furniture, but do make sure to have the different rooms of the home outlined and labeled as indicated in figure 6.5.

Step 2

Determine the center point of your home.

Finding the accurate center of your home is very important, so conduct this step carefully. To begin, you need to identify the footprint of your home. A home's footprint is the outline or the surface area of the entire home. For an area to be part of the footprint, it must meet these two requirements:

- It must be under the same roof as the rest of the home.

- It must have walls completely around it.

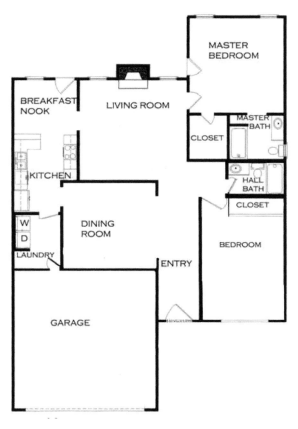

Figure 6.5

Hence, balconies and patios are *not* included in the footprint because they have open sides and/or aren't under the roof of the home. Garages *are* part of the footprint if they are connected to the house and share the roof with the rest of the house. However, carports are *not* included in the footprint because they lack walls on all sides. As an example, the footprint of the floor plan in figure 6.5 appears in figure 6.6.

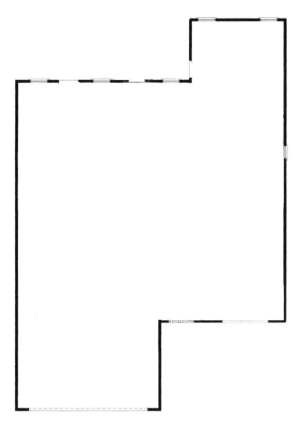

Figure 6.6

Finding the Center Point of a Square or Rectangular Home

If the footprint of your home is a **complete** square or rectangle, finding the center point is easy. There are two ways to do this:

1. Measure the length and width of the home, and find the point where the lines intersect. Remember to include the garage in your calculations, if it's attached to the home. Once you've found the center point, mark the spot with an "X."

2. You can also find the center point by folding your accurately drawn floor plan. Hold the floor plan up to a bright light or a sunny window, and fold the floor plan vertically by lining up the exterior side walls of the home. Now, unfold the floor plan. Next, fold the floor plan horizontally by lining up the exterior front and back walls of the home. The place where the folds intersect is the center point of the home (see figure 6.7). Mark this spot with an "X."

Figure 6.7

Determining the Center Point of a Home with an Irregular Footprint

Not all homes have a footprint in the shape of a complete square or rectangle. In fact, most don't. Usually, a home has an irregular footprint because the garage or another room extends out from the basic shape of the home. It's important to consider this situation carefully because if the footprint of your home is not a complete square or rectangle, your home may have either a "missing piece" or an "extra piece" from a feng shui perspective. These factors determine where the true center of a home is and how the occupants will experience that space.

If your home has an irregular footprint, you need to determine whether the shape creates a missing piece or an extra piece. To do this, divide the home in half. The easiest way to divide it is to fold the floor plan vertically by lining up the exterior side walls. Hold the floor plan up to the light to make sure that it has been accurately divided in half (see figure 6.8).

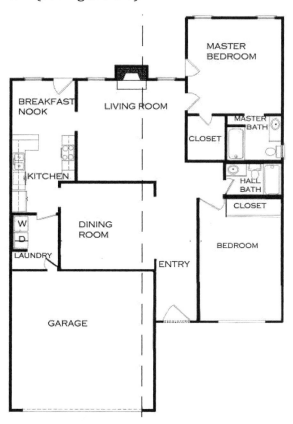

Figure 6.8

Once you've folded the floor plan in half, you'll be able to determine whether the irregular shape of your home creates a missing piece or an extra piece. A missing piece is indicated when the **width** of the protruding room extends *beyond* the center line of the home, as the garage does in figure 6.9. Notice that the width of the garage (measuring from left to right) occupies more than 50 percent of the exterior front wall. The missing piece is indicated by the heavy dotted line. In this case, the outdoor area must be carefully energized in order to enhance the overall feng shui of the home. If a home has more than one missing piece, each missing piece must be enhanced, since missing pieces are energetically weak areas of the home and the Pa Kua.

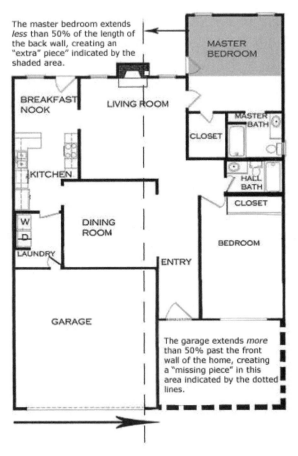

The master bedroom extends *less* than 50% of the length of the back wall, creating an "extra" piece indicated by the shaded area.

The garage extends *more* than 50% past the front wall of the home, creating a "missing piece" in this area indicated by the dotted lines.

Figure 6.9

An extra piece is indicated when the width of the protruding room *doesn't* reach the center line of the home, like the master bedroom in figure 6.9. The master bedroom occupies less than 50 percent of the exterior back wall of the home. The shaded area indicates the extra piece. An extra piece means that there's additional energy in this area of the Pa Kua and is generally positive.

With the missing and extra pieces defined, it's easier to see how the home in figure 6.9 would look as a complete rectangle. Having the complete footprint makes it easier to determine the home's center point. The floor plan can now be folded horizontally to match the edge of the back wall with the edge of the front wall. Since the master bedroom is considered an extra piece, the edge of the back wall would be the wall that runs from the breakfast nook to the bottom of the shaded area. The place where the horizontal and vertical lines intersect is the center point of the home and may now be marked with an "X" as seen in figure 6.10.

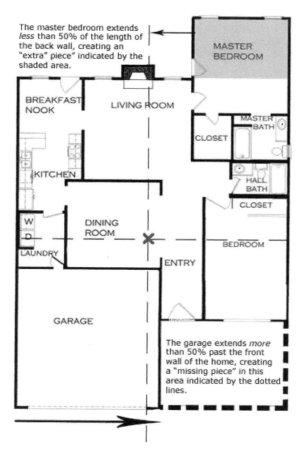

Figure 6.10

Now, taking one of the copies that you made earlier, mark the center point of your home with an "X" on a clean, unfolded copy of the floor plan (see figure 6.11) so that you can proceed to the next step.

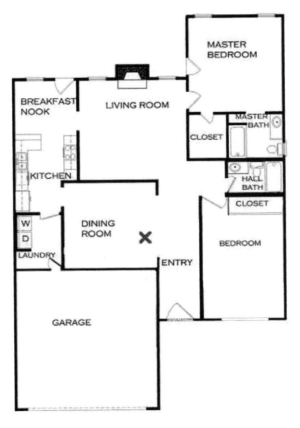

Figure 6.11

Step 3

Take your compass readings.

Taking your floor plan and compass, walk to the actual, physical center of your home. Make sure to orient the floor plan exactly to the point at which you're standing. In other words, the front door of your floor plan should be facing the same direction as the font door of the actual home. When taking your compass readings, avoid standing near anything made of metal or near electrical equipment, as the magnetic fields may interfere with the accuracy of the compass. Remove any heavy, metal jewelry and accessories as well. If you live in a building constructed with a lot of metal supports, you may have difficulty getting accurate compass readings. I've consulted with clients in high-rise buildings where the compass spun every which way, making it impossible to take a reading. If this is the case for you, be sure to step outside the building to verify your compass directions. Important: You *must* use a compass to determine your directions. Don't assume that you know which direction your home faces. *Accurate compass readings are crucial to your success!*

Step 4

Draw the eight compass directions, and define the Health area.

Place the compass directly over the center "X" on your floor plan. Orient the compass properly so that you can identify each direction on the compass. If you need help using a compass, ask a friend to help you or search online for assistance. There are plenty of web sites and videos that show how to take a compass reading. Some compasses are printed with just one indicator that specifies north at 0°. If this is the case with your compass, here are the degrees associated with each direction:

- North 0°
- Northeast 45°
- East 90°
- Southeast 135°
- South 180°
- Southwest 225°
- West 270°
- Northwest 315°

Using a **pencil**, lightly draw a dot on your floor plan to indicate each compass direction. Label the dots with the letters of the directions as you go (i.e., N, NE, E, etc.). When you're finished, lift the compass off of the floor plan. Using a ruler, line up the north and south dots with the center "X" in the middle. Connect the two dots by drawing a straight line and extending that line past the dots to the edges of your floor plan. Do this with each of the following pairs of directions, making sure to intersect the lines at the "X":

- East and west

- Northeast and southwest

- Northwest and southeast

When you're done, the lines will look like wheel spokes. Now, draw a larger dot where each compass line intersects the outer wall on the floor plan. Write the corresponding compass direction of each dot next to it. (See figure 6.12.) By the way, you may discover that your home doesn't face one of the eight directions precisely. This is often the case and nothing to worry about. Just make sure to draw

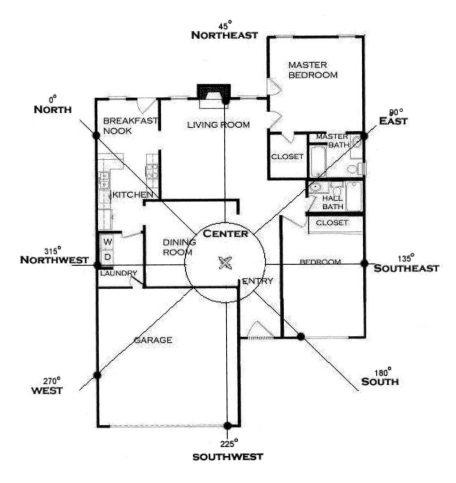

Figure 6.12

the lines accurately, so you'll know where each compass direction is located on your floor plan.

The easiest way to demarcate the Health area on your floor plan is to measure the width and length of the floor plan and then divide each by 3. For example, let's say that your floor plan is 15" wide by 12" long. To calculate the width and length of the Health section, divide the total width and length by 3, as follows:

$$15 \div 3 = 5$$

$$12 \div 3 = 4$$

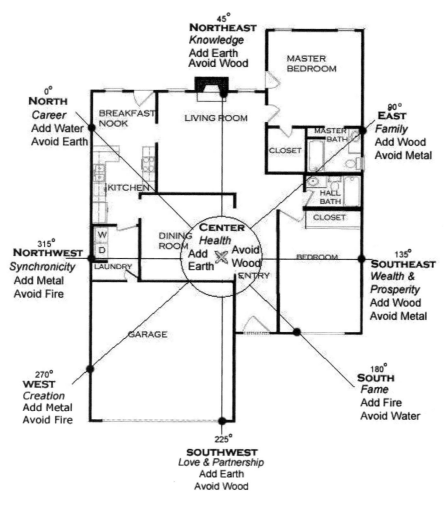

Figure 6.13

Therefore, the Health area is 5" wide by 4" long with the X, or center point, located in the middle. You may define the Health area using a circle, a square, or a rectangle; all are acceptable.

Step 5

Label each Life Aspiration Area with its corresponding elements.

Using the Pa Kua diagram in figure 6.4 on page 198, identify the Life Aspiration Areas on your floor plan and write them down. Next, write down the main element and the destructive element within each area (see figure 6.13). It's helpful to put a plus (+) sign next to the elements that need to be added and a minus (–) sign next to those that should be avoided

When enhancing the Life Aspiration Areas of the home, place elements as closely as possible to where the compass line intersects with the outer wall of the home. For the Health area, place the earth element as closely as possible to the center point (marked with an X) of your home. Sometimes this is impossible, especially if the center of the home is a hallway, a stairway, or a closet. In this case, place the earth element as closely to the center point as possible, and be sure to keep the location free of clutter. Also, be sure that any plumbing located in the center of the home is kept in perfect working condition.

Step 6

Enhance and energize your home using the five elements.

Now you're ready to begin the process of energizing your home. Using your completed feng shui floor plan as a guide, go to each room and carefully note what elements you need to add or remove in order to optimize each area. Consider adding artwork and other symbolic enhancements that relate to each Life Aspiration Area. While symbolic enhancements are not substitutes for the actual elements, they can serve as visual reminders of what you wish to achieve in a specific area of life.

Doing a Home Walk-through

My students and clients often ask where each area of the Pa Kua begins and ends. Basically, each of the nine areas of the Pa Kua occupies approximately one-ninth of a home's total area. Figure 6.14 illustrates how more than one room, or just a part of a room, can fall within an area. Sometimes, a portion of (or all of) a Life Aspiration Area may be missing because it lies outside of the home's footprint.

In figure 6.14, notice how the eight compass directions actually fall in the *middle* of their corresponding Life Aspiration Area. In the figure, each meridian is marked with a dot to indicate where the compass point intersects with the outer wall of the home. When energizing an area with its main element, try to place the element as closely as possible to the point where the compass meridian line meets the outer

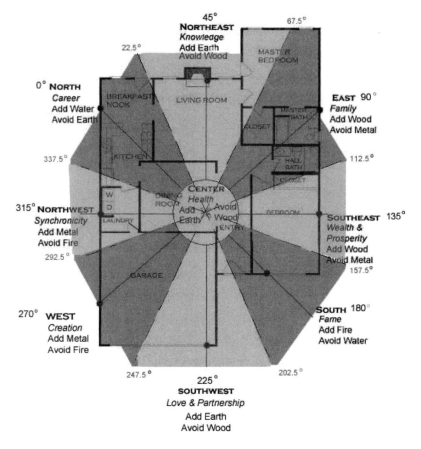

Figure 6.14

wall of the house. The Health area, however, is the exception to this rule. Because the Health area is located at the center of the home, the earth element is placed as closely as possible to the home's center point. If the center point falls in the middle of a hallway, on a staircase, or in a closet, place the element as closely to the center point as you can without the placement seeming awkward, and be sure to keep the area free of clutter. Any plumbing in this area should be kept in top working order. If the floor in the center of the home happens to be cement or tile, the earth element is already present, so there's no need to add more unless you wish to.

Remember that the further away you go from the meridian point, the less effective the element becomes. The closer you can place your elements to the exact meridian point, the more energy you will be giving to that area. If you live in an apartment or an attached home, place the elements on the meridians that intersect the outer walls of *your* space only, *not* the outer walls of the entire building.

While elements located on the exact meridian points are the most effective, be aware of the positive and negative elements within each area of the Pa Kua. For example, let's say that the southeast meridian line runs through your dining room. Not only would you want to include a healthy plant where the meridian point intersects the wall of that room but you'd also want to consider the furnishings of the room as they correspond to the necessary and unwanted elements. Wood is the preferable element in the southeast, while metal is undesirable in this area. Therefore, if your dining room is located in the southeast, you would want to include a table made of wood rather than metal because wood is desired in the southeast and metal is not. By using the elements as a guide, you can make choices regarding décor and furnishings that will help reinforce the energy of each area.

To clarify the process of enhancing the Life Aspiration Areas in your home, I'm going to do a walk-through of the floor plan illustrated in figure 6.14, starting with the west and working my way around the Pa Kua.

West/Creation

Location: garage

Elements: add metal (main) and earth (supporting); avoid fire (destructive) and water (depleting); wood is neutral.

Having the garage in this area is a bonus because the main element is metal. Cars and many materials found in the garage are also made of metal. The floor of the garage is concrete, which represents the earth element. The only downside may be that the water heater (representing water and fire) is located in this area, but it's one of those things that can't be avoided.

I'd suggest parking the car on the west side of the garage, storing metal items like rakes and bicycles on that side as well, and choosing metal shelves if storage is needed. As always, this area must be kept free of clutter. If a family lives here, the west wall of the garage might be a fun area to post paintings and artwork that the children have created.

If there's enough space outdoors on the west side of the home, it would be a great place to store metal lawn tools, metal trash cans, or anything else made of metal.

Northwest/Synchronicity

Location: laundry room and a small portion of the dining room
Elements: add metal (main) and earth (supporting); avoid fire (destructive) and water (depleting); wood is neutral.

The majority of this area falls in the laundry room. The good news is that the laundry room has two large items made of metal (the washer and dryer), and metal is the element needed in this area. The bad news is that the laundry room also has heat for the dryer, which represents the fire element and is destructive to metal. The washing machine adds water to this area, and water depletes the metal element. This is one of those situations when you don't worry about what you can't change. I'd suggest that, if anything needs to be added to this area such as storage racks or trash cans, it be made of metal. Adding the element that's needed can help mitigate the effects of the undesirable elements in an area. Earth is the supporting element for metal, so a tile floor would be a positive influence in the laundry room.

A small portion of the Synchronicity area falls in the dining room. Since the intersection of the meridian point and the outer wall of the home is located in the laundry room, this is the most potent location for the element enhancements. If desired, the northwest area of the dining room may also be enhanced with the metal element, such as a metal corner table, picture frames, or storage for metal items like silverware and metal candleholders.

Any outdoor space on the northwest side of the house would be a suitable space for storing metal garden tools or adding metal garden ornaments, tables, or lawn furniture. A metal wind chime is also a great enhancement for both the west and the northwest sections of the yard.

North/Career

Location: kitchen and breakfast nook
Elements: add water (main) and metal (supporting); avoid earth (destructive) and wood (depleting); fire is neutral.

The point where the north meridian intersects the outer wall of the home is located in the breakfast nook. Flowing water needs to be located here to activate the Career energy. A tabletop fountain would be the best enhancement for this area, but it may be difficult to place it exactly on the north meridian due to space constraints or aesthetics. In that case, the fountain can be placed on the kitchen counter, as close to the meridian point as possible. The fountain should be kept running twenty-four hours a day, unless you'll be away for more than two days (in which case, the fountain should be turned off). Using distilled water will keep mineral deposits from accumulating. However, if a pet is going to drink out of the fountain, filtered drinking water is the next best choice to distilled water.

If space allows on the north side of the home, a fountain or birdbath can be placed outside near the meridian point. However, if there's little room or the area is not conducive to a water feature, then the indoor fountain may be enough water to activate the area. Both the outdoor space and the upstairs area of a home offer secondary opportunities where elements can be used to enhance the energy, but the interior main floor is the most important area to enhance.

Northeast/Knowledge

Location: living room and part of master bedroom

Elements: add earth (main) and fire (supporting); avoid wood (destructive) and metal (depleting); water is neutral.

The northeast meridian intersects the house at the fireplace. This is fortunate because the fireplace is a feature that represents earth and fire (occasionally). These two elements are positive in this part of the house. Wood is undesirable in the northeast, so if a plant is needed for décor purposes, a silk plant would be a better choice than a live plant.

Due to the floor plan of this house, there's an extra piece in the Pa Kua in the master bedroom. This extra piece is split between the northeast (Knowledge) and the east (Family). As long as the earth element is located on the main meridian point (the fireplace), it's not necessary to enhance the area in the bedroom with more earth. If desired, however, a salt lamp placed in the bedroom within the Knowledge area would make a good addition. Plants should be avoided in the Knowledge area of the master bedroom but can be added in the Family area of the master bedroom, where wood is compatible.

Outdoors, a patio made of slate, tile, cement, or brick would enhance the northeast, as would an outdoor fireplace or garden statuary made from cement or stone. For aesthetic reasons, plants will likely be occupying the northeast area outside, even though wood is undesirable here. As long as there aren't too many plants in the outdoor area of the northeast and there's plenty of earth, the plants shouldn't pose too much of a problem in activating this area.

East/Family

Location: master bedroom, master closet, master bathroom, and hall bathroom

Elements: add wood (main) and water (supporting); avoid metal (destructive) and fire (depleting); earth is neutral.

Due to the extra piece in the floor plan created by the master bedroom, this home has added beneficial energy in the Family area. While wood and plants are undesirable in the northeast (Knowledge) area of the master bedroom, plants and wood may be located on the east side of this room. This is an example of one room containing two or more Life Aspiration Areas. When this happens, add and avoid elements in the room according to where they belong. It's nice to add family pictures in the east, but since the east falls in the master bedroom and in the bathrooms, it's best if family photos are displayed in other areas of the home.

The meridian point for Family intersects the wall of the home in the master bathroom. This is actually a benefit because water is the supporting element for wood. Healthy plants should be included in the master bathroom, perhaps on the vanity to be as close to the meridian point as possible. Metal needs to be avoided here, so a plastic or wicker trash can is preferable to a metal one. Plants may be added to the hall bathroom and to the master bedroom for extra impact, but they definitely need to be present in the master bathroom, as that's where the Family energy is concentrated in this home.

Outside, the entire backyard of the home is ideal for a water feature, such as a pool, a hot tub, or a fountain because water is ideal in the north, neutral in the northeast, and supportive in the east. If there's room along the east side of the home to plant flowers, trees, or bushes, these can help activate the Family energy outdoors. The east side of the home is not a good place to store metal items. If metal items (like trash cans and lawn tools) need to be stored outdoors, the west side of this home is preferable to the east.

Southeast/Wealth & Prosperity

Location: second bedroom
Elements: add wood (main) and water (supporting); avoid metal (destructive) and fire (depleting); earth is neutral.

Whenever an area needs to be enhanced with wood, healthy growing plants are the best solution, energetically. Almost the entire Wealth & Prosperity area for this home is located in the second bedroom. Ideally, a healthy growing plant would be placed on the meridian line in the room, but in this case, the line intersects the wall where the bed will go. The plants, then, should be located either on nightstands or as close to the meridian as possible without feeling awkward.

As discussed in chapter 5, a bed should always have a solid wood headboard, regardless of whether or not it's located in an area where wood is needed. Fortunately, a wood bedframe happens to enhance the east (Family) area of this home. Metal needs to be avoided as much as possible in this room, so picture frames, curtain rods, artwork, and window blinds made from wood are better options here.

Reality Check

Myth: *Plants should never be located in a bedroom.*

This is another common myth in feng shui. I've read many different views on why people think plants should be excluded from a bedroom. One of the sillier reasons I've come across is that plants "take energy away from people while they are sleeping." Plants are not evil zombies that rob human beings of their life force during sleep.

Another excuse I read in an article on feng shui stated that, "Plants emit carbon dioxide at night, and they will deplete the oxygen supply in the bedroom." How ridiculous is that? While it's true that plants do emit a small amount of CO_2 at night (when photosynthesis is not occurring), it's a negligible amount and is certainly not going to reduce the oxygen in a bedroom to a dangerous level. If this were true, people living or camping in forests all over the world would die in their sleep because they're surrounded by an abundance of plants. Ridiculous!

The truth is that adding a plant is just fine in the bedroom. As long as plants are healthy and don't have spiked leaves, there's no reason to avoid them in the bedroom or any other room where wood is an acceptable element.

South/Fame

Location: second bedroom, entry, and front yard.

Elements: add fire (main) and wood (supporting); avoid water (destructive) and earth (depleting); metal is neutral.

Due to the shape of this home, a large portion of the Fame area sits outside the home's footprint. This creates a weakness in the energy balance of the home. With the Fame area missing in the footprint, those living here may have challenges related to growing their business, receiving raises or recognition at work, being the target of gossip, or having others undermine their efforts.

In this case, a portion of the Fame area still falls inside the home, so that area must be energized. In figure 6.14, you can see that the south compass point intersects the wall in the second bedroom near the window. To best energize this area, place a lamp that's connected to a lamp timer, and program the timer for at least three hours a day. Turning on the lamp for at least three hours a day enables the energy of fire (the electricity in this case) to activate this area.

Since the majority of the Fame area falls outside the home's footprint, it's essential that the outdoor area be energized. While energizing the outdoor area is not as effective as doing so indoors, it's important to give the area as much attention as possible since it's considered a missing piece, indicating a weakness in the energy of the home. To activate the Fame area outdoors, lighting should be installed in the area under the front bedroom window. If there's no electrical lighting outdoors in this area and installing some is impossible, solar-powered lights can be easily placed here. They will go on at night and off in the morning and cost nothing to run. Wood is the supporting element for fire, so adding healthy plants and lighting under the bedroom window would be a positive enhancement. Additionally, no water features (fountains or birdbaths) should be located in this area because water is the destructive element for fire.

Southwest/Love & Partnership

Location: garage, a small portion of the entry, and front yard
Elements: add earth (main) and fire (supporting); avoid wood (destructive) and metal (depleting); water is neutral.

As with the Fame area, part of the Love & Partnership area lies outside the footprint of the home as well. When this happens, it can indicate that those living here may experience challenges in partnerships (such as marriages or business partnerships). With the Fame and the Love & Partnership areas lying outside the footprint, those living here may experience scandal in their relationship (such as infidelity or legal trouble). It's very important to properly energize these areas as much as possible, both inside and outside.

The Love & Partnership meridian runs directly through the garage and intersects the home at the very edge of the front of the garage. The cement floor in the garage brings the necessary earth element to the area. Most likely, the driveway that borders the garage and the walkway that leads to the front door are also made of concrete or stone—adding the earth element outdoors. The challenge here is that earth is the required element, but wood is undesirable. The absence of plants in the front of the home leading up to the front door might look unattractive and cause the front area to feel depleted. In this case, a few plants will not deplete the strong earth energy of the garage floor, the driveway, and the front walkway. If plants *are* placed along the front walkway, use river rock as ground cover between the plants to bring in the earth energy. The plants, while not the desired element, are needed to soften the area visually so that the front of the home looks and *feels* pleasing. I'd also suggest adding a pair of cement or stone statues outside in the Love & Partnership area. They don't have to be large nor do they have to be human figures; they could be two birds, two cats, two rabbits, or two large beautiful rocks or stones. Fire supports earth, so lights along the walkway leading to the front door will boost the earth energy of the southwest area outside.

Since a portion of the Love & Partnership section is located outside and is therefore a weak area of the home, those living here may wish to display images of pairs (including photos of themselves together, if they are a couple) throughout the home. These images may serve as visual reminders of the positive energy of partnership.

Center/Heath

Location: dining room, portions of the entry, and a tiny part of the garage

Elements: add earth (main) and fire (supporting); avoid wood (destructive) and metal (depleting); water is neutral.

The center of this home is located in a fairly open area, which is considered positive because the energy can flow more easily. If those living here are considering what type of floor to add in the entry, they may wish to add tile or stone, as the earth element is positive in this location. If the floor isn't made of an earth element, the element can still be integrated in creative ways by including stone or ceramic artwork (such as sculptures, vases, or urns) or furniture with stone tops. A salt lamp could be added to bring in the earth element as well. Another enhancement would be to display a large, decorative stone or mineral in the Health section. Amethyst is a stone that has been traditionally associated with health and healing, so a beautiful amethyst crystal would be a beneficial addition to the Health area.

Since the center point of the home is in a high-traffic open area, adding the earth element on the exact center (other than as stone flooring) may be challenging. In this situation, it's best to add the earth element enhancements as close to the center as possible without it looking odd or out of place. The Health area must be kept free of clutter, with everything (especially plumbing) in tiptop working condition. The Health area is not a good place for plants (especially dying or dead ones). If the look of plants is desired in the center, silk plants are a better choice here.

FAQs on Enhancing the Life Aspiration Areas in Your Home

If I live in a two-story house, do I have to enhance each area upstairs too? What about the basement?

If you live in a two-story house, the rooms directly above each Life Aspiration Area have the same requirements as those on the main floor. In other words, you have two opportunities to enhance your home with the elements. The main floor of the house is the primary area to focus on, but the other floors offer secondary opportunities to enhance the energy of your home. For example, if you have a garage in the southeast/Wealth & Prosperity area and it's impossible to keep a plant in the garage, then you can place a plant in the room directly above the garage. The same is true with basements.

Do I need to do an individual Pa Kua for each room in my house?

No, that's unnecessary and definitely overkill. Applying the Pa Kua to the entire house is much more important and helpful than applying one to each room individually. The only exception to this would be if you're renting a room in a home, and the only space you have control over is your own room. In this case, you would enhance your room as its own space, much like one would do in an apartment.

Other feng shui books tell me to arrange my home differently, and now I'm confused. Which method should I use?

As stated in chapter 1, there are many different philosophies and approaches to feng shui and many that contradict each other. With so much conflicting information, it can be difficult to decide which method is right for you. I've been practicing feng shui successfully for over twenty years and have shared the methods that I have personally found to be very effective. My clients and students also have applied these techniques with great success. Ultimately, it's up to you to decide which method feels and works best for you.

Variety is the spice of life, and there's no "one size fits all" approach to feng shui (no matter what others may wish you to believe). Trust your intuition as you go through this process. Your feelings will help guide you. If something doesn't work for you or doesn't feel right, don't give up on feng shui, just keep experimenting until you find something that feels good and gives you the results you're looking for. Life, like feng shui, is a process of balance and flow.

How much of each element do I need to add in each area?

It's possible to have too much or too little of an element. If finances are an issue, you don't need to turn the southeast area of your home into a jungle. At the same time, a tiny houseplant won't be enough. Remember, balance in all things is important. When in doubt, use your intuition and employ the Goldilocks Principle: Everything needs to feel just right.

I have a very large yard. How much of the outside area do I need to concentrate on to enhance the outdoor Life Aspiration Areas?

Don't worry about what sits more than twenty feet away from the home. The inside of the home is the most important area. However, incorporating the required elements outside with patio furniture, garden ornaments, statuary, and landscaping can support the efforts you make inside, especially if the home's footprint has a missing piece. In some cases, the outdoor area may be the only opportunity to include the required elements.

What if I have an element where it doesn't belong and I can't change it?

Sometimes you'll have destructive or depleting elements that can't be moved from an area. For example, you may have a bathroom or a swimming pool in the Fame area. Since fire is the main element for the south and water is the destructive element, it's not optimal to have your bathroom or pool located in this area. Of course, I'm not going to advise you to move your bathroom or fill in your pool! It's not required that you completely eliminate the negative element from an area, especially when it's impossible or impractical to do so. If you have a situation where a large, undesirable element cannot be changed, just be sure that the main element is well-represented, perhaps in a greater quantity, and add the supporting element in order to give the energy a boost.

In the case of a bathroom being in the south, a healthy plant (wood increases fire), a nightlight, or a light that's on at least three hours a day would help to counteract the water element in the south. When a swimming pool is located in the south, the best solution is to increase the amount of lighting around the pool, making sure it's turned on a minimum of three hours a day. You may also wish to add some healthy red flowers, red cushions, or a red patio umbrella around the pool to increase the fire energy. If the undesirable element is outside, then the inside of the house needs to be carefully energized. If the undesirable element is inside the house, then the outside would need special attention.

Can a missing piece be completely made up by enhancing the area outside?

Unfortunately, no it can't. A piece missing out of the footprint of a home is always considered a weakness in the energetic pattern of the home. Before you jump to conclusions as to whether a piece of the footprint is missing or not, be sure to CAREFULLY follow the instructions in Step 2 on page 220. If the area is indeed missing, add the necessary elements for the missing piece outside and minimize the undesirable elements in that area as much as possible.

When a Missing Piece Cannot Be Improved

Every once in a while, I meet a client with a home that has a missing piece which cannot be improved. Several years ago, a client named Melissa called me in desperation. She told me that both she and her husband had been very successful in their respective careers and had finally made enough money to buy their dream home. Ever since they'd moved in, however, both of their careers were in downward spirals that showed no signs of turning around. Melissa wanted to know if I could help them figure out whether or not the house was having any influence on the reversal of their career success.

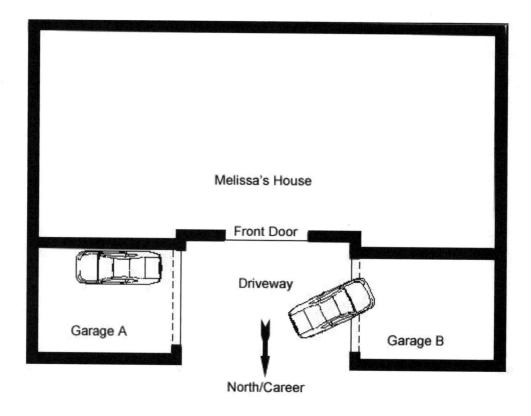

Figure 6.15

When I arrived at Melissa's house, I was dismayed at what I saw. The house was U-shaped and faced due north (see figure 6.15). When a home is shaped like this, I add the combined width of both garages to determine whether they comprise more than 50 percent of the front width of the home, thus creating a missing piece. In Melissa's case, the Career area was completely missing from her home. Normally, when an area is missing, we try to improve the energy by adding the main element outside. At Melissa's house, two garages in front of the home opened onto a single driveway, and there was no way to add the main element (water) in the north because both cars needed to be able to move in and out of this area. Furthermore, the driveway was made of beautiful stone pavers, the north's destructive element (earth). There was very little that could be done to remedy Melissa's situation without doing major construction—something that the homeowner's association wouldn't allow.

I helped Melissa enhance the other areas of her home as much as possible. After about six months, she called to tell me that they had decided to sell their home and asked me to help them find their next one. I'm happy to say that Melissa and her husband moved into a home with no missing pieces, and their careers are going strong. Melissa told me she'll never live in a home with a missing piece again after her dream home turned into a nightmare!

The Life Assessment Inventory

When you first begin energizing the various areas of your home, it's easy to feel overwhelmed and unsure of where to start. While it's important to energize all the Life Aspiration Areas, there may be specific areas that you feel need more focus and attention than others. Progress is made more quickly when you concentrate on one area at a time rather than scattering your efforts. To help you identify where to start, I've created the Life Assessment Inventory, a short survey to help clarify what is and is not going well in your life right now. This assessment can be a very helpful tool in determining the priorities of your feng shui efforts.

Here's how it works: Read each question, and answer it with a number between one and ten. Ten is the highest rating and means that things are as perfect as they can be. Five indicates neutral feelings about the situation. One is the lowest rating and signifies that this area of your life is completely unsatisfactory.

Life is dynamic and changes all the time, so your answers should reflect how you feel right now, at this very moment. Your answers will change from day to day, month to month, and year to year depending upon what's happening in your life. It is more or less a snapshot of your life at the present moment. You may want to use a separate piece of paper to record your answers, or use a pencil. That way, you can take inventory again in a couple of months to see how your life has changed and find out what you may need to focus on next.

Life Assessment Inventory

Today's Date: _____

Rate each question with a number value using the following scale:

Very Dissatisfied 1   2   3   4   5   6   7   8   9   10 Very Satisfied

1. Do you feel respected by the people in your personal life? _____

2. Do you feel respected by the people in your professional life? _____

3. Are you satisfied with your romantic life? _____

4. If you have children, do you have a good relationship with them? _____

5. Do you have time and space for creative activities? _____

6. Are you able to travel as much as you would like? _____

7. Is your social life as active as you wish? _____

8. Do you have people you can count on when you need them? _____

9. Do you find your current occupation emotionally satisfying? _____

10. Do you feel that your life has meaning and purpose? _____

11. Do you take time to learn new things? _____

12. Do you nurture yourself spiritually as much as you would like? _____

13. Do you take time out for rest and relaxation? _____

14. How are your relationships with your childhood family members? _____

15. If you've created a family of your own as an adult, would you say that it's a happy household? _____

16. How do you feel about your current financial situation? _____

17. Is your standard of living at a level that is satisfying to you? _____

18. Do you have a steady income? _____

19. Do you enjoy good health? _____

20. Does everyone living in your home enjoy good health? _____

Now, go back and circle all the numbers that have a value of five or lower. These numbers indicate which Life Aspiration Areas you need to energize the most. If several questions received a value of five or lower, choose the area with the lowest score and focus on that one first. Below, I've indicated which questions relate to each Life Aspiration Area to help you identify which area needs your attention first:

Questions	Life Aspiration Area/Direction
1, 2	Fame/South
3	Love & Partnership/Southwest
4, 5	Creation/West
6, 7, 8	Synchronicity/Northwest
9, 10	Career/North
11, 12, 13	Knowledge/Northeast
14, 15	Family/East
16, 17, 18	Wealth & Prosperity/Southeast
19, 20	Health/Center

Now that you've chosen *one* area of life that you would most like to improve, complete the answers to these questions:

1. As of this moment, my highest priority is improving the area in my home related to (circle one): Fame, Love & Partnership, Creation, Synchronicity, Career, Knowledge, Family, Wealth & Prosperity, or Health.

2. In order to improve this area of my life, I need to concentrate on enhancing the _____ (compass direction) area of my home, which happens to fall in the _____. (Write down the room or rooms that occupy this particular compass direction, with special emphasis on where the meridian point exactly intersects the outer wall of the home.)

3. I will start enhancing this area by adding more _____. (Write down the main element that is needed in this area.) I will do so by _____. (Write down how you plan to bring the main element into the space.)

4. I can also add _____. (Write down the supporting element for this area). I will do so by _____. (Write down how you plan to bring the supporting element into the space.)

5. In order to optimize this section of my home, I must remove _____. (These can be specific elements such as clutter, artwork, or furniture.)

6. My overall goal for enhancing this area of my life is to _____. (Write down what you wish to accomplish or improve in this area of your life.)

7. In addition to the feng shui of my home, I'll help myself reach my goal by doing the following:_____.
(Write down the steps that you will take to reach your goal, such as *networking more, exercising, look for a new job, saving money*, etc.)

You'll find that, as you enhance each area, the success of one area is dependent upon another; they all work together. Feng shui is about life, and life is a holistic process—everything is interdependent and interconnected. The expression, "If you don't have your health, you don't have anything" has important meaning in feng shui. The Health area is located at the center of the Pa Kua, and all areas are connected to it. Physical, mental, and spiritual health must be optimized in order for us to fully benefit from the other eight areas. In the same way, each area is connected to all the others. So, start with your main area of concern, and then attend to the supporting areas. Eventually, make sure to review and enhance all Life Aspiration Areas of your home in order to live a happier, more balanced, and more fulfilling life.

FAQs on What to Expect After Enhancing Your Home

Once I've finished making all of my feng shui enhancements, how long will it take to see results?

Every situation is unique, and there are no guaranteed outcomes or specific timelines. I've heard from clients who've achieved results almost instantly and others who've had to be more patient. One thing I can tell you is that it's very important to implement *all* the enhancements in order to have optimal results. Your results are a direct reflection of the effort you put into achieving them. Feng shui cannot solve all of your problems. You need to do the work, and feng shui certainly seems to help by increasing the energy flow in the environment, bringing to you what's best for your highest good—often in wondrous ways.

I enhanced my Career area to land a job that I wanted, but I didn't get it. What did I do wrong?

Nothing is wrong. Remember that feng shui is always working toward the most positive outcome possible. Sometimes, opportunities are disguised as losses. That is, you may have to let go of relationships, homes, beliefs, attitudes, or jobs that no longer serve you before you can experience all that feng shui and life have to offer. Most likely, you didn't get the job that you thought you wanted because there's something better out there for you. Down the road, you may look back and be happy that you didn't get the job because it might have prevented you from accepting a better position. Be patient, stay positive, and be open to new ideas and opportunities. Make sure that all Life Aspiration Areas in your home are in tiptop shape—not just the Career area—and look forward to something even better coming your way.

My husband [partner, roommate, etc.] thinks I'm crazy for doing this. How can I convince him/her to believe in feng shui?

You don't need to convince anyone to believe in feng shui because feng shui is not a belief system. The feng shui of your surroundings affects you at all times, whether you believe in it or not. The easiest way to explain feng shui to someone who doesn't understand it is to ask him/her to describe two different places: one that feels comfortable and another that feels uncomfortable. Explain that the way he/she experiences both places is due to the feng shui of that place. You can also share my simple description of feng shui: feng shui is the study of the environment and how it affects people. There's no escaping the experience of feng shui.

Your Personal Kua Number

This chapter has taken you through the basic steps of Compass School feng shui. There are more advanced formulas related to Compass School feng shui that I have purposely *not* mentioned in order to make this book as easy to use and understand as possible. Now that you've enhanced your home and are comfortable with the process, you may want to delve deeper into the complex aspects of feng shui.

One place to start is by finding your personal Kua number. Your Kua number is used to identify the best compass directions for you as an individual. The Kua number is calculated using your birth date and your gender. With that number, you can then identify the best direction for sleeping, working, romance, health, and even the best direction for your home to face. If you're interested in learning more about this aspect of Compass School feng shui, please refer to the appendix.

Inner Self and Outer Surroundings

Feng shui is a beautiful, ancient system of environmental design that teaches us how to make our surroundings as optimal as possible. Feng shui, when properly applied, can greatly enhance the quality of our lives while also nurturing our bodies, minds, and spirits. Once you've carefully integrated the principles of feng shui into your home, you will have created a space that supports you in making your life all it can be. I hope you enjoy this incredible process of discovering your inner self through your outer surroundings. Once you've experienced the benefits of good feng shui, you may never see your surroundings or your life in the same way again.

Chapter 7
Home Numerology

The whole history of science has been the gradual realization that events do not happen in an arbitrary manner, but that they reflect a certain underlying order, which may or may not be divinely inspired.

— *Stephen Hawking*

In an effort to teach you as much as possible about how your environment can affect you, I would be remiss in leaving out the fun and interesting subject of numerology and its influence on your particular home. After doing this work for so many years, experience has taught me the validity of numerology.

Like feng shui, numerology has been around for at least twenty-five hundred years. It's thought that the Greek mathematician Pythagoras (570-490 BC) originated the science of numerology. Pythagoras postulated that numbers have unique vibrations and characteristics that influence the qualities of people or places. Much as they did in the time of Pythagoras, many people still look to numerology for insights.[1]

After all these years, it still amazes me to see how often the numerology of a client's home mirrors the qualities of their experiences while living in the home. It's important to remember that a home's number doesn't necessarily make things

---

[1] Peter Kingsley, *Ancient Philosophy Mystery, and Magic: Empedocles and Pythagorean Tradition* (New York: Oxford University Press, 1995).

happen. Rather, the home's number serves as an influence for the experiences that play out in the lives of those who live there. To better grasp this, consider calculating the numerology of places where you've lived in the past to see how much of a correlation exists between the numerology of a past home and the experiences you had while living there.

As with feng shui, numerology is a complex and fascinating subject that has withstood the test of time. There's a lot to learn, so for our purposes, I'll introduce you to a very basic description of how numerology can influence your experience of the places where you live and work.

Figuring Out the Numerology of Your Home

You'll begin by adding the numbers in your house number to produce a one-digit sum. If the sum of your house number is a two-digit number, then add those two digits together until you arrive at a single digit. For example, if your street address is 4371 Main Street, you would add the numbers like this:

$$4+3+7+1=15$$

Since 15 is a two-digit number, add these two digits together to get a single-digit number. In this case:

$$1+5=6.$$

The numerology for this home indicates a 6-type energy. Here's another one for a street address of 68979 Bancroft Street:

$$6+8+9+7+9=39$$

Because 39 is a two-digit number, you need to add these two numbers together and add the numbers in that sum together once more.

$$3+9=12$$
$$1+2=3$$

By continuing to add the numbers in this address until you arrive at a single-digit number, you determine that the home on Bancroft Street vibrates to the energy associated with number 3.

Addresses with Letters

Apartment and condo addresses frequently include a letter either for, or in addition to, the individual unit number. Since each letter in the alphabet corresponds to a number, you can use the following chart to calculate your unit number:

Pythagorean Number System

1	2	3	4	5	6	7	8	9
A	B	C	D	E	F	G	H	I
J	K	L	M	N	O	P	Q	R
S	T	U	V	W	X	Y	Z	

With an address of 206 West Elm Street, Apartment 3B, you'd pay the most attention to "3B" because this is the number that's unique to your particular home or unit. The building number (206) applies to all residents, while 3B is the number that pertains solely to the people living in that unit. In the chart above, you'll see that "B" corresponds to the number 2.

If B=2, then 3+B is the same as 3+2, and 3+2=5

This means that your apartment would be influenced by the qualities that relate to the number 5. Since the building number is 206, you add these together to get the following:

$$2+0+6=8$$

In this case, the building itself relates to the qualities of the number 8. While the numerology of the building will exert some influence, it's the numerology of the apartment (3B) that will exert the most influence on the residents of that apartment unit.

Addresses with Repeating Numbers

When an address has a repeating number, such as the number 2 in 7221 Maple Street, the repeating number carries a secondary influence. Using the methodology above, the house number 7221 adds up to a 3 in numerology (7+2+2+1=12 and 1+2=3). This home will vibrate primarily to the energy of the number 3 but will have a secondary influence relating to the number 2 as well.

Characteristics of Each Number

Once you've calculated the single digit that corresponds to your home, it's time to find out what it means. Below, you'll find the basic qualities of each number as they relate to a home.

The #1 Home

The #1 home is a great home for individuals and for establishing independence. It's an optimistic, future-oriented number, focusing more on the aspirations and goals of the individual rather than of the team. Couples who move into a #1 home need to be conscious of nurturing their partnership, as the energy can promote independence to the point of excluding a partner.

If the resident of a #1 home is single and wants to attract a partner or if the resident is in a partnership but doesn't want to drift too far apart while also doing his/her own thing, it may be necessary to place artwork and items depicting pairs throughout the home to help ground the energy of partnership.

The energy of a #1 home is that of new beginnings. It's a great house for fresh starts. If a resident experiences a setback, there will likely be another avenue to explore. Residents of #1 homes will want to affirm their intentions of what it is they'd like to achieve while living in the home—be it a new job, a new venture, or a new fitness program. If you've recently set new and important goals for your life or career, a #1 home may be just the place to achieve them.

The #2 Home

Unlike a #1 home, the #2 home focuses on partnership and teamwork. It encourages cooperation in love and friendship. It's a wonderful home to share with a loving partner. In a #2 home, residents may feel more empathetic than usual to their partners and/or children. Women, in particular, need to remember to take care of their own needs and be careful not to give too much to their spouse and/or children while living in a #2 home.

A #2 home can foster peace, harmony, creativity, and an appreciation of the beauty found in nature among plants, natural materials, birds, and animals. If you're looking for a home that feels peaceful, a #2 home may be a good choice. This home promotes relaxation, and its residents may reflect that energy in their décor with candles, soft fabrics, music, and mood lighting.

The #3 Home

The #3 home can enhance communication. Residents may find themselves on the phone, checking email, and receiving visitors more frequently while living in a #3 home. There's a tendency to take short trips, give impromptu parties, and strike up new friendships in a #3 home.

This home can have an upbeat, light energy that's fun, especially for people who enjoy an active social life or communicating via written or spoken words. The downside of a #3 home is that residents can feel overly optimistic. An attitude of "play now, pay later" can creep in, so it's important to take care of responsibilities like paying bills on time, maintaining household schedules and chores, and tending to the more mundane aspects of life.

To make the most of a #3 home, provide comfortable areas for conversation and entertaining. This is an ideal house for a pool table, a home theater, a game room, or any other activity that promotes fun and togetherness.

The #4 Home

The #4 home offers a solid foundation and a sense of stability, since this number is associated with security—like the four sides of a square. This is a great home for anyone who desires a feeling of protection.

People who live in #4 homes often find that the focus of their lives becomes work and responsibility. This can be either career-related work or work around the house, including chores, repairs, or home improvement projects that take center stage.

The downside of a #4 home is that life can take on a very serious tone. While living in a #4 home, it's important to get out of the house and have some fun. Take a trip, go to a movie, or visit friends to avoid feeling like your life is "all work and no play." This is especially important for residents of #4 home who also work at home.

In order to lighten the feeling of responsibility while living in a #4 home, be sure to include whimsical artwork and items that promote feelings of fun and enjoyment. Bright colors, prints, and décor that enhance joyful feelings are great for balancing the serious nature of a #4 home.

Reality Check

Myth: The number four brings bad luck.

The Chinese will often avoid a home if the number four is prominently featured in its address. We in the west have often misunderstood the reason for this. For the Chinese, the word that represents the number four sounds like the Chinese word for "death." You can surely understand why the Chinese may not want this number displayed in their address. For Westerners, there's no reason why the number four should have a negative association, since the word "four" doesn't have the same connotation in English as it does in Chinese.

The #5 Home

The #5 home is the party house! This is a busy, busy home where life never stops moving and can feel like a whirlwind. This is a wonderful home for people who love being the hub of activity and for those who really enjoy entertaining.

If there are children living here, this home may become the place where all the kids in the neighborhood want to hang out and play. Conversely, parents may find themselves driving their kids around constantly to a multitude of activities, from sports to piano lessons to friends' homes.

A #5 home can help us embrace change for change's sake, so residents of a #5 home will want to take the necessary time to think things through before making hasty decisions that they may regret later.

The main complaint that I hear from clients living in #5 homes is that their lives feel chaotic, and they never feel a sense of peace. One way to soothe the kinetic energy of a #5 home is to decorate in warm earth tones and select artwork that depicts peaceful, calm scenery.

For families living in #5 homes, it's important to keep a centrally located calendar where family members can write down their schedules. Be sure that each child has a place where toys and possessions may be easily stored. Because of the hectic nature of this home, it may be difficult to stay organized.

The #6 Home

The #6 home is ideal for family life and raising children. It is, overall, a peaceful, loving, and nurturing home. I'm astonished at how often I meet people who have lived in their #6 homes for decades. A #6 home is frequently the "family homestead," where a couple gets married, raises children, and even after the children grow up and move way, Mom and Dad remain in the home for thirty or forty years.

A #6 home is the ideal location for gathering the family together to celebrate holidays and special occasions. Family photos and mementos are a nice addition to the décor of this home. As with a #2 home, residents of a #6 home need to be aware of taking time away from nurturing others in order to nurture themselves.

The #7 Home

The #7 home has philosophical energy and can promote spiritual development. This is an ideal home in which to reflect on the meaning of life. And while a #7 home promotes spiritual development, it isn't necessarily the best space for a partner or for socializing, as the feeling here is more reclusive and contemplative than social.

Frequently, I find that clients who live in a #7 home prefer staying home to going out with friends. Even if they share the home with family members, they often enjoy spending time alone either reading or watching television. If you live in a #7 home with a partner, it's important to reconnect from time to time. This is a home where a couple can grow apart based on their individual interests, if they're not careful to give time and energy to the partnership. Residents should keep pictures of friends, family, and partners throughout the home in order to balance the "alone time" that a #7 home can promote. It's important for those living in a #7 home to accept invitations and to go out, instead of embracing their inner homebody to the point of reclusiveness.

The #8 Home

In numerology, the number 8 is associated with abundance. Some people call it the "money number." In China, the number 8 is considered very auspicious. Many Chinese go to great lengths to use the number 8 whenever possible. The date of the Opening Ceremonies for the 2008 Summer Olympics in Beijing, China was August 8, 2008 or 8/8/08 and chosen specifically because the number eight is associated with prosperity. Even more powerful was the fact that when all the numbers in the date were added up (8+8+2+0+0+8=26, and then 2+6=8), the result was 8, making August 8th, 2008 an especially symbolic day for the Chinese.

However, just because you live in a #8 home doesn't mean that you're going to be rolling in dough. What it can mean is that the issue of abundance may take center stage while living there. While the number 8 can bring prosperity, it can also bring issues regarding money to the forefront. The emphasis in this home will be on material advancement and power. If you have an unhealthy attitude toward material advancement, you may have to face this issue before you can reap the benefits of the #8 home's energy.

One of my clients, who lives in a #8 home, is married to a man who had issues regarding self-worth and success. Although he received plenty of job offers, he would often sabotage himself so that he failed to either get the job or keep it. His career (or lack thereof) and money were problems in their marriage. So, living in an #8 house wasn't bringing in money per se, but it was forcing them to deal with attitudes regarding success and prosperity. Through counseling, my client's husband finally overcame his self-defeating attitudes regarding abundance, and this couple went on to live quite nicely in their #8 home.

To make the most of a #8 home, you may wish to decorate with luxurious fabrics, thick carpets, artwork featuring lush landscapes, and rich jewel tones like royal blue, forest green, purple, burgundy, and gold. This will increase the energy of success and abundance in this home.

The #9 Home

Nine is the number of universal compassion. People living in a #9 home may find that their attitudes toward humanity become more focused in positive ways. Residents may become more philanthropic and interested in being of service to others, such as helping the poor, healing the environment, or volunteering at a soup kitchen or a hospital. Nine is also the number of completion, of tying up loose ends, and of letting go of the old in order to welcome the new. A #9 home is a good place to identify what's helpful and necessary in your life as well as what's obstructing your growth. It's a home where people may decide to leave a long-term career or a relationship that no longer serves them.

To make the most of a #9 home, include artwork and items made of natural materials as well as those made by folk artists or craftsmen. Artwork that helps to sustain cultural or humanitarian groups is also suited to a #9 home as are images of world leaders or spiritual figures.

No Need to Move

There's much more to numerology than just your home address, and I encourage you to explore the subject further. If the numerology of your home address doesn't have all the qualities that you'd like, there's no need to fret—and certainly no need to move! Remember, each number has unique properties and brings with it specific experiences. Whether or not you choose to make the most of those experiences is completely up to you.

Chapter 8
Space Clearing and House Blessings

Not only can your home help to strengthen and heal you but your home
can be a template of harmony within which you and all who enter
can be invited to step up to a higher level of spiritual frequency.

— *Denise Linn*

One of the most important things you can do to properly align the energy in your home is to conduct a space clearing followed by a house blessing. Space clearing is a practice used to remove negative or residual energy from a space, replacing it with fresh, positive energy. After a space clearing, a house blessing can help you establish the intent for what you'd like to experience and attract while living in your home.

Almost every culture and spiritual practice in the world employs some type of space clearing or purifying technique. In the Catholic Church, spoken prayer and incense are used. Monks chant in monasteries. Buddhist temples ring bells. Hindus recite mantras. Native Americans drum and smudge with sage, and African tribes sing and dance. Each of these relies on sound and ritual to purify and uplift the energy of a space, enhancing the atmosphere and bringing people closer to their spiritual source.

I first learned about space clearing from Denise Linn,[1] an amazing writer, spiritual teacher, and space clearing expert. I've found the process to be an essential component of creating optimal feng shui in a home or workspace.

The Science behind Space Clearing

In the seventeenth century, a Dutch scientist named Christiaan Huygens noticed that two pendulum clocks hung side by side would eventually synchronize and begin to swing in the same rhythm. Huygens called this process *entrainment*.[2] Entrainment occurs as two objects, each with their own vibratory pattern, transfer small amounts of energy between them, eventually settling into a rhythmic relationship. Everything in the universe, including human beings, is made up of molecules and atoms that are vibrating at different frequencies. Even objects that appear solid and inanimate, such as walls, ceilings, and floors, are made up of atomic particles that constantly vibrate.

Science has proven that human emotions and thoughts have electrical frequencies.[3] Different emotions have different vibratory patterns. The stronger the emotion behind the thought, the more intense the vibration is. Perhaps you've experienced walking into a room where there's been an argument and felt tension in the air. The tension is a result of the emotional energy released during the disagreement. When someone experiences strong emotions or thoughts repeatedly in a space, they send out vibrations that are *picked up by* and *projected back from* the solid materials in the surroundings, including walls, ceilings, floors, and furniture. Through the process of entrainment, the room itself begins to match the vibration of these emotional frequencies.

---

[1] Denise Linn, *Sacred Space: Clearing and Enhancing the Energy of Your Home* (New York: Ballantine Books, 1995).

[2] Hans van den Ende and others, *Huygens' Legacy: The Golden Age of the Pendulum Clock* (Isle of Man, UK: Fromanteel Ltd., 2004).

[3] Richard Gerber, MD, *Vibrational Medicine: The #1 Handbook of Subtle-Energy Therapies* (Rochester, VT: Bear and Company, 2001).

Let's imagine, for example, that you have serious financial trouble, and your thoughts and emotions are focused on money worries, loss, and financial ruin. When you're at home, these thoughts and emotions constantly send out specific frequencies into your surroundings. Through the process of entrainment, the energy of your worry and stress influences the vibratory rate of the molecules and atoms in the walls, ceilings, and floors, synchronizing the house to the energetic pattern of financial difficulty.

Eventually, you move out of the home, but your energetic imprint remains, still vibrating in the structure of the house. Since energy is in perpetual motion until something interferes with it, the home continues to vibrate at the same frequency, even though you're no longer living there.

The next owner of the home may have had no previous problems with finances but may begin to experience more and more issues in this area after moving into the home. Why? Once again, through the dynamic process of entrainment, the energetic imprint of the home influences the energetic vibration of the new resident. A home is much larger than a human being. Therefore, the home's energy surrounds the new resident, and over time, the new resident often experiences similar life patterns as the previous occupants. This is one reason why, in analyzing the feng shui of a home, it's important to learn about the history of the home itself and of the people who have lived there. Fortunately, a space clearing can work wonders to cleanse the home of unfavorable influences.

In order to clear the way for optimal energy flow in your home, it's necessary to rid the house of any energy that may impede your efforts. You can create the most comfortable and beautiful space, place all the elements in their proper locations, and arrange everything according to its best position, but if your home or place of business has any residual energy that's negative, you're going to have a difficult time attracting positive experiences into your life. In addition to feng shui, space clearing is an extremely important component of creating the best environment possible.

Using Sound to Clear a Space

There are many techniques that can rid a home or a workspace of unwanted energy. Experience has shown me the benefit of using sound and the process of entrainment to clear a space. Sound is very effective in elevating the energy of a room and clearing any negative energy that may be interfering with your best feng shui efforts. Sound waves travel well through solids and liquids which is why you can hear sounds so well under water. By introducing sound waves into a space, you can influence the vibrational frequency of the walls, ceilings, furniture, and other objects in a room.

Space clearing through sound not only improves the energy of a building, it can also improve the energy of the human beings that dwell in that space.[4] Positive energy vibrates at a faster frequency than negative energy. By using high-frequency sounds in a space, you can raise the vibration of your home and workspace relatively easily. Through the process of entrainment, the space's previous energy imprint is eliminated and replaced with high-frequency energy, which is more conducive to positive experiences.

When to Conduct a Space Clearing

Conduct a space clearing whenever you feel the need to improve the energy of your home or workspace. I find that when my life feels stuck, a space clearing does wonders to get it back on track. Specific situations that call for a space clearing include the following:

- Upon moving into or out of a home
- After an illness, a death, or an accident in the home
- After an argument or a bout of depression
- Upon a change of residents, including roommates, spouses, or houseguests
- When your life feels stuck or stagnant
- Before and after parties
- When you sense a spirit or "presence" in the home
- To welcome a new year, a new relationship, or a new season

---

[4] Jeffrey D. Thompson, DC, BFA, "The Clinical Use of Sound," (Encinitas, CA: Center for Neuroacoustic Research, 2007).

Once your home has been cleared, you'll most likely feel a freshness and vitality that wasn't there before. I often find that my home feels cooler and that the colors seem brighter after a space clearing. The investment of time and effort to properly clear a space is well worth it, and improving the energy of your home further enhances your feng shui efforts.

Procedure

The first item needed to conduct a space clearing is something that makes a sound. I prefer to use energy chimes. (See the appendix.) Energy chimes simplify the process and allow for a gradual introduction of higher frequencies into a space. If you don't have energy chimes, then consider the use of singing bowls, bells, drums, clapping, or virtually any other percussion-type instrument that's available.

In her book, *Sacred Space*, Denise Linn recommends moving through the house in a clockwise direction until every room has been cleared.[5] I've found the front door to be an excellent starting point because people tend to dump their energy at the front door. Think about the many times you've walked into your home after a long or difficult day and just dumped everything at the front door—keys, coat, cell phone, and shoes—along with a big exhale to rid yourself of the day's energy. The front door or main entrance of a home may take a bit longer to clear, due to the many times that people come and go through this area each day.

If you are using energy chimes, start with the lowest tone first (i.e., the longest chime) and then make three passes through the house using the next highest tone each time. If you're using a singing bowl, a drum, a bell, or a clap of your hands, there will be only one tone, so you'll make only one pass through the home.

Start by standing in your entryway facing the front door. Then clap, ring a bell, beat a drum, play the singing bowl, or strike an energy chime. Direct the sound toward the door and the surrounding walls. Listen for a clear pitch that continues to resonate. "Stuck" energy will sound dull and flat. If this is the case, keep making the

---

[5] Denise Linn, *Sacred Space: Clearing and Enhancing the Energy of Your Home* (New York: Ballantine Books, 1995), 115-137.

sound in that area and don't move along until the sound begins to resonate and/or until the energy feels lighter and more positive.

After you've cleared the area by the front door, continue directing the sound toward the walls as you move in a clockwise direction into the next room. Be sure to direct the sound into the corners of each room, as energy tends to stagnate in corners. Sound waves travel out from their source, so you don't have to be close to the ceiling to clear that area. Older homes and/or those that have had many different occupants or negative experiences may take longer to clear.

Make your way systematically through all rooms on all floors of the home until you end up back at the main entrance where you started. Be sure to include garages, closets, basements, attics, and bathrooms. If you're using energy chimes, you'll make a total of three passes through the entire home, moving up a tone each time: On the first pass, use the longest rod; on the second pass, use the middle rod, and on the last pass, use the smallest rod. If you get tired, sit and rest and then pick up where you left off.

Pay attention to any impressions or experiences you may have while conducting your space clearing. While uncommon, I have had clients react during a space clearing by crying, feeling nervous, sad, or even (rarely) nauseous. More often, people experience a subtle gurgling in the stomach. This is nothing to be concerned about and is simply a result of experiencing the moving and releasing of energies that have been trapped in the space. If you experience any uncomfortable feelings, they will pass quickly and are usually followed by feelings of happiness, clarity, and a lightness of being. I highly recommend that anyone present in the house during the space clearing drink a lot of water for the rest of the day. Water helps the body cleanse and process any energy that's been released during the space clearing.

At the end of the space clearing, stand with your back to the main entrance, face the interior of the home, and strike your instrument. This is when I like to say a blessing or a prayer to complete the process. After a space clearing, a house blessing is a wonderful way to set an intention for your space. The following section offers some ideas on how to carry out a house blessing.

Helpful Tips for Space Clearing

Clear your clutter before a space clearing! Clutter equals stagnation, and it's very difficult to do an effective space clearing in a cluttered environment. Any time that you remove clutter, follow with a space clearing to rid the area of the stagnant energy imprint that the clutter may have left behind.

Give yourself plenty of uninterrupted time. The larger your home, the longer the space clearing will take. Aim for monthly space clearings. Do them more frequently if there have been any negative experiences or energies in the home that need to be cleared.

Clean your home. A clean home has a lighter, more positive vibration than a dirty one, so make sure that your home is very clean before you conduct a space clearing. Consider taking a shower or a bath before a space clearing to cleanse your own energy and to put yourself in a positive mind-set.

Be mindful during a space clearing. Reschedule your space clearing if you're in a bad mood, ill, or depressed. A positive mind-set while space clearing is essential; otherwise, you'll be adding negative energy to your home as fast as you're clearing it.

Dense cloth furniture, such as mattresses or sofas, tend to hold more energy because people spend a lot of time on them, leaving more of their energetic imprint on those objects. Space clearing can be used on furniture to help rid it of previous energy. Likewise, it's very important to clear any antiques used in your décor, as they carry the energy of their previous owners.

House Blessings

A house blessing is a beautiful complement to a space clearing. While a space clearing *erases* an energy imprint, a house blessing *creates* an energy imprint. The purpose of a house blessing is to set the intention for your home by consciously welcoming positive, loving energy into your space in order to make the experience of living there as optimal as possible. The clearer you can be with your thoughts and your intentions, the better you and your space will feel.

As you've learned from this book, a home is far more than just a place of shelter. It's an energetic environment that can impact daily living—either positively or negatively. Happiness, security, love, health, success, friendship, safety, and financial well-being are just some of the aspects that can be influenced by a house blessing.

Don't worry too much about correct procedure when blessing your home. There's no right or wrong way to conduct a house blessing. You can keep it simple or conduct something elaborate. For some people, a house blessing is religious or spiritual in nature. For others, it's not. The blessing can be almost anything you want it to be. For example, you can imagine your house filled with beautiful white light or with angels bringing positive and loving energy. Some people read a prayer, a poem, or a meaningful passage from a book, while others enjoy playing music or singing a favorite song. A clear heart and a loving intention are all that's required to conduct a successful house blessing.

Ways to Bless Your Home

As with space clearing, I recommend that the house be as clean as possible before a house blessing. It's best to clean the home, clean your body (bathe and put on clean clothes), conduct a space clearing, and finish with a house blessing.

Who attends is up to you. You may do the blessing yourself or invite friends and family to join you—whatever feels comfortable. If you have a religious preference, you may invite your minister, rabbi, or priest to officiate. This is your home, and the important thing is that you feel good about the process.

Some people enjoy making a house blessing into a ceremony and/or setting up a house blessing altar. In this case, the process of gathering materials for the blessing becomes part of the blessing itself. Materials such as a special cloth, candles, flowers, photographs, incense, sage, music, stones, or representations of each Life Aspiration Area may be used as meaningful objects during house blessings. For my own house blessings, I place a representation of the five elements and a ring of beautiful stones around a candle. What you choose to do and how you choose to do it are completely up to you.

Most house blessings take place in the main gathering room of the home, but any room where you feel the most comfortable is fine. Some people conduct the blessing in one room; others like to go throughout the house. When I do house blessings in my own home, I go to each Life Aspiration Area of the home (see chapter 6) and set my intention for each area.

You may wish to do house blessings periodically. I suggest doing them in concert with space clearing. If you conduct a house blessing each time you conduct a space clearing, you'll be doing yourself and your home a big favor. Like energy attracts like energy. By space clearing and then consciously blessing your home, you are creating positive attraction energy. I highly recommend conducting a space clearing and a house blessing when you first move into a new home and annually on New Year's Day to set your intention for the year to come.

The Process I Use to Bless My Home

As I mentioned earlier, there's no right or wrong way to bless your home. The goal is to focus your intention on the energy that you'd like to attract into your home and life. Here's what I like to do as a house blessing:

First, I set aside a day when I'll have enough uninterrupted time to do a complete job of cleaning, space clearing, and blessing. Before the day arrives, I plan ahead by gathering representations of the five elements: a metal tray (metal), a new votive candle (fire), a few favorite rocks and stones that have been cleansed and rinsed under cold, running water (earth), a small glass bowl of purified water (water), and a beautiful flower (wood). I like to burn sandalwood incense as well when I do a house blessing, so I have some of that on hand, too.

I begin with a thorough cleaning of my home. This includes washing all the sheets and towels. After the house is clean, I start a bath. I add Epsom salts and a few drops of therapeutic-grade essential oil to the water (see the appendix). I use eucalyptus, geranium, lavender, or whatever oil I feel like adding at the time to help me relax and put me a positive mind-set. After my bath, I dress in something clean and comfortable, and then I conduct a space clearing of my entire house using energy chimes.

After the space clearing is done, I light a stick of sandalwood incense and arrange the five elements mentioned above on the metal tray. I do the house blessing in my living room, so I place the tray on the hearth. I say a quiet prayer for my home, blessing it as a place of peace, protection, rejuvenation, and happiness. Sometimes, I pray for one of my Life Aspiration Areas, and other times, I pray for someone in my life. I light the candle and focus on feeling love and gratitude for my home. I like to picture angels surrounding my home with protection and white light. I stay with this process until the house really feels cleansed and protected. *Remember, safety comes first. If you're burning anything during your blessing ceremony, be sure to do so in a safe place and don't leave burning things unattended or within reach of children and pets.*

While this is the process that feels best to me, you need to identify what feels best to you. If you'd like more ideas on ways to bless your home, there's a lot of information available in books and on the Internet about house blessings. Yes, it takes time to do all the cleaning and clearing, but the effort is well worth the result of creating a home of beauty, comfort, and positive healing energy. Through space clearing and blessing your home, you are truly clearing the way for, and amplifying, the energy of your feng shui efforts.

Final Thoughts

I sincerely hope that you've enjoyed reading this book and have found the information useful. Armed with a new understanding of these basic concepts, you now have a solid foundation from which to work as well as the confidence necessary to make positive changes in your life. My wish is that you continue to explore feng shui in more depth, enjoying the journey as much as the destination.

Appendix: Resources

For help in finding items mentioned in this book or for information about Cathleen's workshops and classes, please visit:

www.FengShuiThatMakesSense.com

Index

About the Author

With over twenty years' experience, **Cathleen McCandless** is a highly respected and sought-after expert, author, teacher, and speaker on the subject of feng shui. Cathleen's work and no-nonsense approach to feng shui have been featured in the *New York Times,* the *Washington Post,* the *Los Angeles Times,* and many others. Her radio and television appearances include everything from prime-time newscasts to a starring role in the television series, *Feng Shui Living.* Cathleen's clients range from busy homemakers to top executives of Fortune 500 companies. Her students delight in her warm, relaxed, and entertaining teaching style and benefit from her many years of research and first-hand experience in the fields of feng shui and environmental psychology.